VOID IF DETACHED

The Writings & Musings

of

Mark Richard Green

ISBN 978-0-9962676-0-1

Void If Detached is available for bulk purchase and special promotions. For information on reselling and special purchase opportunities, contact the publisher at dcdesignteamvt@gmail.com | 802-380-1121

Visit the author's website: moosevt.wordpress.com
Proceeds to benefit The Mark R. Green Trust and Accelerate Brain Cancer Cure (ABC2)

Moose VT | DCDesign Books
Brattleboro, Vermont

COVER PHOTO: "Lovers of Valdaro" (detail)
Archaeological Society SAP / AP

TITLE PAGE PHOTO BY THE AUTHOR:
Morning in Walpole, Friday, August 19, 2011

AUTHOR PHOTO: Rachel Portesi

Printed on recycled paper
in the United States of America at Thomson Shore.

About MooseVT

earth air water fire aether

wind rain snow sun

see hear smell taste touch

Mark Richard Green

NOTE: Mark's blog contained a number of music and video clips, as well as illustrative materials and references to other writings. . . . A reader may wish to consult those entries to enhance appreciation of the contents of this book. See…moosevt.wordpress.com.

Dedicated to my daughters

Libby and Hannah

FOREWORD
Dealing with the Weight of a Diagnosis

WHO would have known that the young boy pictured sitting with his younger sister in the photo so many years ago would later be dealt a heavy blow with a diagnosis of stage III anaplastic ependymoma brain cancer?

The day I was told I had a 4.3 cm tumor in my head was as if someone had tossed on top of me a hundred lead blankets, the kind you wear during x-rays at the dentist. It was a train wreck of epic magnitude. But I quickly decided I would do my best to get the train back on the rails. Since the initial chaos I have endured three surgeries*, radiation and chemotherapy.

New Desire – Helping Others

I have found a deep desire to help push brain cancer over the cliff. My desire to live was equaled by my desire to help others do the same. I quit my job at an independent school in Vermont to work for Accelerate Brain Cancer Cure (ABC2). I am VP for Strategic Partnerships working to create a collaborative network for those who seek to support us, which, in turn, helps support organizations like CERN (Collaborative Ependymoma Research Network, funded by ABC2) by providing funding to researchers and institutions seeking to find a cure for brain cancers such as ependymoma.

I spend my free time camping, canoeing, kayaking, biking, cooking, Nordic skiing throughout New England and Canada with my family. We also like to attend concerts such as Avett Brothers, Wilco and the Lumineers. My family participates in cancer awareness and fundraising activities and my daughter, Hannah, started the organization, All Shades of Cancer, whose goal is to fight to end

*Mark endured two more surgeries after writing this.

cancer. As of the date of publication, Hannah is a sophomore at Middlebury College, Middlebury, VT and Libby is a junior at The Putney School, Putney, VT.

Please enjoy my blog and book and support the great work of CERN in any way you can. This is the lodestone for those affected by and afflicted with this disease and the people involved deserve a standing ovation for their service.

Inspirational Quotes

A few random quotes and one of my favorite poems to share that I hope will help you as much as they help me. I think it's the simple beauty of the poem and the simple humanity of the quotes that help keep me strong.

> I can get sad, I can get frustrated, I can get scared, but I never get depressed—because there's joy in my life.
> —Michael J. Fox

> Some days there won't be a song in your heart. Sing anyway.
> —Emory Austin

Inspirational Poem

The Red Wheelbarrow

so much depends
upon
a red wheel
barrow
glazed with rain
water
beside the white
chickens.
—William Carlos Williams

Sadly, Mark lost his battle on February 27, 2015

VOID IF DETACHED

Andy Warhol's Factory or MRI?

Posted on August 15, 2011

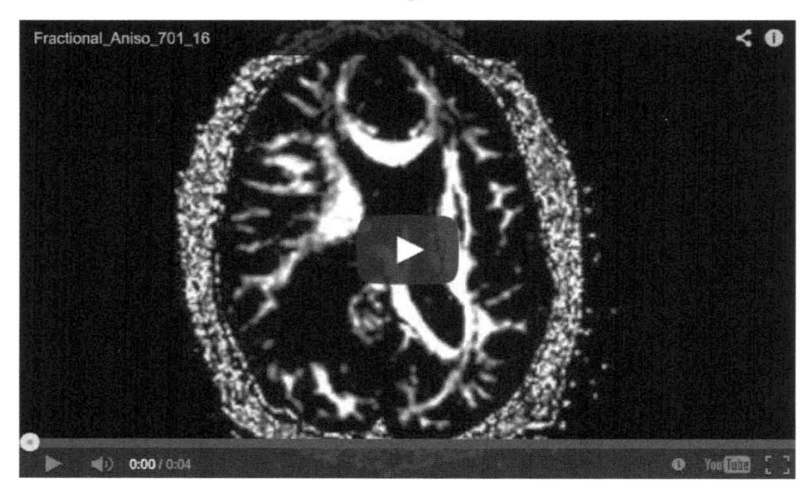

world within

Posted on August 15, 2011

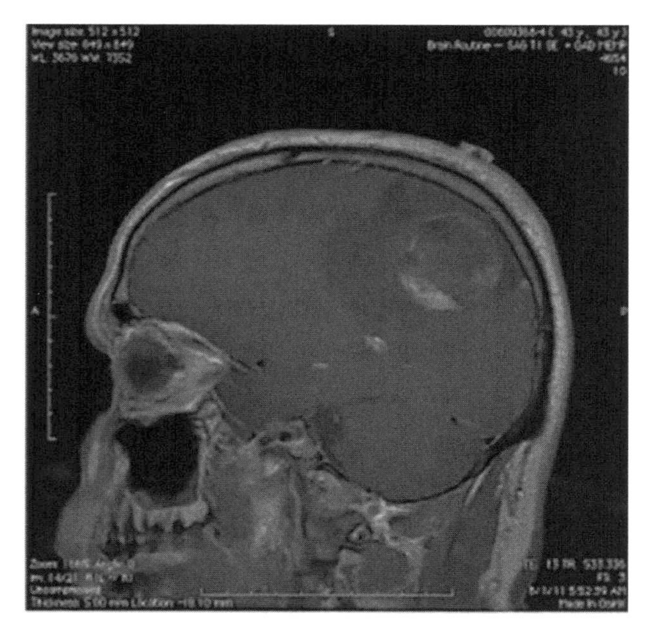

INTRODUCTION
Two Worlds Collide

Sunday, August 14, 2011

Welcome to the Journey. Thank you for reading. This is good therapy for me and I hope a good read for you...and it is also written for those who are afflicted with this cancer, those who have family and friends with brain cancer (or any cancer or related illness for that matter), and those incredible doctors, researchers, scientists, and others working towards finding answers...

First Steps:

There are moments in life that are completely out of our control. Some are minor disasters, and others are of epic proportions. We experience moments that are truly beyond our grasp and often defy our ability to comprehend. There is a particularly unstable glass shelf in our medicine cabinet loaded with various medicine-cabinet items—medicine bottles, shaving cream, cologne, razors, and so forth—which from time to time comes loose, sending the objects sliding and crashing to the sink below. It's an awful mess. It's loud and it's bothersome. And it remains one of those little things, those small projects that nag and bother, that we just don't seem to be able to get to. Of the more catastrophic events which come to mind, there are two that gnaw at my heart.

On September 11, 2001, I was working as the development director at the Greenwood School in Putney, Vermont, a junior boarding school for boys with learning differences. When news of the first plane hitting the North Tower of the World Trade Center arrived, the faculty and staff went into lockdown mode, shutting off the media from the young children, many of whom had family in the New York City area, until more news came in. I went to a friend's apartment on campus to watch the events unfold on television. Like so many, I had friends in New York, including classmates from college who worked near or in one instance, as we later found out, at the World Trade Center.

With the newscaster standing in the foreground, I watched the second plane fly into the South Tower. Like so many, I felt sick to my core. What appeared at first to be a horrific accident was now a new nightmare of unparalled proportions. The world had changed in an instant and would never, ever be the same. One hour and thirteen minutes later, yet another unspeakable, surreal moment occurred. As the South Tower collapsed into itself, I rose from where I was sitting holding up my hands and screaming, "*No! Stop!*"

This instinctive reflex, trying to somehow magically stop the building from falling with my hands, haunts me to this day. All of those people pulverized into dust. The jumpers. The mass of destruction. Another moment seared into memory was watching the effects of the tsunami in Indonesia, and one particular piece of news footage that showed an elderly couple, stranded on a structure of some sort, literally holding on to each other for dear life. Despite rescuers attempting to offer a helping hand, the terrified couple, with a look of despair in their eyes, was out of reach and helpless. Eventually, as the waters raged, whatever they were holding on to gave way, and they both tumbled into the murky abyss of the raging waters, never to be seen again.

My name is Mark Richard Green. I live in the small, idyllic New England village of Walpole, New Hampshire, located along the Connecticut River. Living here, to paraphrase artist Maxfield Parrish, I can "get a better view of Vermont." I will turn 44 this Thursday, and I have two beautiful, remarkable daughters. I am a major gifts officer for the Putney School, in Putney, Vermont, and live in a wonderful, supportive, loving, and diverse community full of educators, artists, writers, entrepreneurs, builders, farmers, and other professionals. My family—sister, father, mother, niece, and nephew—live in Philadelphia. I have relatives in Florida, Kentucky, Chicago, New Jersey, Georgia, and California. We are a small but loving clan.

What has unfolded these past two weeks can only be described in metaphor. Imagine sitting peacefully in your kitchen eating breakfast when, without warning, a locomotive train plows through your home. You are still sitting there, bowl of cereal before you, and you sit bewildered as the debris from the destruction swirls around you. It's been like that.

When I was a child, there was a short piece on *Sesame Street* in which a child spills his milk. When his mother asks him what happened, he explains the mishap through a series of little lies. As he shares how the milk spilled, his imagination comes alive. At one point he tells his mother, "A heard of rhinos came through the kitchen, and they knocked it over!" Here the camera cuts to an enormous herd of stampeding rhinoceroses, and we see the kitchen shake and his milk spill. It's been like that

A giant boulder. A meteorite. In real terms, a golf ball–sized tumor. A golf ball is 4.26 cm in diameter. My golf ball was 4.3 cm. And I'm not even good at golf! A rare form of brain cancer normally found in pediatric cases: stage III (WHO grade) anaplastic ependymoma. Of all cancers, brain cancer makes up 1 percent. Of these, 2 to 3 percent are in the form of ependymomas.

Of these ependymomas, 95 percent are found in children, 30 percent under the age of three. 90 percent of ependymomas in children occur in the brain. In adults, 60 percent occur in the spine. Mine is in the brain. Just writing the word brain is strange. It *sounds* strange. Like the words *putrid, vomit, goulash*, or *moist*.

Math was never my strong suit, so forgive me for not having the figures, but let's just say it's rare. But cancer is cancer, and in the end the numbers don't change the facts or the course of the disease. Except to say that because of the rarity, there is, understandably, not as much data or resources to help with research and cures. But there is hope, and there are doctors and scientists in the field who are working to help find a way out—the CERN (Collaborative Ependymoma Resource Network) Foundation is one such organization. I am heading to Houston soon to see leading doctors in the field at MD Andersen.

My moment of truth came on June 28. I was home alone. The kids and Barb, my partner, were in St. John, and I was getting ready to walk or bike down to Burdick's, an ambience-filled, French-themed restarant run by world-class chocolatier Larry Burdick. I figured I would use this time alone to sit at the bar, read the *New York Times*, and have a nice, relaxing meal.

What happened next occurred over a span of about twenty minutes. I was outside, getting something from the car perhaps, when I slowly fell to the ground. Crumpled is more like it. Like a marionette whose strings had been let out. I felt a bizarre wave wash over me, as if someone were covering me with a lead blanket, and I felt enormously weak. I felt as if I had been shot by a tranquilizer dart (not that I would know).

I realized I had lost function of my body. I literally crawled into the house, pulling my legs over the threshold. As I rose, my hands were uncooperative. I tried to button my shirt. My hands ignored my command. I tried to put on my shoes only to find them unwilling to go on my feet. I actually laughed. I wasn't in pain. I was just more uncoordinated than usual.

As I sat down, I imagined a trippy film, like something Warhol would have shown at a Happening, with melting celluloid images and psychedelic swirls. Or something by Luis Buñuel. I realize now that when films show someone in the throes of an acid trip or under the influence of a hallucinogen, they have it down pretty well. *Clockwork Orange, Fear and Loathing in Las Vegas, Trainspotting, The Big Lebowski, The Wall, The Doors*—the filmmakers must have some experience to be able to translate this feeling so accurately.

I tried to dial my phone, but my fingers were spastic. I finally managed to speed-dial my ex-wife, Laura, with whom I remain close. She talked me down. Told me to relax. Suggested I call an ambulance. In my stubborn and ignorant state, I resolved to push through this. Frightening as it was, I still wanted to go have dinner. Was it a mini-stroke? A TIA? Lyme disease? My blood pressure had been running consistently pre-hypertensive, not alarming but borderline concern. As the minutes wore on, I regained function. I was weary but eager to get going. Rather than walk or ride my Holland-made Union "town bike," of which I am so proud, I hopped in the car for the half-mile drive. When I arrived, I shared with the host that I'd had a dizzy spell, and said not to be alarmed if I seemed more woozy than normal. I ordered a margarita and dinner and sat down to work my way through the newspaper. All was well again.

I followed the family to St. John two days later and spent the week there without incident, as far as I can recall. Looking back, perhaps I felt "off " on some level, but being used to ignoring pain and discomfort—we all have some sort of discomfort somewhere as our bodies age—I carried on. After all, I'd been known to bruise and bleed and not realize it until someone said, "Hey, Mark, what's that blood on your arm?"

When I returned from vacation, I started my new position at the Putney School as major gifts officer. After a wide and sometimes wild journey with a variety of institutions, all of which I found rewarding and fulfilling in their own way, I felt that I had taken everything I'd learned and come "home." Being back at Putney, where I'd worked in the early '90s, felt good to my very core. The school, stronger and healthier than ever, was a place to which I felt a deep connection, due in part to my Quaker schooling. Its progressive roots were deep and strong. I was eager to get going and rise to the challenge.

As I started my new role, my body and mind continued to feel out of order. My normal high-energy self felt sapped. My balance was off. Even my keyboarding, particularly on my left hand, felt stiff, and finding the proper keys proved difficult. At one point I went to sit down and fell off my chair, having missed my target. My co-worker Carla came in, inquiring about the noise. "I'm just a klutz sometimes," I shared. We had a good laugh.

But looking back, things were deteriorating. I couldn't focus. (Many who know me will argue that this was nothing new.) After speaking with friends and visiting my primary physician, we all started assuming these were symptoms of Lyme disease, and I had my blood sent out for testing. I started a course of antibiotics, and told my colleagues I was sorry if I seemed "off "—again, how would anyone know the difference?—and that I was convinced it was Lyme. I could sense the frustration of my boss when I'd ask a question and she'd smile affectionately but with some understandable perplexion, "Well, Mark, as I thought I had previously shared...." She was very gracious and kind, and I was sad that I was acting so flaky. I was not making a great first impression. Even my words, which normally flow with ease, would seize up, like sand being poured into a Caterpillar-engine crankcase à la ecowarrior tactics from Edward Abbey's *Monkey Wrench Gang*. Another week passed, and I had another vertiginous incident at the opticians in Lebanon, New Hampshire. The optician suddenly started to bend and sway like a funhouse mirror, and I felt dizzy. "Vertigo! Must be vertigo!" they exclaimed with concern. This passed, and I was on my way.

The next week I attended the Green River Festival with my two daughters, Hannah and Libby, and the Kitfields, from the nearby Northfield Mount Hermon School. I was eager to enjoy the music and share a drink with my newfound friends. The Carolina Chocolate Drops and Toots and the Maytals were among the acts, and normally I would be whipping up a storm of dance and play, but instead I spent a good part of the time in the first aid tent with a headache, lying on a cot with a nurse spraying me with misty water from a bottle. "Heat exhaustion," we concluded.

Sunday evening was when the landslide occurred. As the evening wore on, a dull headache I'd had for most of the day turned into an epic migraine. Barb and I tried to watch an episode of *Breaking Bad*, but I had my hand over my eyes the entire time. Then I started to vomit. Things were going downhill quickly. I had spent the past two days painting the deck in the hot sun. We figured I was just dehydrated. Tests were underway for detection of Lyme disease, based on my previous headaches and spells, but it got worse. Barb and I drove to the emergency room at Cheshire Medical Center in Keene, New Hampshire. What happened next felt like being pulled into a vortex, an energy field of the most powerful type.

I was given a CT scan, and within twenty minutes the doctor on duty delivered the news. I had a golf ball sized tumor, and it was a serious matter. Already on intravenous pain meds, I experienced a series of events that oscillated between stop-motion photography and riding on some awful carnival ride with sickly colored lights and the din of machines and people. It was a circus of nightmares. The bad dream commingled with reality to create a horrific, numbing, bewildering episode, and this was only chapter one. The feeling of shock and bewilderment Barb and I felt at that moment will never leave us. Was he kidding? In between feeling shocked and tearful, I think we even smiled, or laughed in a sad, sickly manner. Surely he was just kidding...

Ironically, the tumor is but a mere flesh wound. I am absolutely blown away by the fact that at 6:00 am on Tuesday, August 2, my skull (that word alone makes me tingle) was opened up, a tumor removed, titanium screws and plates inserted, I was sewn back up, and on

Friday night I was holding court at Burdick's, albeit quietly and sans martini (six weeks or more before that can happen again...seizure meds and steroids don't mix well with alcohol). Before this, when I thought of brain surgery I thought of references to the ancient and ill-informed art of trepanning, "perhaps the oldest surgical procedure for which there is forensic evidence," which involved drilling a burrhole in the skull to treat health problems.

Consider how far we have come from the days of the Civil War, where as many, if not more, soldiers died of infection from wounds as from the wounds themselves. Bleeding, purging, and unproven drugs led famous poet and physician Oliver Wendell Holmes to share, "I firmly believe that if the whole materia medica as now used could be sunk to the bottom of the sea, it would be all the better for mankind and all the worse for the fishes."

But the most profound thought I can share in this foreword to the story is that I am blessed by and grateful for the immense love, support, good wishes, prayers, and friendship of my family, friends near and far, colleagues, excellent medical establishment, and my communities: Saxtons River, Walpole, Twin Lakes, Abington Friends, Hamilton College, BAJC (Brattleboro Area Jewish Community), Sojourns, the Grammar School, the Putney School, Dartmouth College, Dartmouth-Hitchcock Medical Center, Friends of Norris Cotton Cancer Center, CERN Foundation, and countless others. If love makes a family, I am indeed a rich and lucky man, and wish I could share it all with those in need. If love helps healing, I've already traveled far.

That this is a condition normally affecting children, as many have said, explains a lot. No wonder I have a disturbing affinity for Buddy the Elf, Willy Wonka, *Caps for Sale* and *Miss Rumphius*, the Muppets, Stuart from MadTV, and madcap pranks and childlike behavior.

As I prepare for battle (more on the language of war, valor, courage, struggle, winning, losing, and cancer later), I will be arming up not just to protect myself and carry on, but to raise awareness of this cancer in the hope that the lives of children affected shall not suffer.

More to follow...the story continues, and so does the music. The music never stopped...nor will it.

Magazines my friends brought me and a few nuggets

Monday, August 15, 2011

Harper's, Harper's Weekly, Time-Life's 100 Places to Visit in Your Lifetime, The Beatles Special Issue, Rolling Stone, Mountain Bike Magazine, Fame-Tiger Woods, (adult-comic series), Groundpounder, BikerChick Mag

And thank you friends for flowers and food! I will never look at those "1000 or 100 Paintings to See, Foods to Eat, Video Games to Play, Gardens to Visit, Music to Hear, Places to See, Golf, Fish, Visit, Have Sex, Dive, Swim, Ski, Hike, Kayak, Beers to Drink, Wines to Taste, Books to Read, Sports You Should Play, Things to Know... before you...." books again in the same way. I mean, who has the time?! Jeezum! Too much pressure!

There are nearly 10,000 entries on Amazon for such titles with "...before you..."

According to witnesses, when I was under anesthesia I was joking that I wanted to see more rainbows and unicorns on television and less garbage and violence. There indeed is a need for a hospital-stay Zen movie channel showing nothing but deer drinking from a stream, sunsets, sunrises, moonscapes and paint peeling. Much more soothing than the pabulum and din. Give me the NYC public access Yule log anytime!

My resolve is strong and my outlook bright, but I also have been thinking about those left behind...Jill Noss, Brigid Maire Clark, family members, Hugh Roberts, David Rothschild, and so many more...

A friend on the MRI of tumor: "is that a planet in your head?"

Letter to President of DHMC

Monday, August 15, 2011

Dear Dr. Weinstein,

I write to share my deepest gratitude and profound humility while being in the care of every single individual with whom I came in contact during my recent health cataclysm.

On On August 1, 2011, I was admitted to Dartmouth-Hitchcock with an immediate diagnosis of a brain tumor. The next morning a 4.3 cm spherical, malignant tumor was removed and identified as a WHO grade III anaplastic ependymoma. I will begin radiation shortly. I am a healthy, vibrant, fun-loving 43-year-old father of two beautiful daughters and am blessed by a cadre of supportive friends and family. That family now extends to DHMC.

As a former employee of Dartmouth College (working in advancement for the Dartmouth College Fund and at Thayer) and having served briefly but happily as a board member of the FNCCC, I had already been enamored with all things DHMC. A three-time, 100 mile Prouty participant, I became involved when a friend's father passed away of cancer and was cared for at DHMC.

I suppose my first connection, albeit somewhat circuitous, occurred when I was just a child. Dr. C. Everett Koop operated on me for an inguinal hernia (one of 17,000 such operations he performed in his career) at Children's Hospital in Philadelphia. Years later, when he was at DHMC, I shared with him that I recalled sitting on his lap thinking he was Santa Claus.

What I have relayed to friends and neighbors about my experience at Dartmouth-Hitchcock has become a mantra: not only did I receive the very best care from the very best professionals, but throughout the entire journey (one which has only begun), I was treated with care, kindness, and humanity. It is difficult to express in words how strongly I wish to extend my gratitude.

There are names I sadly will omit (I suppose I have an excuse with the anesthesiology team!) but to attempt the impossible I wish to mention and thank directly those I recall who were there for me and my family 110 percent:

Dr. Erkmen, Dr. Fadul, Dr. Mody, Dr. Spire, Dr. Bekelis, Dr. Kakoulides, Dr. Evans, Dr. Merlis, Dr. Guerin, Dr. Hampers, Dr. Jarvis, Amber Merrill, the entire neuro ward including nurses Debra Fitzpatrick, Wren, Maddie, Mike, Josephine, Patricia, Brett and Diane and the MRI team, the path lab, the records folks, the transport team, Lindsay, Rachel, Linda Mason, and those who brought me food, cleaned my room, and put up with my bad jokes. I know there are many more, and I wish I could thank them all personally.

Kindly share my note with any and all parties. I have copied a few friends and family members who have also been a part of this new unknown, and for whom I am grateful. Thank you to DHMC from the deepest depths of my heart and soul.

Sincerely,

Mark R. Green

"Laugh as much as you breathe and love as long as you live."
—Author unknown

Surgery redux: "Turn your face to the sun and the shadows fall behind you" —Maori proverb

Wednesday, August 17, 2011

"I am thankful for laughter, except when milk comes out of my nose."
—Woody Allen

Thanks again all for the love and support. I have so much to share and am grateful to those willing to listen. This event will *not* define me. It is *not* who I am. I will define it! Today's post leans heavily on the reportage and technical side of things. I have other things percolating, including the role animals seem to play in my spiritual world. So thanks for tuning in. I tried in vain to stream Mozart No. 6 K14 in G Major, but to no avail. Photo project en route as well.

There is, somewhere in my home, an illustrated children's book called *It Could Always Be Worse*, A Yiddish folk tale in which a beleaguered villager from the shtetl seeks spiritual guidance from his rabbi about the stressed state of affairs in his cramped, one-room domicile, where he lives with his six children, wife, and mother. As the story unfolds, the rabbi instructs the man not to clear his house but to fill it with more and more animals until chaos unfolds beyond the gentleman's ability to comprehend. Each time the man returns to the rabbi for more advice, he is told to collect more animals. At the very end, when the man is about to break, the rabbi tells him to now clear his house of all oxen, sheep, goats, chickens, and so forth. The refrain "it could always be worse" takes on new meaning as the man is given a fresh perspective on what he considered to be a miserable life. It could always be worse.

~

Yesterday was a visit to Dr. Fadul, professor of medicine and director of the neuro-oncology program, and Dr. Jarvis, assistant professor, radiation oncology. A kind, gentle man originally from Colombia, Dr. Fadul warmed my heart and soothed my soul. He was impressed with my speedy recovery and expressed concern for my family—my daughter Hannah in particular, who had been with me from the very beginning. He asked Barb if I was behaving, and she assured him that she had the taser set to high.

He then explained again that he was intrigued by the rarity of my cancer. It reminded me of a favorite quote I used to use when anxious, overprotective parents (I plead guilty to the crime… we all let our daddy-bear/mommy-bear claws out from time to time) armed with swaths of bubble-wrap would give teachers and staff headaches, thinking that their child was rare, super-special, and deserving of more attention at the expense of their peers. We call them scorched-earth parents, and fortunately for those of us working in the field, they represent a tiny fraction of the population—but account for 99 percent of the headaches.

"Each child is unique, just like all the rest."

All cancers are unique in their own way, as is the way in which individuals, friends, and family deal with the crises. While I am now armed with reams of literature on how to cope, deal with, address, manage, ameliorate, defend, protect, help, support, and care for this new reality, there are no rules or steadfast answers on "how to." Ultimately you just do what comes naturally. Some fight, some surrender. Some laugh, some cry, some withdraw, some seek others. Most, I believe, combine all of these elements, as it is indeed a roller coaster ride of emotion.

Moving away from the statistics and numbers, Dr. Fadul shared that he may see a case like mine once every two years or so. That this is a disease normally affecting children makes this rare. That the cancer did not occur in the spine, as it often does, makes this rarer.

That the tumor, normally found near the cerebellum, was growing in the supratentorium makes this rarer still. In many ways, I am my own statistic, as there is little data on these tumors in adults.

So the good news? The cancer is not in my spine, and thus I will probably not need a lumbar puncture. The PITA news? (PITA is a nickname coined by a friend whom I harassed in loving fashion. It stands for Pain in the Ass.) It is highly likely that, because the best outcome for this cancer is a "total gross resection" of the tumor, and because postoperative scans showed that while most of the tumor was scooped out (my words), there are signs that a small amount (2 to 4 percent) is still left inside, radiation alone (more on that in a moment) is not enough to kill what's left. So while I now have a few titanium screws and a plate in my skull (I am really beginning to dislike that word *skull*), they did not put a hinge on the replaced bone, which means a second surgery. Lord knows what they will find in there. I may ask them, in true *Wired* magazine fashion, if they might not consider installing a one-terabyte hard drive and a USB port when they get back in. My guess is that this idea will not seem completely absurd in a matter of years. Imagine going to work and installing your "work flash drive" with no need for a laptop! At the end of the day you replace it with your 500GB flash drive of music. Want to watch a movie? Have them install a wireless chip. Actually, forget the flash drive. It should all be wireless. Movies, GPS for driving, hiking, bicycling, recipes, music. I'm ready.

Here is a scan of my now empty space where the tumor grew...

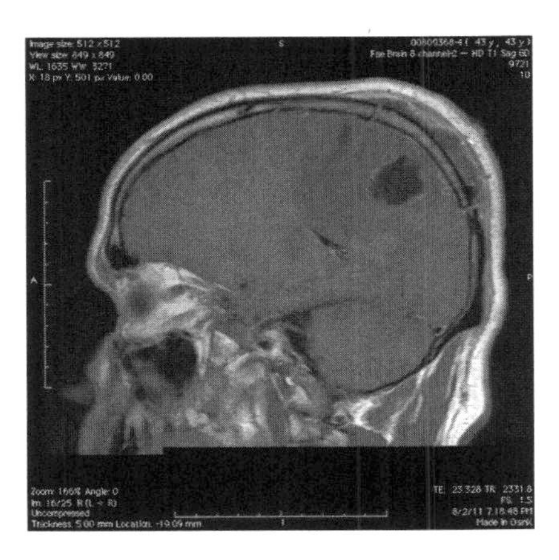

…and the bummer, on the image below: the white spot on the lower left near the "hole" is not scar tissue but the remnants of the tumor. Dr. Erkman is a master doctor and craftsman. At the time of surgery they had no idea what kind of tumor I had or whether it was benign or malignant, and they erred on the side of caution since getting at the tumor too aggressively could have resulted in serious consequences. It *is* brain tissue after all. While I am told the cancer will indeed grow back, there is no telling when or how fast at this point, but getting what's left will be an investment for the future. I may have some permanent left-side "deficit" depending upon what happens, but hopefully this will mean nothing more than that I need to be careful around fire and ice, as I might not be able to sense injury, heat, or cold. No big deal.

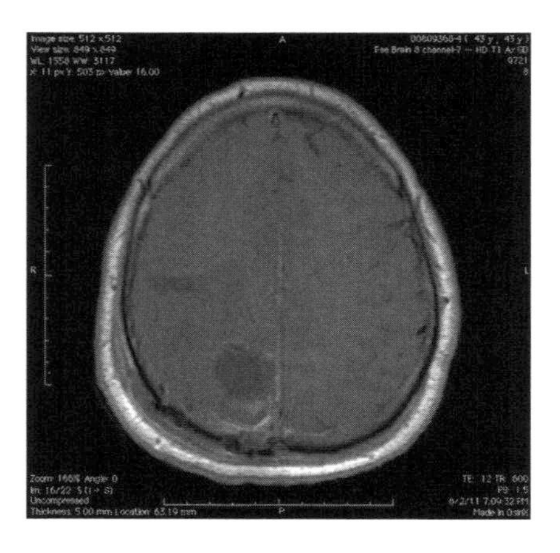

I was told that I would have been dead in a week, because the tumor, which was bleeding from within as aberrant cells sought blood sources, would have "herniated into my brain stem." Deep breath. Leos, being felines, have nine lives, and I've got a few left.

The next part of my visit was with the radiation team. I will endure six weeks of radiation after my second surgery. If that happens. I will lose my hair (not a big deal!), feel tired and perhaps nauseous, and look like I have a bad sunburn. It is very strange to receive material entitled "Brain Irradiation: Information for Patients." Yikes! For some reason the cult-film *Toxic Avenger* and Bruce Banner from *The Incredible Hulk* come to mind…

While there is risk of a secondary "radiation tumor" down the road, the risks are of course outweighed by the benefits. The dead and dying cells, called radiation necrosis, can be difficult to discern from growing cells on the MRI (I think I have this right), and I will have an MRI every three months for a year, every four months for another year, and every six months thereafter to keep an eye on things. If the cancer returns, we will cross that bridge when we need to. Since radiation treatment is usually a one-time gig, chemo or clinical trials, for which I will be eligible, are possible options.

So I left feeling a little like a character in a boxing movie. Up and fighting but perhaps a little punch drunk. "He's up, he's down, he's up again!" Dang, they have to go in again! As anyone who knows the film *Rocky* or who grew up in Philadelphia remembers, there was a time when every kid who had the chance would run up the steps of the Philadelphia Museum of Art and pump their fists in the air. If you were authentic, you might even wear a grey hooded sweatshirt and speak with a thick Rocky Balboa accent, screaming, "Adrian! Yo, Adrian!" I was there once, just for a moment. (My, how the Philly skyline has changed!)

In radiology they fitted me with a very cool Freddy Kruger-esque hockey mask, which will be my fixture for radiation. Designed to keep my head in place (okay, add ironic comment here:_____), it will also help target the appropriate beams.

All I could imagine was the agony of waiting endured by movie stars undergoing mask creation for such movies as *Planet of the Apes* back in the Roddy McDowell day. According to my old sci-fi mag *Starlog*, those masks took hours to create. This took less than 30 minutes. And yes, I felt like one of those crazy Mexican wrestlers à la *Nacho Libre!*

In other technical news, within the sixty pages or so of the initial report is an enormous amount of biological data. A few intriguing pieces include the pathology report detailing "right parietal brain tumor, fresh, with several tissue fragments of white-red neural tissue with areas of hemorrhage and necrosis," with "all pieces of brain tissue" (words together that do not sit well with breakfast), submitted in three cassettes. Because there was some question of additional cells different from the anaplastic ependymoma, possibly "oligodendroglial differentiation," they have sent the samples to the Mayo Clinic for further research.

The surgical report is equally fascinating. I know this may have a "look at me" voyeur/exhibitonist quality, but I am amazed at the science and carpentry. And I hope it helps understanding. The surgery was labeled "CRANI, for tumor, supretentorial, stereotactic computer-assisted navigational cranial intradural microscope use" for a hemorrhagic right parietal mass. Choice phrases like "hemorrhagic mass with surrounding edema" and "after prepping and draping in the usual sterile fashion, a local anesthetic of epinephrine was infiltrated into a linear incision. This was carried down with a #10 blade." Retractors, burr holes, elevating dura, "opened in a horse-shoe shape," "bone on back table was prepared with Leibinger-set titanium [my favorite!] plates and screws. This was used to affix patient's bone flap to his skull."

So I am off to Houston soon to see those who will offer their own experience and wisdom as to what lies ahead.

I cry, I laugh, I am irritable. I can't sleep very well. Steroids and seizure meds can have this effect as well as the usual adjusting-to-new-harsh-reality stress. I can't wait to get back to work, ride my bike, ski, kayak, and have a finely crafted margarita with fresh lime, Patron Silver, Cointreau, and a splash of Grand Marnier. All in due time.

That my head needs to be opened up again so soon is a drag, but I'll be paying it forward. My love goes out to friends and family and especially to the parents of children who suffer from this particular cancer.

Two thoughts to leave you with...

"The journey is the reward"
—Tao Proverb

"It goes to 11."
—Nigel Tufnel, *This is Spinal Tap*

The Swath and a debt of gratitude

Thursday, August 18, 2011

MRI of Love

"I have a simple philosophy: Fill what's empty.
Empty what's full.
Scratch where it itches."
—Alice Roosevelt Longworth

I don't know if you've heard of such incidents, but every once in a while there's a story of some mentally unstable individual who either hijacks a tank from an armory or takes an up-armored bulldozer and goes on a destructive rampage. Sadly, most of the time that person meets an untimely death, either by their own hand or by the authorities. But the image of an enormous bulldozer plowing over everything in its path is an apt metaphor for the past few weeks. And my guess is that Lord Voldemort or Sith master Emperor Palpatine was at the wheel of our uninvited assault vehicle.

Barb has described the experience as if we were trapped inside of a snow globe, turned upside down and shaken. The liquid and snowflakes are a whirling storm in which we are stuck. We are upside down. Those snowflakes will, of course, settle. But when? In time… in time.

The first thing that concerned me when the news was delivered of tumor/cancer, the thing that ripped me into shreds, shattered me into a million shards, was the well-being of my children, Hannah and Libby. I didn't care about anything else. My stomach became stone and my heart numb. And I all can think of now are the calamities suffered by families who have endured trauma. It hurts my heart. Soldiers back from war, environmental disasters, terrorism, victims of heinous crimes, accidents, disease, genocide. These are global horrors experienced daily with an impact zone that ultimately touches all of humanity. I believe this deeply.

By comparison, thinking along these thought-lines, I am happy, overjoyed, to be alive. Today I celebrated my birthday, and today was indeed a day to celebrate: I had a birthday! (Okay, without my desired margarita, but I can deal… six to eight more weeks… I think.…)

Yes, I cry. But to be honest I have not yet given myself enough time to mourn, it's been so much, so hectic. So much new information to download, a new language to learn. When tears do come, they come at night, alone, when I go downstairs, when I can't sleep and don't wish to keep Barb up. The steroids for swelling are fighting against my body's desire for sleep. Ultimately, with the help of the right music, I can find that place again and get back to the center. But sometimes I feel like I want to lift a house or a car and toss it over the bank. Some of that is the medicine, some is deeply seeded fear and anger. I know this, and I accept it, and in time will face and deal with it. In time…in time…and I will fight this, like the cancer, with love and humor. Loving your enemy has a new twist.

I have flashbacks of watching *The Incredible Hulk* on TV as a kid. Watching the trailer now, it's pretty freaky actually. Dr. David Banner, "physician, scientist," experiences his transformation into the Hulk as a result of overradiating himself during research. But in some strange way—and I think partially because as hokey as that show was, Bill Bixby (Courtship of Eddie's Father, etc. who sadly passed away in 1993 to prostate cancer)—played David Banner with a certain ’70s era humanity, I identify with the Hulk. He is large, green, grunts a lot and likes to run around with no clothes on, after all. On some level I would bet that many, especially men, identify with the subcutaneous rage of testosterone that sometimes simmers beneath. We all have our inner Hulk, as played by Lou Ferrigno (who is in real life a professional, partially deaf body-builder of note, but that is another topic entirely). So the landslide of events, combined with the steroids, combined with the physical trauma of having your head opened up and resealed with titanium plates and screws, certainly leaves one with some modicum of desire to release anger and frustration. Not toward someone, thankfully, but perhaps toward some inanimate object, with no harm done.

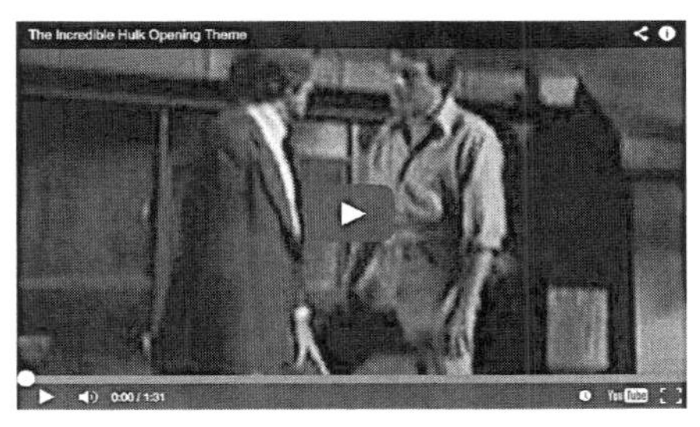

“Don’t make me angry.
You wouldn’t like me
when I’m angry.”
—David Banner, *The Incredible Hulk*

Ironically, I have recently taken to hitting golf balls as a form of relaxation and release. Given the toxic golf ball removed from my head, I now have a new reason to take out my aggression on golf balls (normally bicycling, music, food, skiing, and friends are my preferred drug of choice). That I must have another surgery bluntly sucks. But I am in great hands with the very best. And, as I have shared before, opening up my head again and electrocauterizing what is left of the tumor, followed by six weeks of radiation (which, according to what I’ve been told, will leave me nauseous, extremely tired, and without hair), pales in comparison to the dark cloud I will learn to live with for the rest of my life. In a larger sense, I am just damned lucky to be alive. Those crazy cancer cells! Bad cells. Bad cells.

The swath of chaos and destruction an event like this creates cannot be underestimated. Barb, a mother of two of her own and stepmom to mine, has a job. She has a life. A house to tend to, friends and family, her own day-to-day challenges that life brings us all. And now the tank has rolled through our home. It's all quite terrifying. I, half serious, have simply apologized. Hobbies, desires, dreams, vacation plans, calendars all thrown out of whack (but not canceled forever!). Countless hours on the phone tending to the details of the next visit to the doctors, life insurance issues (Word to the wise: lightning can strike at anytime; get whatever you can afford, now, pronto especially if you have children. *Now*. Did you hear me? *NOW*. Once you are diagnosed with such an illness you become uninsurable for life insurance.), retirement issues, financial concerns, a desire to get back to normal, or settle in to the new normal, whatever that is.

My parents, sister, aunts, relatives have been rock solid. My mother and father were here the day of the surgery and through the week. Dad, a steady, calm, loving presence, deeply concerned. Mom, dogged in her loving pursuit of ensuring I was receiving the very best care. My sister Kerrin, from afar, sending love and her own knowledge and access from her work as an editor for the National Comprehensive Cancer Network to help direct me to the right folks with this rare cancer. They have been more amazing than anyone could imagine. But they too are all blown to bits. Laura, my former wife and amazing mom to our amazing children, has also had her life turned inside out as the father of her children faces an uncertain reality. She has been there too from the start. Her partner and my friend, Dave, lends a steady hand of support.

My daughter Hannah, who on the second day of the event was on the eighth floor at DHMC talking to friends at Norris Cotton about helping to raise awareness of ependymoma cancer, has endured and seen more than any fifteen-year-old needs to as I slid downhill on August 1, vomiting and dizzy as the tumor exerted pressure within my head and began hemorrhaging. Libby, who came back from being away at Lochearn Camp for Girls to find her dad had a tumor and cancer, has been full of love and concern. Friends, former classmates, neighbors, colleagues new and former from near and far continue to be the wind in my sails as I glide into the unknown. And I am forever grateful.

This crummy turn of events has an impact on so many. Not only do I owe my friends and family a debt of gratitude, I owe it to them to live a full life and do what I can to help make the world a better place.

Last fall, Barb and I were on the subway in New York City. A seemingly homeless man waltzed up and down the subway car singing and chanting. I don't recall if he was fundraising, but I think he was, because I remember thinking here was a man engaged in the same work I was in, employing similar tactics in an upbeat manner. He didn't seem to bother anyone. He was polite and sweet. As he paced up the aisle, he looked at Barb. His eyes opened wider. He stopped. Looked at her. He looked at me. Looked at her again and turned to me and smiled a broken but gracious smile. "You're a lucky man. You're a lucky man," he repeated.

Later that evening, on a different subway car from a different station, there was that very same man. Again, he caught our eye, looked at both of us, turned to me and repeated what he'd shared earlier. "You're a lucky man. You're a lucky man." I think he was a shaman.

I am indeed a lucky man. In a million ways. And while right now I feel like the baker in the old Sesame Street clip—the one in which he proudly announces the pastry he's holding… until he trips and falls down the stairs in a mess of pies, cakes, and shakes—I will continue to make more pies. I will fall. But I will get up. Again and again.

...a rough one but helps smooth the jagged edges...

Sunday, August 21, 2011

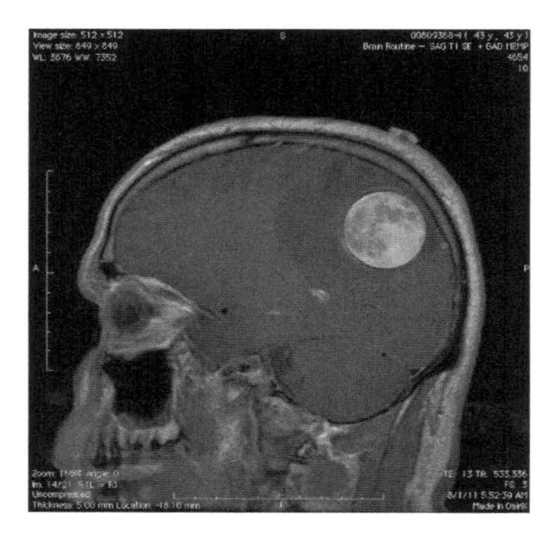

"Mark's Moon" by C. Bennett (Auntie C)

I have every intent on joining my friends, family and comrades-in-cancer to fight the good fight and push this boulder as close to the cliff as possible even if it will not fall off into the abyss without taking me with it. It's funny how much I wrestle with the language of cancer: battles to be fought with valor, courage, ferocity. Nearly every day an obituary shares the passing of a loved one who, after a "valiant, courageous, or brave" battle with "XYZ" disease/illness, mental or physical, was "laid to rest, met his/her maker, or shed his/her mortal coil." It's a harrowing thought, and since the moment the tiny meteor in my head decided to show itself, it has been a struggle to find the right language without falling into cliché. My years of Quaker schooling have made me wary of language with militant overtones. After all, I was raised, gratefully, in a household that banned even water pistols. While it seemed silly at the time, I salute my parents for raising me with conviction. At Abington Friends, as part of our Quaker studies, we participated in a seminar on how to register for CO (conscientious objector) status should we be drafted into one of Reagan's crazy escapades.

So implementing the language of war with my diagnosis was at first awkward. How quickly I realized what it was: a good war. There *are* good fights. A battle. I'll take it. That said, one of the most valuable pieces of advice I've been given was shared by a friend who visited recently with her own story of struggle, pain, and loss: "the hardest thing is to embrace the unknown." How true. It's a refrain that has been with me now every day and every hour.

As an aside, there have been, and will be, many words of wisdom and advice. So many of us have been touched by struggle and loss. Frankly, I really don't mind, since intentions are heartfelt even if when someone is suggesting that I partake in a raw-food diet (no, thank you!) or that using a cellphone will result in a tumor in the shape of the cellphone itself (iTumor?).

Actually, two of the sections I most desire from my daily bread of the *New York Times*, aside from Tuesday's science section, Wednesday's food/dining section, and the Sunday Book Review, are the wedding announcements on Sundays and the daily obituaries. The juxtaposition is often poetic. People beginning new lives, and existing lives coming to a close. I find it especially intriguing to read of the passing of individuals most of us have never heard of who have left some sort of indelible mark on the world. In just the past few weeks, we lost Robert Breer, a "pioneer of avant-garde animation"; Nancy Wake, "proud spy and Nazi fighter"; Ruth Brinker, who "gave AIDS patients meals"; and Marshall Grant, Johnny Cash's bass player. Locally, we may read about the life of a neighbor we never knew, or maybe did, and their passing makes us appreciate their own journey, whether filled with struggle and challenge or joy and happiness.

Yesterday was the first time I lost all control. It started last evening when I went to Harlow's Farmstand to see Rusty Belle play their terrific folk-boho (love them!). Two of the band members, Matt and Kate, also happen to be the children of my former boss and continued confidante Steve Lorenz and his wife, Nancie. The scene was perfect: beautiful music, fine food, great company, and a beautiful sunset accented by the green hills and farm fields. I took a walk. I was at peace but emotionally fragile. I began to contemplate my eldest daughter's words as she shared her feelings one evening. She wanted me to promise that I would be there for her wedding. To see my grandchildren. Not that this is anywhere near the immediate horizon, thankfully, but events like this tumor surgery/cancer force-feed all of us to think about the past, present, and future in ways never imagined. I bawled as I looked out upon the fields of corn and squash. It was a moan I don't think I've ever heard myself make. I felt nauseous, and my body began to shake. And suddenly I stopped. I had to. I'm still not ready for this, and not ready to let it all out. I'm scared as much as I'm strong. Sad as much as I'm happy. To draw on that fear and sadness every time I see friends, neighbors, and family would be physically, emotionally, and spiritually impossible. It would drain me to nothing. So this website is a way for me to share this experience as a purging, a purification, and a tool for learning as I try to unbury myself from a library of material that I did not ask for, with hope that it might help others understand. We have all been touched by loss, and we all need to be touched by the human element that makes us just that: human.

While I know I can be exceedingly sentimental and even mushy, I seldom cry. Yet I believe it would be of great benefit if we all had a good, solid cry on our emotional calendar now and then. Some are better at this than others. It feels good, a release. All that submerged emotion spewing out of the normally dormant volcano.

I can think of a few catalysts, right now, that invariably make me quake with sadness. A certain strain of Mozart, Bach, or Haydn. Cello Suites, violin sonatas. It's a physical and spiritual reaction, and given the right circumstances can send me over the cliff. Or the scene in the final episode of M*A*S*H, in which Hawkeye has been institutionalized with PTSD and is speaking with the beloved psychologist Sidney Freeman (expertly played by Allan Arbus, former husband of photographer Diane Arbus) after recalling a horrific incident on a bus.

Another scene, also from M*A*S*H, shows the very dear, paternally loving Lieutenant Colonel Henry Blake's honorable discharge, in an episode titled "Abyssinia." The resonance here is multifaceted: M*A*S*H reminds me of my youth and my parents as we all watched the series as a family; then there's Alan Alda, an avuncular figure, so acutely channeling his beloved character to a place we all fear—that of losing our minds; and there's the loss of a fictional yet very real character in Lt. Col. Blake. (who reminded my mother of her father, Captain Arnold Bennett, DDS). Really good television, of which there is little, is often best when there is an ensemble you feel a part of, rather than apart from.

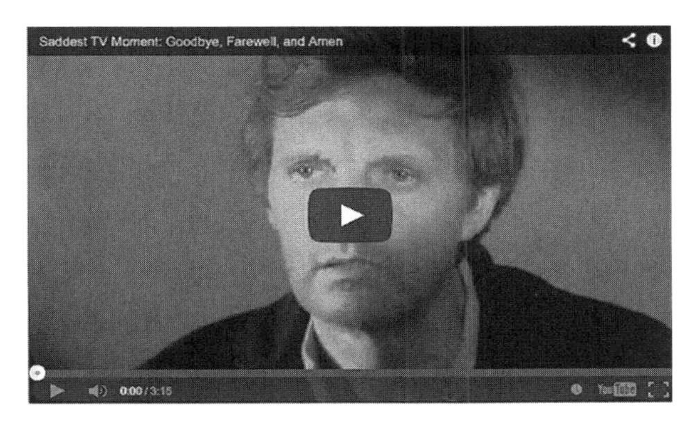

Another overwhelming moment that pushes my insides to collapse is the last scene in the last episode of *Six Feet Under*. The song "Breathe Me," by Sia, alone is exceedingly powerful. The ensemble cast of the series, which deals directly with our own mortality (among other themes), is extraordinary. In the end, that last episode looks into the future and shows the final moments of each cast member. It's quite simply awful, and moving, and is a trigger for an avalanche of emotion.

Finally, since I am on a tangent of digging into a space I normally cover up with humor and strength, I want to share, before Barb and I head out for some Tex-Mex in the very hot, humid, concrete sprawl of Houston (we go to MD Anderson tomorrow), that in the June 13 issue of the *New Yorker,* there is a piece of writing by Sarajevo-born, Chicago-based author Aleksander Hemon (Guggenheim Fellow, MacArthur "genius grant" winner, and author of *The Lazarus Project, The Question of Bruno, Nowhere Man,* and *Love and Obstacles*) that shook me to my deepest core.

His essay "The Aquarium: A Child's Isolating Illness" is a sink-to-your-knees account of his nine-month-old daughter succumbing to a rare form of brain cancer and his family's devastation. I held on to this piece, ripping it from the magazine. It was a brilliant and profoundly devastating work. With a sad twist of irony, at the time I read the piece, riveted, I had no idea of my own expanding tumor/cancer, one that normally afflicts children in their earliest years. Last night I read the entire piece aloud to Barb. It was midnight, and we cried together until 2:00 am, even though we needed to rise at 6:00 the next morning for the trip to Texas. The tears, I suppose, were a major step away from the sticky web of shock, fear, bewilderment, and denial in which we are still caught. I cannot think of any loss in any form, of any kind, like that of losing a child. None. Ever.

Having read Aleksander's horrific journey into the abyss of loss, along with that of his wife Teri, his other daughter Ella, and the beautiful Isabel, I have every hope of raising awareness of such brain cancers (which represent 1 percent of all cancers) so that others might gain knowledge, power, and resources to fight the good fight. As Aleksander emailed me today, after I shared with him my gratitude for his moving, painful share: "I hope you beat the bastard soon!" Thank you, Aleksander. I will. I will.

❧

Aleksander Hemon excerpt from *The Aquarium* as appeared in *The New Yorker* 6/13/2011:

> "One of the most despicable religious fallacies is that suffering is ennobling—that it is a step on the path to some kind of enlightenment or salvation. Isabel's suffering and

death did nothing for her, or us, or the world. We learned no lessons worth learning; we acquired no experience that could benefit anyone. And Isabel, most certainly did not earn ascension to a better place, as there was no place better for her than at home with her family. Without Isabel, Teri and I were left with oceans of love we could no longer dispense; we found ourselves with an excess of time that we used to devote to her; we had to live in a void that could be filled only by Isabel. Her indelible absence is now an organ in our bodies, whose sole function is a continuous secretion of sorrow."

"All life is an experiment.
The more experiments you make, better"
—Ralph Waldo Emerson

Monday, August 22, 2011

"Any idiot can face a crisis—it's day to day living
that wears you out."
—Anton Chekhov

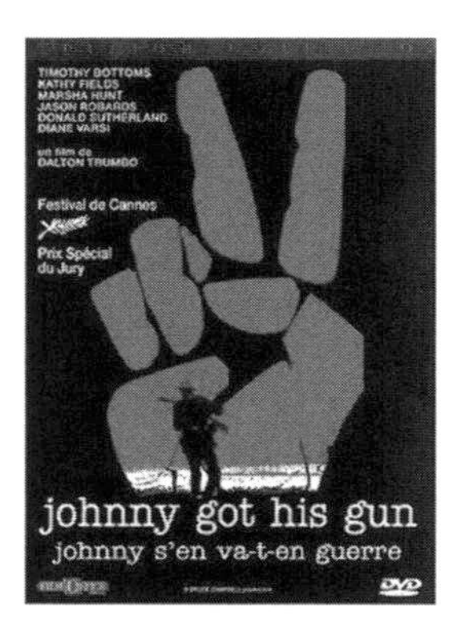

Of all the books I have read and films I have seen, none has left as indelible a mark on my heart as Dalton Trumbo's *Johnny Got His Gun*, perhaps one of the most virulent, passionate anti-war novels ever written. I recall I was a high school student at Abington Friends, where it was assigned by a passionate but deeply troubled teacher and Vietnam veteran, who years later took his own life. He assigned us other life-altering books, including Peter Singer's *Animal Liberation*, a book that was ahead of its time on the topic of animal rights, much as Upton Sinclair's *The Jungle* brought to light the horrid conditions for workers as well as animals in the Chicago stockyards (although Sinclair's intention was to write a tale of poverty and corruption of power).

Blacklisted during the McCarthy era in 1947, Trumbo, who later spent eleven months in a federal prison for contempt of Congress, was pushed to the sidelines of the literary establishment years after the book's publication on the eve of World War II in 1939. During this vicious era of fervent anticommunism, the very sad and undemocratic witch hunt of political activists, artists, musicians, writers, and the like touched all corners of the country. It was an ugly time for America—and such passionate fearmongering and hatred continues to rear its ugly head via Fox News, the Tea Party, Palin, Bachmann, O'Reilly, Limbaugh, and the rest of the extremely nasty side of the Republican party (the "hate-wing") anytime someone's ill-focused version of patriotism is perceived to be threatened, America's policies are questioned, or the status-quo is challenged (see: Freedom Fries, the NRA, Iraq War, gay marriage, etc., etc., ad nauseum).

In the novel—put to film in 1971 by Trumbo himself, with uncredited support from Luis Buñuel—a World War I veteran named Joe returns home from battle with the thoughts, memories, and images of the war still burning inside his brain. He is less than a corpse but, with the assistance of tubes and medicine, still breathing. He's a slab of meat, a torso with a brain, although nobody believes he's capable of thought, assuming he's a vegetable. It's brutal and very real. He has lost his limbs right up to the shortest of stumps. His face is gone (in the film, beautifully rendered in black and white, he's covered in gauze so we never see the gruesomeness) and he can't hear, speak, see, or taste. He has no mouth, no tongue, no teeth, no eyes, no ears, and no nose. He's able to move his head, and ultimately communicates by banging it in morse code. He can feel the touch of a hand, and I recall a scene in which a small spot on his forehead is caressed lovingly, leading his imagination to run to places he can now only dream of in between nightmares.

He replays his life in vivid detail despite his hopelessness. All we hear throughout the book, is the voice inside his head and flashbacks to the past. It is pure torture in its rawest form.

If there was ever a convincing argument against the savage machinery of war, the use of violence to solve problems, this book is it. (The films *Ghandi, Slaughterhouse Five, The Deer Hunter,*

Apocalypse Now, Fail-Safe, Catch-22, The Killing Fields, and *Romero* also come to mind, among many others).

I am again grateful to Abington Friends School: when I was in high school, they once rented an entire movie theater and gave us the day off from school to attend the three-hour and ten-minute epic film *Ghandi*, by Richard Attenborough, about one of the world's greatest heros, Mohandas Karamchand Gandhi. We followed up with a day of discussion and assignments. It was a brilliant and courageous "out of the box" educational effort.

If only the generals, criminals, terrorists, and warlords were able to watch these films with an open heart and mind—but then if this were the case, they probably wouldn't be generals, criminals, terrorists, and warlords. *Johnny Got His Gun* came to mind because ever since this whole strange event began to affect my functioning—due to hemorrhaging and the buildup of pressure from the expanding orb of aberrant cancer cells whose DNA had run amuck—I have been, with no irony intended, *thinking* a lot about that strange, gray matter giving me so much trouble. And I think about Joe the soldier. The what ifs, the what coulds, and the impossible thought of having my own brain waste away. It's sickening, frankly, but it only makes my resolve stronger. As I have shared, I will not let this cancer fight me or define me. I will define and fight it.

The human body is an astounding creation with a powerful dichotomy: we are as vulnerable as ants on the pavement. Our fate can be met at any moment and our existence obliterated. A piano could fall from above while we're walking down a city street. Lightning could strike. We could fall into the Grand Canyon or over a waterfall, as sadly occurs in our great parks with alarming regularity. And not much would be left. A red splotch. A mess of skin and bones. I simply cannot fathom how rescue workers, soldiers, military medical personnel, and others in health care and law enforcement, particularly those in the ER, on accident scenes, or on the battlefield cope with the grim and haunting devastation of managing the retrieval of bodies and parts. My guess is that no matter how strong or how numerous the coping tools provided, the emotional and spiritual scars never, ever fade. We owe a debt of gratitude to those who sacrifice their own well-being to clean up the aftermath of such devastation.

What a waste, many must think. What was once someone's daughter or son is no more. A woman carried this person in her belly for nine moths or so and created the person who is now being shoveled into a body bag. Recent heinous crimes in our small community, resulting in senseless death, have tested our collective resolve and my own continued inner conflict about the death penalty and punishment as, sadly, the march of unspeakable acts fills our airwaves, invades our print media, and scrolls across the screen.

Here I am, pontificating about the horror of war, while my first reaction to the news of two recent shootings was frontier justice: those who murder should be met with their own fate, perhaps in the same manner or worse.

And then I think of the quote "an eye for an eye makes the whole world blind." No easy answers here....

We are mere mortals, and our existence is no more or less important than the next creature. Believing otherwise is a foolish exercise, because in the end it's all the same. Ashes to ashes and dust to dust, whether you're a human, an ant, a squirrel, or a mountain lion. We are all just bodies, hopefully in motion.

On the other hand, we can endure and survive through astounding adversity. Sharks may rip off our limbs; we may lose our hearing and faculties of speech, sight, taste, and touch; and we may suffer great trauma to our hearts, brains, and bodies, and somehow through a fine blend of science and nature, blessings and miracles (if you so believe), we can come out the other side relatively intact. Our bodies are capable of compensating to a remarkable degree.

In a book that was required reading for Putney School faculty last year—at the recommendation of the most remarkable head of school, Emily Jones, who endured her own challenge with a brain tumor—*The Brain That Changes Itself: Stories of Personal Triumph from the Frontiers of Brain Science* takes on the notion that our brains are fixed and the mapping is permanent. Not so. It is now known that the brain is more elastic and malleable than we imagined. Those who lose sight do in fact compensate: their brains adapt and become stronger in other areas such as smell and touch. Space, as William Shatner quipped before every episode of Star Trek, may be the final frontier, but I think that space includes what lies within the quarter-inch-thick dome resting on our shoulders. (Funny new fact: "the average thicknesses of the skull in men was 6.5 millimeters, but 7.1 mm in women.") Our brains are the greatest unknown and we are learning more (with our brains, no less) every day about this vastly uncharted territory. Let the journey begin.

I'm off to MD Anderson to see, with the endorsement of the DHMC team, Dr. Mark Gilbert, a leader in the field of this particular cancer. Much thanks for reading and joining me for the ride…

Too much perspective...

Wednesday, August 24, 2011

Nigel Tufnel:
"It really puts perspective on things, though, doesn't it?"

David St. Hubbins:
"Too much, there's too much @#$%ing perspective now."

—From *This is Spinal Tap* (scene at Graceland)

I took an aptly named sleeping aid aptly named Ambien and went to sleep, settling into an ambient state of mind and body. My steady cocktail of Dilaudid (Elvis's drug of choice) for pain, steroids to reduce swelling from surgery, and Keppra for controlling potential seizures had created a sleepless monster out of me. I love the description for Keppra, also known as levetiracetam: used for "decreasing abnormal excitement in the brain." Abnormal excitement?! What, pray tell would that be? Fortunately I am now tapering the use of the painkiller and steroids until the next surgery, though I'm continuing the anti-seizure meds. But I had to take the Ambien. I. Had. To. Sleep. My brain, overwhelmed with the download of several terabytes of new information and a language I knew not how to speak, along with the emotional torrent from stress, fear, sadness, and anticipation, was keeping me awake. My body was exploding with more than normal energy, but since having my head sliced, burr holed, repaired with titanium screws and plates, and sealed with a medical-grade caulk called Durabond ("weather sealed for your protection!"), I've been unable to participate in normal, strenuous physical activity and have had to be cautious about too much blood flowing too fast to or from my brain (written with a slight grin).

Walks and careful wades in the pool and swimming hole have been the most I can muster safely. I was pleased to hear that the best outcome after radiation is the level of physical activity a patient engages in during and after treatment. As I noted earlier, there is something I love, for lack of a better word, about the excerpt from the surgical report that reads "the bone on back table was prepared with Leibinger-set titanium plates and screws. This was used to affix patient's bone flap to his skull." Cool, I think. Wow. How very...cool.

I had taken Ambien once before. An old and dear high school friend I was visiting in Seattle had offered it as a salve for the red-eye I was about to take back to New England. He warned me, "You won't remember anything, so be careful." How true. I had to change planes in Chicago around 3:00 am. To this day, I don't remember waking up, rolling my carry-on off the plane, getting to the next gate, or settling into the connecting flight. Apparently the things that can happen under the influence of Ambien include walking, eating, emailing, texting, and other "activities," with no recognition later of said acts. That's a *big* "hello how are ya?" isn't it?

Knowing that the best outcome relied on sufficient, quality rest, I waved the white flag of surrender to modern pharma, having never been one to enjoy taking pills of any kind save for those sickly-sweet but yummy-flavored Flintstone vitamins. (Yabba Dabba Doo!) The sleeping-pill biz is an incredible, multibillion-dollar industry, and I dined with, at the late Lever House in NYC, the very funny, nattily dressed Englishman David Southwell, owner of Sepracor, maker of Lunesta, on one my fundraising junkets. He's just a savvy businessman doing business, quite well, I might add. (He's also very philanthropic.)

Even after a lifetime of asthma, I still resist taking in the daily recommended inhalation of Advair 250, to which I owe relatively stable lung function after years of feeling like I was breathing through a coffee-stirrer. Asthma, pun intended, sucks. After too many visits to the ER unable to breathe, I leave behind a tattered laundry list of medications and alternative remedies spinning like a whirling dervish of trash on a city sidewalk.

Theo-Dur, Prednisone, Azmacort, Singulair, all stored in pill form or contained, aerosolized, within a colorful delivery system, a contraption apparently designed by some stoner-engineer-artist with a CAD machine to mimic, in plastic pastels, the smoking paraphernalia found at your local head shop. "Duuuude, nice...i-n-h-a-l-e-r!"

Of my more memorable ER visits, including those in Sedona, Arizona, Keene and Littleton, New Hampshire and Philadelphia, Pennsylvania, the midnight run to Fletcher-Allen Hospital in Burlington, Vermont, was perhaps the most Woody Allenesque. (Why does so much of my life seem Woody Allenesque?) It was just after midnight, January 1, 1990, and I had been seeing an artist fifteen or so years my senior. I was twenty-three; she, probably forty or so, was what would now be considered a "cougar." She looked and dressed like a mash-up between Joni Mitchell and Rickie Lee Jones. She was fun to be with, on a post-divorce tear and completely insane. But I was just out of college and living near a terrific city, working multiple jobs, so to me we were simply having a pleasant time... I think we went to the Front (now defunct) or Nectar's (where I had seen an as yet relatively unknown band called Phish several times), and then to her apartment in downtown Burlington. Cats, or rather their dander, are the death of me, but being smitten with her, I chose to ignore this known danger (among other signs I ignored, but never mind). Almost immediately, her feline friends sent me into a full-blown asthma emergency. I was sweating profusely, red-faced, as I gasped for air. My lungs were in high gear, and my throat was closing. I couldn't breathe. We raced up the hill to the hospital. As she sat next to me in the hospital bed, stroking what was then a fuller mane of hair on my head, the doctor asked how old her son was. "Oh. He's not my son. He's my boyfriend." For a variety of reasons, the romance didn't last.

During this "postgraduate year," in which I declined a teaching position and applied to the Peace Corps, leaving me in a state of career limbo, much to my parents' chagrin, I was a part–time ski bum at Smuggler's Notch, which got very old very quickly. When I wasn't working or skiing, I was busy hiking, fishing, and bicycling on my own, hanging with happy-go-lucky but not-that-motivated kids from Johnson State College, or riding the chair lifts with sad, alcoholic, divorced guys who were the age I am now (44), who only talked about moguls, house-painting jobs they had or wanted, the careers they used to have, and the ski bunnies they had "had." It quickly became depressing. They skied for free as "Ambassadors of the Mountain" or with the ski patrol. But I loved hanging at the Plum and Main and the Vermont Studio School in Johnson and at Jana's Cupboard and the Brewski in Jeffersonville. I worked waiting tables at Smuggler's and Banditos Mexican Café with a cast of characters worthy of a reality show and an owner who snorted his profits up his nose. Yikes.

When the snowstorms were bad, rather than go back to Jericho, where I lived, I would drive my faded blue, rusty, completely unsexy bread-box of a Toyota SR5 4WD wagon (those were ugly cars) covered with the requisite political bumper stickers up the mountain road of Route 108 as far as it could go before the snow blocked passage. The sound of crusty ice, rock, and snow scraping the undercarriage as I barreled up the climb signaled my stop. I would recline the seats to make a bed, unfurl my sub-zero down midnight blue North Face sleeping bag with that sleeping bag smell of wood smoke and faint mildew, pop Neil Young (Everybody Knows This is Nowhere, Zuma or Decade) in my boom-box, and settle in for the night with a journal and a Catamount ale. Ensconced in my little world, with the moon bouncing light off the milky ice-covered fields and road, I was in bliss.

This car didn't even have a built-in cassette player. I had arrived in Vermont with my beloved emerald-green VW Scirocco, a graduation present purchased used in upstate New York for $2,000. It was a two-door sporty thing and had a great stereo and sunroof. As I negotiated with the seller, an old farmer who had a used-car business on the side, I heard a phrase for the first time that I will not forget: when I offered a lower price, he smiled and exclaimed with no hint of meanness "Well, buddy, don't try to Jew me down, it's a fair price." I think I was too bewildered by the comment to realize just what he was saying, and realizing the guy was an idiot anyway, I bought the car. Later the moment sunk in. Wow. That was really bizarre. Ick. Why? "Jew me down?" *Really?* I should have showed him my horns.

Scirocco means desert wind, and you will be hard pressed to see many of these sports cars on the road anymore, although I believe Volkswagen may be reviving this model. My car, after only six months of ownership, met its sad demise when I slid on black ice down an embankment, rolling over softly, gracefully, down a short, frozen, grassy knoll, landing upside down in a creek bed on my way to a small acoustic concert at the Daily Bread Bakery and Café in Richmond where I also worked part-time. Just before the accident, I had inserted a tape and hit rewind. As I crawled out of the partially submerged car, the Tailgator's rockabilly song "Brown Eyed Girl," with a great, fuzzy, raucous guitar intro, blared from the speakers. The engine was off, but the battery still worked, at least for the moment. With the headlights piercing the steam from the boiling engine, now partially submerged in water, and the moon above, the scene was surreal. I recalled the movie version of Stephen King's Christine. The car was still alive! Sadly, it did not survive. My Scirocco. My desert wind was still.

I was living in Jericho, Vermont, diagonally across from Joes' Snack Bar ("#16 your hot dogs and fries are ready!" I could hear from my window) and writing local newsworthy bits part-time for the "The Mountain Villager—Made in the Shade of the Mountains," whose offices were in the basement of an old red mill. I got to know the ghost of Snowflake Bentley and interviewed local Vermonters of note, including a wonderful artist-author, Tracey Campbell Pearson, and then-governor Madeleine Kunin while watching a performance of "L'Histoire du Soldat" by Igor Stravinsky at the Inn at Essex. What an amazing, wonderful woman she was (and is!).

I did a stint waiting tables at Chequer's Restaurant in Richmond where the owner Forrest, a mad, crazy chef, would often cook in an apron and no pants, chasing the waitresses around with an artfully carved, phallic carrot (the largest he could find) while his sweet but beleaguered and significantly younger wife Melissa ran the business and resisted the temptation to drown him in the fryolator. Ben Cohen and Jerry Greenfield, of Ben and Jerry's, were neighbors and would often stop by for a meal. This was during the height of the company's fame, before they ditched the "no employee makes more than seven times the lowest-paid person" policy and the Dutch conglomerate UniLever bought them out. They often ordered, gluttonously, an entire side of the menu. Thankfully, I think they are living a much healthier lifestyle now and their arrangement with Unilever, unique at the time, has allowed for some autonomy. Ben and Jerry's as a company has not, thankfully, lost its soul.

I was also a bank teller at the now defunct Bank of Vermont, a pool cleaner with a business that seemed to serve mostly wealthy

Canadians, and a construction worker on the I-89 span over the Winooski River bridge. In construction, I spent the days making good money for risking my life, wearing a hard-hat, goggles, and earplugs with a 200-pound drill bit pounding the concrete into the river not too far from my head—illegally, I'm sure. My job was to place the large chunks into a front-end loader with dust and debris swirling around me. I was tethered, rock-climber-style to some random piece of the bridge lest I fall off (sorry, Mom!).

One of my most memorable moments from any workplace was working alongside an enormous, cue-ball-bald construction worker with several missing teeth and no shirt, adorned in what was probably an XXL pair of sweat-soaked, filthy denim overalls. He looked like a cross between Curly from the Three Stooges and Mr. Clean, but not as handsome. Not at all, in fact.

At one point he stood there, looking eight-feet tall, like an extra from a slasher film, shouting in a southern but mysterious drawl over the din and chaos of heavy equipment to a group of grunts, including myself: "Yuh boys! Yuh boys know where I ken geet sum pooooon-tang? Whas thu mattur w' yuh boys? Are yur wimmen all corrrrn-fed?" And he said it again just for good measure. Louder this time, to be sure we heard him. I don't think any of us "boys" were able to respond. It took a long time for me to fully comprehend what he was saying. I don't believe I'd ever heard anyone use that word in a sentence (okay, maybe when I was in middle school and experimenting with touching the edges of filthy words, as many kids do), nor did I at first interpret the allusion to the fact that perhaps he felt, erroneously, that all of the women of Vermont were fed corn like our bovine population. Holy smokes, I thought, I am in the twilight zone.

Back to the dream. The Ambien. My dislike for taking medication. The visit to Houston.

Soon after the Ambien, I was carried away, flying, soaring, floating, and drifting through the air and down rivers unknown. I knew not which direction I was headed, with all of my inner navigational components set to autopilot. I was at the mercy of the medicine. The problem is that I'm still not sure, as I write on the flight back to New England, whether any of this is real. Am I in a dream state? At the very least, I want my month of August back. The planned vacation with Hannah and Libby to California with my cousin. The weekend getaway to Maine with Barb. Getting back to my wonderful job at Putney. Seeing my friends and family under different circumstances. That's all on hold as I climb out of the wormhole in which we seem to be stuck.

The Ambien did wear off this morning, but my head is awash in fear of the great unknown, hope for what could be (what *will* be… I *think* I can, I *think* I can…I *know* I can, I *know* I can!), and heretofore incomprehensible compassion for what I witnessed.

In Texas, everything is bigger: big cars, big trucks, big horns, big horns on cars and trucks, big hats, big boots, big (fake) breasts, big steaks, big highways, big universities, big oil, and big medical centers. There is virtually no easy public transportation. Whereas taking a train to the Sea-Tac airport from downtown Seattle costs less than five dollars, there is really no way to get from Bush International to downtown without a sixty-five-dollar cab ride. It is the land of the great automobile. But going to MD Anderson for a second opinion was supported by the great doctors at Dartmouth Hitchcock and was unquestionably the right thing to do.

There is an adorable joke about a Texan and a Vermonter. A Texan, with his big hat and boots, is boasting to an old Vermonter about how big things are in Texas. "You know, old man, where I come from, my land is sooo big that I can get in my car and drive all day and not reach the other end of my property! *That's* how big Texas is." The Vermonter, nonplussed, looks at the Texan and says, in a humble Vermont accent, "Ayup, I used to have a car like that too!"

Having arrived at MD Anderson, I still wasn't sure if I'd awakened. Perhaps I was still under the cloudy effects of the Ambien.

MD Anderson is the largest cancer center in the world, the largest hospital in the United States, and one of the leading centers of research and treatment of all cancers, including mine. There are over 17,000 employees. In 2010, there were nearly 24,000 hospital admissions; 1,132,338 outpatient clinic visits, procedures and treatments; 61,783 surgery hours; 538,514 diagnostic imaging procedures; 7,884,053 pathology/laboratory medicine procedures; and 1,009 total active clinical research protocols. With $3.3 billion in revenue in 2010, they also received nearly $550 million in research funding through grants, contracts, and philanthropy. The complex resembles a small city. It is, in every way, remarkable. Mind you, I love my DHMC.

Annually, in this country of 312,000,000 people, less than 100 will have a WHO (World Health Organization) grade III anaplastic ependymoma. Of those 100 or so, even fewer will have it in the brain, as it often goes to the spinal column. Looks like I won the brain cancer lottery. I will continue the expert treatment at Dartmouth-Hitchcock, to which I owe a deep debt of gratitude. I am a lucky man. But visiting MD Anderson was a critical step in this early stage of the journey as we amass information and expert opinions.

"It was like entering a frenzied airplane terminal, except everyone there had cancer," exclaimed Barb. We left the hotel in an enormous black van with a pair of four-foot-wide Texas Longhorns affixed to the grille. It was hot. Houston has been experiencing 100-degree weather for over a week. Water mains had been cracking daily. It's hard to breathe. The place isn't so much a zoo as a busy airport terminal at its peak.

Walking inside, I was overcome by yet another wave of emotion. My legs became weak (again), and I held back from breaking down. Everywhere were people either being cared for or caring for cancer-afflicted people: children, the elderly, and the middle-aged. People of all colors, races, ethnicities, women in burqas, orthodox Jews, women in saris, and families in Native American dress. It was a sea of cancer. People with masks covering up cancers of the face, tongue, jaw, neck, and head. Partially shaved heads, odd fixtures and contraptions. A parade of IV trees, liquids offering sustenance, remedy, stopgaps, and pain relief.

I recalled the scene from *Toy Story* in which a mean, disturbed child named Sid has mutilated, desemboweled, and reconstructed his toys into objects of horror and despair. It was the Island of Misfit Toys, with cancer. Or perhaps I was watching, with the various styles and patterns of shaved heads, outtakes from Penelope Spheeris's paean to punk rock, *The Decline of Western Civilization.* There were hundreds of internists, nurses, doctors, volunteers, and staff milling about, all there for the same purpose: to help others.

Mind you, I do not intend for this to be a critique. It is not. Nor am I making fun of what I saw. It was not at all grim. I would argue the opposite. It was hopeful. People were there quite literally from all over the globe, at one of the best cancer centers in the world, for the same reason: to get better. To buy time. To inspire. To give and to receive. But it was an enormous, undeniable, unavoidable reality check. It was a shock to the system. I'd been initiated into a club to which I did not apply nor wish to become a member. And suddenly, I am a member. Overnight. A tumor. A cancer. In this case, one that's incurable, for which there is little data, and that requires fighting the odds with every fiber of my body and soul. And I will win. With a total gross resection (full tumor removal) during craniotomy, there's a 60 to 70 percent chance the cancer will return based on eight-year outcomes. That's all the data they have. But this also means that 30 to 40 percent of adult ependymomas after TGR haven't recurred after eight years. (This data is from those who have participated in the Outcomes project, which is why the work of CERN is so critical.)

With a sad irony, one Barb immediately recognized, the name of the hospital section we were in was "the Aquarium," just like in Aleksander Hemon's New Yorker piece. It was haunting. Walking into the cafeteria, an enormous food court, one could have everything from Asian to salad bar, Chik-Fil-A (an obscenity) to Texas-style BBQ. When you have cancer, as much as one should eat as healthfully as possible, I suppose there is also a place for guilty pleasures. I had the brisket, be damned!

We spent two days winding our way through the maze and haze of insurance protocols, living wills, scheduling, and amassing even more information. A sweet woman from Jewish Family Services came by with mandelbrot (just like grandma's!). A social worker called. We spent hours sorting things out with the business office.

And finally, we met with Dr. Mark Gilbert, the man we had come to see. He and his team were remarkable in their knowledge, care, and concern. He shared that he had two primary findings and questions. First, he discussed the need for a higher-resolution MRI using a 3-Tesla rather than the usual 1.5-Tesla MRI. Even MD Anderson, we were told, does not always use 3-Tesla MRIs. It all depends upon what's available at the time and what's needed. A better MRI will help gauge whether the white spot inside my brain is residual tumor, requiring another craniotomy to complete the removal, or simply necrotic (dead) tissue or blood. The second critical piece was to determine whether proton or photon radiation is necessary. This morning we saw a radiation oncologist, Dr. Brown, another excellent, kind, top doctor, who, after studying my case, thankfully shared that he felt that photon therapy, a more generalized and widely used radiation therapy, would be appropriate given the location and nature of the cancer. Proton therapy, which is available in only thirty-seven locations worldwide and only nine in the United States, including MD Anderson, University of Pennsylvania, and Massachusetts General,is a more precise way to deliver radiation and promises better results, depending on the type and location of cancer. In my case, photon therapy will work just fine, so Dartmouth Hitchcock, where my friends and new family are, it will be. So, (1) determine after the next MRI if surgery is needed (probably) and (2) begin, after time to heal following surgery, six weeks of radiation therapy to try to destroy what remaining cancer cells are left hiding. And then we wait and see. Forever. And ever. Amen.

At the end of our first very long and taxing day at MD, we called the hotel for our shuttle. Again, a black SUV with ginormous long horns attached to the front of the car pulled up. (Barb and I have decided that our next car will be a Mini-Cooper with similar gargantuan long horns attached.) There was another couple returning to the same hotel in the car, and they obliged when we asked if we could join them. It was clear at the outset they were together in a way that only couples (at least, some couples) walking through trauma can look. Close. In love. Slightly sad. And holding each other close as if protecting each other from the elements. They were perhaps five or ten years older than us, early fifties perhaps, with a warm presence. They were both survivors, even if only she had cancer. They beamed love and hope. As we chatted, we learned quickly that we were all part of this strange new club, the one to which we did not apply nor wish to be members. But the humanity between us was so real, so moving. They were veterans of sorts. They looked at us knowingly, lovingly. With tears welling up between us, we shared our stories.

She had an extremely rare form of breast cancer and had come from Kentucky to MD Anderson for treatment. Afterwards, they had rented an apartment in Houston so she could undergo the requisite six weeks of radiation therapy. Now they were coming to MD every three weeks from Kentucky for a clinical trial that will last through November. They nodded knowingly as we told them our story.

The freight train that had crashed through our home only a few weeks ago had been on the same path as the one that passed through their home. They'd picked up the pieces and glued them together with hope and love. By the time we arrived at the hotel, we had exchanged phone numbers and were holding each other close, tears welling up between all four of us as we said our goodbyes with warm embraces. We could all barely hold it together. These sweet, dear people we had never met were now kindred spirits. We were part of a new family. We promised each other we would get together again should we find ourselves back in Houston. Or Kentucky. Or New Hampshire. Or anywhere. Because now we know. We are not alone. We are not alone.

Life is funny, but not ha ha funny
—EELS, "3 Speed"

Saturday, August 27, 2011

I will show you fear in a handful of dust.
—T. S. ELIOT, *The Waste Land*

Imagine being told that tomorrow morning you are leaving for a remote, faraway land where you don't speak the language and you must learn to read, write, and comprehend the mother tongue. You have less than 24 hours.

Or imagine you're in a library looking for books in your favorite section. Perhaps architecture, music, political science, environmental studies, or prose. There's a tremor. The lights above you begin to flicker, and before you can do anything about the earthquake, you find yourself trapped beneath several bookcases. You are quite literally being smothered by books, magazines, and brochures. And the worst part? It's a section you normally avoid.

It that shall be named!

A friend, who experienced her own tragic loss years ago, shared with me that, just as Albus Dumbledore convinced Harry Potter to "own" Lord Voldemort ("He Who Must Not Be Named") and speak his name, it was important for all of us to speak the name of that which afflicts and has invaded our lives. For us, spoken with the sickly, Voldemort-esque hissing undercurrent of resentment: "Cancer. Tumor. Brain Cancer. Anaplastic Ependymoma grade III."

"Always use the proper name for things. Fear of a name increases fear of the thing itself" explained Dumbledore to Harry in *The Sorcerer's Stone.*

In my black, overstuffed, Timbuk2 messenger bag, on our night stand, on our kitchen table, and in the car, which now overfloweth, we have a new library from which Barb and I come up for air when we can.

Magazines from DHMC and MD Anderson as well as a free (bonus!) subscription to *Cure: Cancer Updates, Research, and Education.* Pamphlets on "Patient Advocacy," "Social Work," "Oncology and Your Diet," "Ependymoma: Focusing on Brain Tumors" (from the American Brain Tumor Association), and, my favorite, "Ways of Giving to MD Anderson." As a development professional, I winced and smiled simultaneously. A perfect captive audience. Good work, advancement team!

Also included were several nicely produced brochures, some fifty pages or more, tabbed and indexed: *At Your Service Handbook for Patients, Welcome to MD Anderson: Where Your Needs Are Our Concern*, *Patient Handbook from the MD Anderson Brain and Spine Center, The National Cancer Institute's Support for People With Cancer Series: Taking Time,* and another from the same series titled *Radiation Therapy and You* (published by NIH and the US Department of Health and Human Services), *ABCs of Cancer at MD Anderson*, and perhaps most remarkably, and inexplicably, a beautiful package from the American Cancer Society with organizational folders for bills, insurance, medical questions, reports, and so forth, as well as a very thorough sixty-page booklet on *Brain and Spinal Tumors in Adults.* This was received three days after my initial surgery, and the shock value was akin to receiving, unsolicited, your first mailing from AARP.

Along with the trove of printed material, the online resources are daunting, impressive, scary, and ultimately a useful tool if applied with caution. We all have differing abilities to sift and sort through the web. Whereas one friend might find an exceptionally obscure but relevant medical abstract, another might find some well-intentioned (or not) but completely out-to-lunch holistic remedy. The internet has sadly become a monster for the marketplace, and cancer as an industry, including online, is a multibillion-dollar enterprise. Following the initial trauma and subsequent overwhelming diagnosis, we were told by many friends, family, and medical professionals to stay off the internet until we know more lest we become sucked into the vortex of misinformation that begets fear, confusion, and loathing. I did my best to abide, save for one moment early on when my eyes locked on the grim statistics of morbidity for this particularly cunning and rare disease. I have had no problem downloading and processing the thousands of virtual information trails leading to answers, as I feel I have a fairly capable BS meter. I have even watched medical videos on brain surgery and the removal of similar tumors. It helps me understand the nature of things. Yes, sometimes it makes me queasy, but the benefits of learning outweigh any induced nausea. Watching how the head is stabilized, it's no wonder my temples hurt as they clamped me into a Mayfield halo!

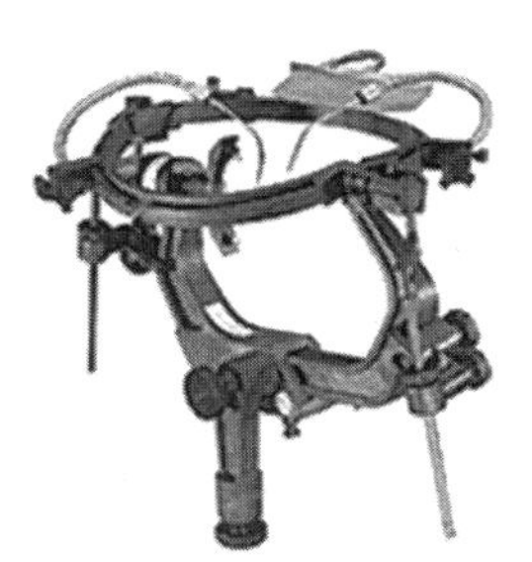

Brain surgery appears to be akin to trying to cauterize and sew up a moving jellyfish, as the brain is indeed moving during surgery, pumping blood to keeps things going. This is one organ they cannot shut down during a procedure. Watching surgeons carve out a bone flap was like watching very sophisticated sculptors or master carpenters at the peak of their craft. And now my head has more titanium than my beloved bike. Buzz, drill, cut, saw, screw. Dr. Erkmen and his team are not only deft, brilliant surgeons, they are master craftsmen and women. Art and science in matrimonial bliss.

Wordplay: My empty space is now filling up with a whole new language. Words that have been woven into my newfound dialect include: craniotomy, Mayfield halo, dura, skull, 1.5-Tesla and 3-Tesla MRI, salvage therapy, proton beam, photon beam, chemotherapy, clinical trials, nausea, radiation burn, radiosurgery, grade II, grade III, anaplastic ependymoma, glioblastoma (GBM), metastatic brain tumor, oligodendroglioma, glioma, astrocytoma, glioblastoma IV, subependymoma, cerebral spinal fluid (CSF; I *dread* that phrase), oncology, radiology, debulking, DuraBond, survivor, palliative care, living will and testament, prior approval, intensity-modulated radiation therapy, 3D, catheter, IV, leviticeram, hydromorphone, total gross resection, supratentorium, posterior fossa, ventricle, social workers, CT scan, cancer. And of course if I were to sum up everything I have written, to its most base, primal level? Apologies to those offended by foul language, but here it is: F**k. F**k. F**k… F**k!

I am blessed and grateful to so many people for their outpouring of love and support not just to me but to Hannah and Libby, Barb, my parents, and Laura. I know I have been included in countless prayer circles, prayers, love expressed in cards, food, flowers, texts, emails, phone calls, and visits. I wish with every fiber of my being I could repay these gifts tenfold, for I am humbled.

Among the well wishes, prayers, and gifts, two comments left me laughing aloud. One was a text sent to my phone immediately after surgery from a close friend and former colleague who had interrupted his vacation on Nantucket to fly back to New Hampshire/Vermont and visit me and family in the hospital. "Now that you have a new hole in your body, may I suggest keeping your fingers away from this one?" Another was from a former student and friend with whom I still keep in touch. He is a sculptor living in Rhode Island and creates incredible art using industrial-grade cables, literally knitting them together into art forms with enormous construction equipment. His email read, quite simply:

"Dude! Brain cancer? A tumor the size of a golf ball? F**k!

Seriously, f**k! Wow. Umm…f**k!"

What I am trying to learn is that it's okay to let it all out…but how? And when? And to whom?

Oh, and by the way, my visit to Houston at MD Anderson was nothing short of breathless, in every way. Upon returning, I received another, higher-resolution MRI (3-Tesla) in addition to learning that photon radiation, not proton, is necessary. Monday morning I meet with the incredible Doctors Erkmen and Fadul to decide on next steps: the possibility of a secondary surgery to remove what is left of the cancerous tumor and then determine the subsequent course of radiation.

The scans below, which are eerily beautiful, appear to show residual tumor, but that is my observation only. We will hear the opinions of the doctors at DHMC as well as Dr. Gilbert in Texas by the end of the day Monday. Bon voyage mes amis!

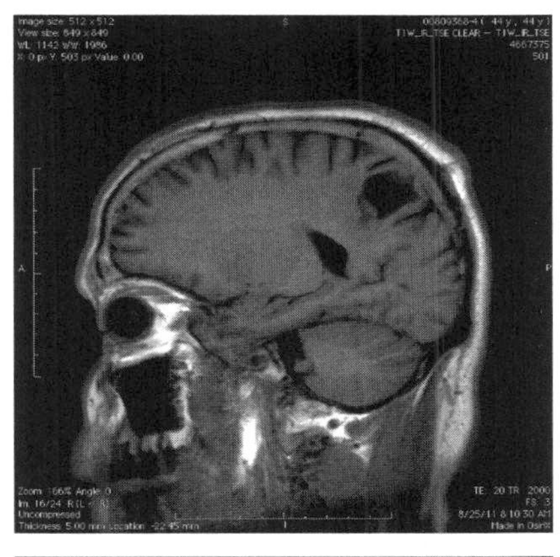

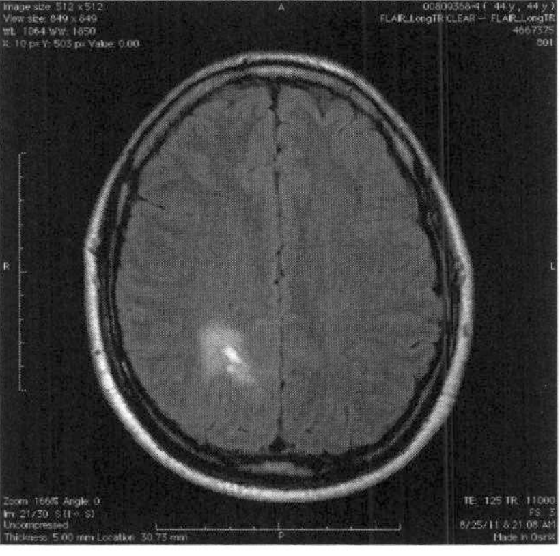

The image on the next page, while not showing tumor as it is at a different phase of the MRI, is a work of art…I am *not* implying, by the way, that *I* am a work of art but the brain itself…and presumably, we all have one…

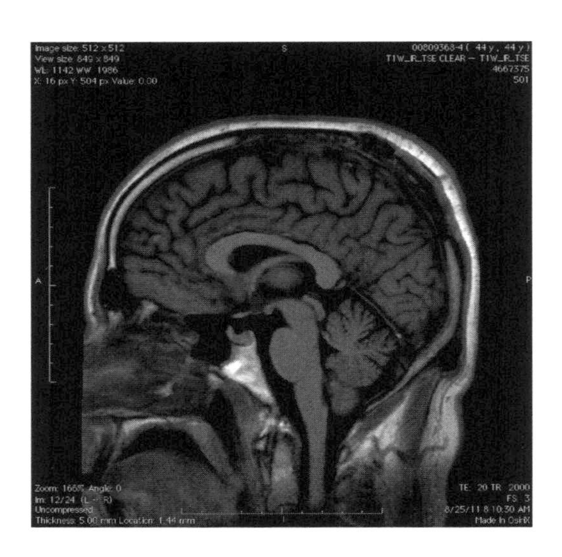

Laugh. Love. Live.

—MRG

Our deepest fear is not that we are inadequate. Our deepest fear is that we are powerful beyond measure. It is our Light, not our Darkness, that most frightens us.

—Marianne Williamson

Regnum Animale

Saturday, August 27, 2011

I am in a deeply wooded forest, perhaps somewhere in Alaska or the Rocky Mountains. Walking through the rich, black soil covered by pine duff, I come to a clearing where the contours of the mountains melt into lush, verdant swaths of deep greens. I can hear and see the water from the river ahead as it bends and twists through the mountain valley, not surging but steady, like a summer rain. The sun soaks the scene with warm blankets of light. In the distance there is a large black bear, just standing there in the water with feet partially submerged. It stares at me with a deep and silent gaze. The bear and I know each other. There is awe but not fear. I *feel* that this bear is a part of me. It is a sensation that weakens me to my core. I am overwhelmed with the surging power of this great animal. Yet, the bear is my protector. I feel safe.

When I was young, I used to sleep with a map of Alaska next to my bed. I knew that Point Barrow was the northernmost town in the fifty states, perhaps in the world, and I longed to be a bush pilot. I was once steps away from working in McKinley National Park. Reading John McPhee's *Coming Into the Country* only brought me closer.

For as long as I can recall, that bear has been part of a recurring dream. Many of us have dreams with repeating themes or visuals. Flying, falling, crashing, sailing, swimming. Many of my dreams have involved motion and water. But the bear always returns. The bear is a constant.

The reawakening of the heart and soul that this recent event has offered has also been a catalyst for helping to move me to a deeper place. While the doctors do not know how long the tumor had been growing, I somehow know that its removal, which was slowly killing me from within, has now left an empty space, and my brain is firing on all cylinders again. It is an incredible feeling. Yes, I am tired, achy, and scared beyond measure. I have many mountains to climb and rivers to cross. But I find myself making connections and observations I might have previously ignored.

Since the "event," I have been moved on many occasions by my interaction with the animal world. I suppose the first incident that knocked me to the ground came just a day after returning home from surgery.

It was exactly 7:45 on Friday morning, and I had just clicked the "give" button to support my dear friend Alicia in her quest to replace her handcycle so that she could continue her preparations for competition in an upcoming race in the Paralympics. Paralyzed from the waist down from an accident in high school, Alicia, single mother of a beautiful girl, with a family full of love and support, has been an inspiration to everyone around her and beyond. Just as I confirmed my gift, there was a deafening explosion outside the window. It woke everyone up with a start. Barb immediately thought the worst—that perhaps in an act of despair, I had decided to call it quits.

The power went out. The whir of the refrigerator, the fans, the lights all came to a halt. I slowly moved myself outside, still medicated, to see if there was any indication of what had happened. I walked to the end of the drive and looked up at the transformer. Nothing. But something caught my eye. There, lying on its back, face to the sky, a charred but still bushy tail draped over the edge, was a squirrel. Somehow it had met with exposed wires or created an arc between two electrical paths with its long body and had electrocuted itself.

The death of any creature is a sad occasion but perhaps due to watching too many Looney Tunes and Tex Avery cartoons as a child, my first reaction was of humored disbelief. The contour of its small nose backlit against the morning sky was sad but slightly comical. Squirrels *are* funny (see *Willy Wonka*, Johnny Depp version). While crying is one reaction to tragedy, sometimes so is laughter, albeit of an awkward, frightened sort. It's a defense response. But almost immediately, I was overcome by a different, secondary emotion.

What makes humans different from any other species is not just our ability to walk upright, drive a car, or play music. It's our ability to rationalize. In some ways, I have always felt religion and spirituality are just one big rationalization for why things happen, or don't. And here I was, doing just that. Gleaning meaning from something seemingly mundane. Or was I?

I decided then and there that this squirrel, and its death, was a noble sacrifice. It had decided, willingly or by some other celestial control, to act as a spirit and help me weather the storms just experienced and those ahead. It took a bullet, or rather, absorbed approximately one hundred and twenty volts of electrical energy, for me. Thank you, squirrel, thank you.

There is proof that when properly trained, dogs can detect through smell certain types of cancer. When forest fires, tsunamis and earthquakes occur, there is evidence that animal casualties are significantly fewer than expected because of the additional sense animals have that something is amiss. Deformed frogs are an indication of the earth's waning health due to our poisoning of the land, air, and water. Elephants possess astounding qualities of memory and communicate at a frequency lower than the human ear can detect. Dolphin intelligence is legend, and we know that crows can distinguish between a caveman and Dick Cheney. And most of us (except, perhaps, those who are proponents of creationism or "intelligent design") know of the connection between humans and apes and chimpanzees: human DNA is about 98.4 percent identical to that of chimpanzees when comparing single nucleotide polymorphisms.

So do I believe, despite the inner battle with logic, in animal spirituality? Absolutely. Disbelievers beware... the animals know. I know without question that Aiden, my standard poodle, and Molly, our adopted Yorkie, understand that I have not been well.

The week of the squirrel sacrifice, there was another incident that, whether cosmic or just dumb luck, was alarmingly metaphoric. Days prior to my cranial landslide, an underground bees nest had reared its ugly head beneath the children's trampoline. The bees were pouring out of a hole and were very angry. It was difficult to know how to best battle this unwelcome neighbor. As much as I didn't want to fill the space with poison, it was the best option at the time. I "bombed" it once and tried to cover up the hole the weekend before things unraveled in my head. Upon later research, I found that covering the holes (there were two, we later found out) with mesh and a glass bowl, essentially sealing the bees to die, might have worked.

My attempt did not succeed. When I arrived home from the hospital my mobility was limited, but my resolve was strong. Damned bees. A few days of rest later, I woke up in the early morning, just before sunrise, when the bees were more or less dormant, to see if I could attack with a different approach. Foolish as it may have been, I came out with a red headlamp (as suggested by the experts) and a shovel. Not being allowed to exert more than five pounds of pressure in physical activity, lest my titanium plates and screws pop out of my fragile dome (I write this with semi-comic intent), I was prepared to give up in my attempt to uproot the nest. To my surprise, the shovel slid deep into very soft soil and uprooted an enormous chunk of honeycombed nest. The monster had awakened, and I was destroying its home. Hundreds of bees came pouring out of the ground in the dawn light. I ran, screaming a guttural roar, tossing the shovel. A bee targeted me directly and landed on my head, dead on the swollen scar, and deposited its stinger into my tender flesh. In an effort to brush away the bee, I swatted my head, Three Stooges-style, which only succeeded in hitting myself in the head. Did I forget to mention I was in my boxers? Thank goodness there is no live footage.

The sting swelled my already swollen head, and I immediately slathered on a homemade paste of baking soda and water, which complemented the stitches and encrusted scars quite beautifully. I looked ridiculous. In between the pain of the sting, which, given what my body had already been through, was nominal, and my frantic end run to the house, I found myself laughing. It was a theater of the absurd. And I firmly believe I had ignited the bee-spirits. That damned bee knew *exactly* where to go to inflict the most pain. It's all karma. House destroyed, the bees counter-attacked, strategically and with precision. "Drone strike" took on a whole new meaning.

We all have our animal stories. In my lifetime we have had rabbits, gerbils, hamsters, fish, dogs, guinea pigs. Some of us have been attacked, others have had our lives both physically and emotionally saved or enriched by animals. Anyone who knows the unconditional love of a dog knows of what I speak. If only our human counterparts could express such unrestrained joy every time we walk in the door, what a world it would be.

My childhood rabbits, named Marianne, Ginger, Gilligan, and Skipper, were housed in cages made by my father, rustic as they were, and set on the tiny patch of lawn in front of our row house, our first home, in Philadelphia. In this neighborhood, populated mostly by Italians, Catholics, Jews, and Koreans, we had a wonderful fireplug of a babysitter named Mrs. Fario. A widowed, feisty Italian woman, she would bring us anise cookies, called pizzelles, every time she came to sit. Much to our horror, she would also inquire, "When you gonna eat them rabbits? My husband, may the Lord rest his soul, loved to cook rabbit. When you gonna eat them rabbits?!" Sadly, two of the rabbits met their fate at the hands of a loose German shepherd. The other two died of old age.

Keeping on the stinging-insect theme, I will share a slightly salty tale (all I ask is that Freudians refrain from comment). We were living at the White Mountain School in a large farmhouse in Bethlehem, New Hampshire. Libby was still crawling, and Hannah was four or five. I had a fairly bad snoring "issue" and was quite resonant. Elephants could hear me. I also had, doctors told me at the time, the shortest "sleep latency" period they had ever seen. In other words, falling asleep before I hit the pillow was no exaggeration. The house, provided by White Mountain School, was large and had many rooms. Quite often, I would move down the hall to spare Laura from the cacophony of my rumbling.

It was autumn, I believe, when many animals begin to move indoors. I woke up in the middle of the night with a strange sensation. Something was crawling on me. Or rather, as I soon found out, inside my boxers. Before I could react, a large wasp decided to attack me from within. Swatting it resulted in yet another comically painful moment. What to do? Stop, drop, and roll? Get a fly swatter? Raid? I leapt out of bed screaming, waking the entire family. Laura, bleary eyed, came out of the bedroom and stared down the hallway to see me dancing a feverish jig, hitting myself where one should not and ripping off my clothes. It was not a pretty sight, I assure you, and Laura was caught between a triad of concern, hysterical laughter, and anger that I had awakened the children. Fortunately, my daughters were spared this potentially damaging image. As a coda to this event, in speaking to my mother the next morning, I explained the events of the evening. There was a long pause after I shared my tale. She then exclaimed, deadpan, "Markie, a wasp stung your penis? I told you to stick to Jewish girls!"

Back to the bear. While my nickname "Moose" was bestowed on me by a high school theater director because, apparently, he felt I "danced like a moose" during my number as "Mr. Cellophane" in *Chicago*, and while it is true that moose, like myself, are ruminant mammals, the bear is clearly my avatar, my spirit animal, my shaman.

Replete with symbolism, the bear is a rich source for Native American, Asian, European, and Nordic cultures. Notable thematic qualities include protection, childbearing, motherhood, freedom, discernment, courage, power, unpredictability.

Bees, bears, squirrels, owls, dogs, cats, horses, whales, dolphins, elephants, and chimpanzees all have representation in the spiritual world in many faiths and cultures. As I embark on this journey, I hope to use the pain and heartache, fear and sadness, to my advantage, as an opportunity. I have never, not once, said to myself, "Why me?" It just *is*. To ask myself anything of the sort would be futile and a negative use of my precious energy. If indeed "the beauty is in the journey," as the Taoist proverb states, I will keep my shamanistic bear close at hand, for it is my protection along the way.

"A dog can express more with his tail in minutes than his owner can express with his tongue in hours."
—Anonymous

The Lobster and the Butterfly

Sunday, August 28, 2011

You seek a great fortune, you three who are now in chains. You will find a fortune, though it will not be the one you seek. But first... first you must travel a long and difficult road, a road fraught with peril. Mm-hmm. You shall see thangs, wonderful to tell. You shall see a... a cow... on the roof of a cotton house, ha. And, oh, so many startlements. I cannot tell you how long this road shall be, but fear not the obstacles in your path, for fate has vouchsafed your reward. Though the road may wind, yea, your hearts grow weary, still shall ye follow them, even unto your salvation.

—Blind Seer, *O Brother Where Art Thou*

Woodland Valley State Park, Catskills, Phoenicia, NY. 1982

A spring morning snow outside our tent offered the comfort of a favorite blanket. The cool, moist air mixed with tendrils of smoke from the smoldering campfire of the night before. A rustle of sleeping bags. The call of a blue jay. The sound of the river nearby and trees clattering, branches dancing. As the dawn light cast a green-blue haze through the translucent nylon, Brigid leaned over to me and whispered, "Have you ever had a butterfly kiss?" "No, I don't think so," I smiled, turning my head slowly, our faces so close, noses almost touching. "Don't move. Close your eyes. Imagine a butterfly." I did as told. The faint feathery wisp of Brig's eyelashes brushed against my cheek. She gave me a butterfly kiss good morning.

Mind you, this was truly a love of friendship, completely platonic, and proof that boys and girls, men and women, could be close friends. Brigid was three years older than me: I was a mere freshman in high school and she a senior. I had been taken in by a group of older friends due in part, I recall, to my work in theater. The camaraderie of the stage creates lifelong bonds that remain with me to this day. Among my many theatrical forays: *Chicago*, *Pippin*, Chekhov's *The Seagull*, Studs Terkel's *Working*, *The Night Thoreau Spent in Jail*, Sam Shepard's *Cowboy Mouth*. Classmates Ian, Michelle, and Kiri were part of the same trip. We were all just enjoying our Thoreauian escapade into the wilderness. Brigid, whose mother, Jo, was the school librarian, and whose father, Dennis, was an Irish historian of note, was a dear, dear friend. With red hair aglow, a passion for art and literature, and a raft of quirky sayings and habits, she was a light in my life. She bestowed upon me my other moniker: Mookie.

Brigid went on to Yale, writing furiously, winning awards, and was a rising star. There she met her fiancé, Chris Noël, and upon graduating they returned to Chris's homeland in Vermont. Chris took a role teaching at what is now Vermont College of Fine Arts, and Brigid took an administrative job at Goddard College. When I moved to Vermont a few years later, I met up with them now and then in their downtown Montpelier apartment, with their beautiful dog, Romeo, also known as Romers. They were in love and just beginning their own journey. I loved them both dearly, and they were very kind and generous. Chris kept me laughing so hard I would cry.

Chris's family became familiar friends. He and Brigid were ultimately nominated for a children's show award for their Christmas tale, "The Gingham Dog and the Calico Cat," set to words and video for the Rabbit Ears Radio Series with Amy Grant and Chet Atkins. On their journey to the ceremony in California, Brig and Chris shared the hilarity of these two country bumpkins stepping out on the red carpet in L.A., and of her being mistaken for Molly Ringwald.

It was January 28, 1992, when our mutual friend Kiri called me in Putney. On her way to work, on a snowy Route 12 in Berlin, Vermont, Brig's tiny Honda was hit head-on by a larger SUV. Brigid, our beautiful, loving Brig, was dead. The howling and moaning of loss punctured my heart. My insides collapsed. At her service in Montpelier, at the Unitarian Church, I could only speak of dark clouds. At the reception back at the house, a miniature Irish wake of sorts, I seem to recall that her brothers, all with profoundly Irish names (Brendan, Kieran), each had their own bottle of Irish whiskey to douse the pain. It wasn't enough. Back in Philadelphia, at a beautiful Catholic church, the plaintive wail of Mick Moloney, a friend of the family, and the Uilleann bagpipes echoed through the halls and up past the spires to help us through the emotional debris left behind.

Years later in his book, *In the Unlikely Event of a Water Landing: A Geography of Grief,* Chris writes of the "grenade days." While his is certainly a journey of grief, loss and mourning, it is also a profoundly deep love story. I highly recommend.

> "The split second before it explodes, a bomb will inhale oxygen enough to feed its detonation. If it's in a small container, it will suck at the walls, causing a near vacuum. On grenade days, as I call them, my chest almost caves in. The pin has been pulled but the grenade refuses to explode; it's just about to. The violence would be a relief. Everywhere I go I go gingerly, because although I do want it to explode, I also want to take care of it before it does, because it's a soft little bomb, very very tender somehow at its center, and as crippling in its demand for constant protection as for its threat."

His website speaks eloquently on all things writing, the writing process and on grief itself. Brigid's collection resides at Yale. Her butterfly kisses reside in my heart and on my cheeks, ever since that beautiful morning.

~

Loss is part of life. Without rain, there would be no sun. Most of us participating in this shared exercise, joining me in this journey into the unknown, have lived lives relatively unscathed compared to those who have suffered inexplicable tragedy. The loss of a child. Genocide in Rwanda, Darfur. Famine in Somalia. The Holocaust. Tsunamis, hurricanes, earthquakes, fires. Suicide bombers ripping family members to pieces. 9/11. Rape. Murder. Hate crimes. The list is endless. Despite my own personal earthquake, there has not been a day I do not consider myself lucky. My moments of despair are reserved for my private spaces, either alone, with Barb, or with my family. The dam has cracked, but it has not burst. I'm waiting for that event…I'm not ready. I know it will come. Yes, this cancer is elusive, stealthy, and frankly sucks. But for now I will take in every breath with delight.

There are moments when a surge of tears and emotion pushes through the door, and they come at unexpected times. A certain song, a view of a river or mountain. Anything related to my children, my parents, sister, Barb, or extended family and friends, but especially Hannah and Libby.

Last week, while participating in orientation for faculty and staff at Putney School, I sat between rows of carrots at

a garden plot while the farm manager, Peter, along with his assistant from the farm crew and Marty, from the kitchen, outlined the logistics and benefits of having a source of food right on campus. As I sat in the dirt, I found myself touching the soft, green carrot tops. They were cool. Comforting. I welled up. I have no idea why. The simple beauty in the seemingly mundane. Simple gifts.

They say there are many stages of grief, as first outlined in the book *On Death and Dying*, published in 1969 by psychiatrist Elizabeth Kübler-Ross. A remarkable woman, who by her own death in 2004 had been inducted into the American National Women's Hall of Fame, awarded over twenty honorary degrees, and whose essays and books had become required reading for anyone entering the field of psychiatry. Her work on caring for those with AIDS and HIV, in helping the medical establishment develop a protocol for empathy, and the care of the terminally ill are legend.

In the Kübler-Ross model, the five stages of grief, in no specific order, are denial, anger, bargaining, depression and acceptance, also known as DABDA. Not everyone experiences each stage, nor is there any intended chronological map or rule book. At this early point, I would say I am immersed in such a soup of emotion that I can't fully comprehend, nor do I feel it necessary to obtain, all the answers, which would be futile anyway. "Embrace the unknown," my dear friend Sara shared.

As with divorce, death, or any other life-changing event, each experience is unique, and there's no "one way" to experience or process. It's easy to throw stones—a dangerous tactic, as we all live in glass houses. Nobody has all the answers.

The brilliant and controversial author and self-avowed atheist Christopher Hitchens expresses his own thoughts and approach to death and dying as he faces the realities of esophageal cancer.

Another friend, who experienced two tours of duty with the Vermont Army National Guard in the Ranger Battalion as an Army Lieutenant Colonel, has not yet returned from the emotional abyss of trauma after his second tour. He saw things, experienced events, that have seared themselves into his being like a white-hot branding iron. The death and mayhem he witnessed cannot be spoken of or written about with any fairness or accuracy. There is no "closure." Just night sweats, horror, and the gnawing agony that you are forever changed. I think of him often—his family, and the experiences of which he can speak little.

Such events as cancer, which, sadly, are a common thread that connects us all in some way, at some point in our lives, thrust you in front of an enormous mirror. Or rather, you are suddenly placed in a room made up entirely of mirrors. You are either forced into a state of denial and cover your eyes or you must look at yourself from all angles in ways you never dreamed possible. Unsettled arguments or disputes are placed in new folders: to let go/unfixable and address/fix. Things left undone to do or to let slide. Things to say that you always wanted to say or things to decide not to say.

In a very strange way I feel liberated, empowered. Then there are what I call "Clint Eastwood" days, when steely eyed, hand on holster, I want to wear a t-shirt and have a bumper sticker on my car that reads, "Don't mess with me, I've got cancer."

I *get* the spiritual odyssey thing. I *get*, at its most rudimentary level, the Buddhist notion of being truly in the moment, and I am still a greenhorn, with velvet on my antlers. I have so much to seek and learn. I *want* to. I am a lobster yet to shed its carapace. I will never forget the metaphor applied by then dean of students Lorne Johnson at the Putney School, many years ago, when he spoke at an all-school assembly. I believe he was addressing sexual harassment and homophobia at a time when such topics were rarely raised. I will never forget his words:

> Humans, like lobsters, need to grow. And, like lobsters, in order to grow they need to shed their shell. And in order to shed their shell they need to be in a safe, welcoming environment. If humans, like lobsters, try to shed their shell and are vulnerable, in a dangerous place, they might be injured, or

worse. It is our job as a community to provide a safe place for all of us to shed our shells so that we may grow and prosper both as individuals and as a community.

I am in a safe place. I am surrounded by love and protection. My shell has been shed and I am ready to grow.

Smoke Signals

Wednesday, August 31, 2011

All life is an experiment.
The more experiments you make the better.
—Ralph Waldo Emerson

I was going to write about my love of food and music and the healing powers of both, but I will save that for another time.I compile notes of my thoughts and small, fleeting moments of inspiration—a mess of chicken scratch written on Post-It notes, recycled paper from trash bins, and even inked on my hand. These thoughts are ephemeral, for my mind has been on hyper-drive, and nearly every sound, sight, and moment resonates with new meaning. It's as if someone changed the wattage of all the light bulbs and my vision has been corrected. My sleep is still off, and I await the so-called "new normal." I carry a tiny two-by-four-inch moleskin notebook everywhere I go..

Getting back to work today was perfect, because it allowed me to focus on something else for a change. The fellowship of Planet Putney is a balm, a salve, and the excitement I feel for the tasks at hand carry me down a road I enjoy.

The above image, from one of my favorite films, *Smoke Signals,* written by Sherman Alexie and based on a short story contained within the collection *The Lone Ranger and Tonto Fistfight in Heaven,* captures beautifully both the visual and lyrical movements of what has been burrowing into my body: thinking of my parents and how they must feel. While the film addresses primarily the love and tension between child and parent, son and father, there is a deeper resonance that reflects the fundamental need for love from the person or people who brought us into this world. Parent-child conflict can metastasize into fear, pain, loathing, and violence, but a house filled with love will stand against any storm. I am fortunate to have been raised in such a home, one filled with warm embraces. In the clip, the raging waters, the brutally beautiful force of nature, represent so much more.

Waters such as these have been witnessed and experienced with great tragedy these past few days from the flooding caused by Hurricane Irene. Vermont was hit exceptionally hard and made international news. Neighboring towns were devastated. Lives were lost, including, as I found out today, the father of a dear student's boyfriend. He was trying to secure his boat and was swept away. I watched industrial-grade propane tanks being carried down the torrential, brown waters, bobbing like unmanned canoes. Pieces of homes. A car. A house in nearby Grafton disappeared, leaving nothing but the concrete step where the front door once stood. Roads washed out. In one painful, chilling clip, a historic bridge in Lower Bartonsville, where my veterinarian lives, slipped away, carrying memories and history downstream in splintered pieces. The cries of bystanders wailed into the wind.

Smoke Signals helped me understand and appreciate more deeply what I have. Yes, my parents have had their share of issues. They have, like so many couples, been through struggles and growing pains. Their temporary separation when I was young is as clear as if it occurred today. I recall the carriage house my father stayed in at a friend's farm and the new sheets he bought me and my sister, in a loving gesture, to make a new home. I had owl-print sheets, my sister had cat sheets: black-and-white cats wearing red sneakers. I think they still reside in the lake cottage in Pennsylvania where I spent my summers. I recall a single tear, resting at the end of his nose, not falling, as he sat on the edge of the bed sobbing as things crumbled around him. And I can see my mother crying, throwing herself onto the red shag carpet, next to the wrought iron bull on the Mediterranean-styled coffee table and the plastic plant (god, the '70s were ugly). Somehow they endured. They were young. The era was adrift in post-Vietnam bitterness. Group therapy, Silva Mind Control, and Gestalt must have done *something* right. My parents, worthy of their own sit-com, are still together. And they are beautiful.

I imagine them with the frozen, stunned, deer-in-the-headlights numbness that comes when your own child is faced with a fate that might precede your own. It makes my own bones brittle. This is all still too raw to digest. My mother, a writer and reader, hasn't touched this blog, while my father, also good with the pen, has been able to climb over the fence of despair and dig in. Mom said that she's sorry, but she just can't. Not now. I told her it was absolutely okay. I understand. I know they're there for me every hour of the day, and I for them.

I tell them, "Please don't blame yourselves. It was nothing you did or didn't do. It just is. This tumor, this cancer, just *is*."

An update: my visit Monday went exceptionally well. Neuro-oncologist extraordinaire, Dr. Fadul, with his warm, calm, and highly astute demeanor, laid out plans for radiation therapy following what will be a second surgery next Tuesday. There is indeed residual tumor left, and removing all of the tumor is essential, critical, to keeping the devil at bay. Why didn't they get all of it the first time? Many reasons, among them the fact that doctors don't know at the time what kind of tumor they're dealing with—benign or malignant, aggressive or passive—and err on the side of caution lest they damage healthy brain tissue and cause unintended permanent damage with life-altering results. Dr. Fadul knows Dr. Gilbert and was pleased that things went well in Houston.

After a few weeks of healing, I will receive intensity modulated radiation therapy (IMRT) for six weeks, five days a week. I will feel tired, appear to have a bad sunburn, and lose what little hair I have left. My beard, I am told, will likely remain. Nausea will be treated with medicine. And then we wait, embrace the unknown, laugh, love, and live.

After Dr. Fadul, we met with Dr. Erkmen, the neurosurgeon, and his compassionate nurse, Amber. Dr. Erkmen, a pleasing, kind expert in his field, came highly endorsed: two friends had been his patients and came out of the procedure 100 percent intact and functioning beautifully. He is an artist and a master physician. The prep for the surgery will begin at 8:00 am, and the surgery itself will happen around 2:00, lasting for about two hours barring any complications. I find it both jarring and comforting that just thinking about another brain surgery has become routine, no different from repairing a torn medial meniscus. But more jarring is the immediate realization that this is, in fact, significantly more critical. The brain, an essential organ, is not your knee. I write this with all due respect to the many incredible orthopaedic surgeons who have sewn my medial menisci (plural Greek for "crescent") and ruptured bicep tendon back together. There's a reason for the phrase "it's not exactly brain surgery."

"You should go clubbing. The pink light might come out of your ears and nose," said Eric A., when I shared that they will be injecting a fluorescent pink dye into my veins as part of a process called 5-ALA. It's used to visualize tumorous tissue in neurosurgical procedures. As far as I understand, my brain's cancerous tissue will glow with a phosphorescent pink hue, helping Dr. Erkmen identify what's left. I'm told that I will need to be in a "dark place" for a few days, as sensitivity to light is quite high. Oooh, boy. A dark place... my favorite! After surgery, I will rest and do my best to obey orders and recuperate from having my head reopened once again. Lord knows what else Dr. Erkmen may find in there. After a few weeks, when the swelling resides, it's radiation time.

Beverly Sharon Bennett Green, of the tiny upstate New York town of Narrowsburg, and Stephen Howard Green, of Philadelphia, lovingly brought me into this world on August 18, 1967. My sister, Kerrin Melissa Green, followed in 1970. Cancer be damned, love conquers all, and I have wheelbarrows full. Thank you Ma, thanks Poppa, thank you sister. I love you.

“Call doctor if you experience…

Monday, September 05, 2011

“…mood changes, sadness, depression or fear.”

Are you kidding me? Given the recent turn of events, I, as well as family and friends, have a pass on this one. Add to this the faltering economy, joblessness, recent storm devastation, other friends and family suffering from a variety of maladies, and the specter of having to put up with yet another election-season parade of out-of-their-mind politicians, and there's ample reason to have “mood changes, sadness, depression, and fear.” Thank you, makers of Levetiracetam! (pronounced lev-eh-turr-RASS-ih-tam, an anti-seizure med, also known as Keppra).

ER's Mark Green

The night before, the day after, food and music, Part I

It is the night before a second craniotomy. No midnight snacks for me. Clear liquids tomorrow morning, another MRI, and then, after I take the fluorescent pink dye that helps illuminate residual cancerous and necrotic tissue, they go in again. The operation will be in the same location. I have already been assured that opening up my head along the existing scar line will not result in a Klingon-like ridge atop my scalp. The titanium screws and washers will be unscrewed, the "bone flap" removed, the dura opened again, and the fishing expedition will begin. This is how I understand it, since I'm no doctor. (Eerily, one of the main protagonists on the hit show ER was named Mark Greene. He was balding, with glasses, and was written out of the show after being diagnosed with brain cancer. Egads.)

How poignant that my chosen topic for the moment is food and music. At least I can always eat the music!

"I need my Haydn! My Mozart! My Bach!" I'd pleaded as I sat up in my hospital bed the morning after my initial surgery on August 2. With the room a storm of activity of bells, buzzers, nurses, doctors, friends, and family, I sought refuge in sound. Eating, for the moment, would happen only in a dream state. After multiple MRIs, which emanate a cacophony of industrial noise something like the opening of the Beatles' *Helter Skelter* on a loop, any soothing music was welcome.

The importance of food and music in my life, to quote a past United States president, cannot be "misunderestimated." (Since the initial brain surgery and cancer diagnoses, I can't stop thinking of hapless Vice President Dan Quayle's infamous quote, "What a waste it is to lose one's mind. Or not to have a mind is being very wasteful. How true that is." Thank you, Dan. I *think* I still have a mind, despite the craniotomy and "resection" of the 4.3 cm tumor in my parietal lobe. What was *his* excuse?)

What gives us sustenance? What *feeds* us? What feeds *you*? What makes you feel truly *alive*?

The founder and director of the Greenwood School, Thomas Scheidler, told new and anxious parents that one reason he felt they had chosen to send their young children to such a special and unique school was that these children had "gone to sleep," and that Greenwood would, hopefully, be a place for them to reawaken. Greenwood continues to raise these often closed, emotionally battered, but talented children from their slumber. "Maximizing potential, awakening talents, and transforming lives" is their motto, and they succeed beautifully in fulfilling this mission.

Many of us, caught in the daily maelstrom of life—jobs, children, parents, partners, spouses, finances, homes—have gone to sleep. It can be a struggle to find that space, that place, the time to reawaken.

For some, it is fear of change: leaving a job or relationship, moving to a different town. This all takes courage and strength that can be hard to muster. Others are just too damned busy—or we let ourselves be too damned busy to avoid the harsh reality that change is necessary.

I feel most alive with friends, family, loved ones, community. With travel, a hike, a ski, a paddle, a walk in the woods, or anything that involves music and food.

Faced with the physical and spiritual mountains I have yet to climb, some with sherpas, some solo, I've sought refuge in the comfort of friends and family, but also in food and music. Listening to and playing music is indeed aural comfort food. And food is just that, a comfort. Even the act of thinking about music or food as I delve into my memory bank (which, since my first surgery, seems to have new room for introspection) is a salve. It's as if a window has been opened, the screen removed, and music is pouring in. And the table by that window? Full of my favorite meals.

"Bear in mind that you should conduct yourself in life as at a feast."
—Epictetus (55 AD–135 AD)

"I'm at the age where food has taken the place of sex in my life. In fact, I've just had a mirror put over my kitchen table."
—Rodney Dangerfield

Gastronomy

Oysters. The act of eating oysters is akin to watching a horse race. There's anticipation, palpitation, anxiousness, eagerness, excitement, and then the gates open. Within a matter of seconds (less than the fleeting two minutes of the Kentucky Derby) the oysters, melting like butter, sending your taste buds firing in a neuro-frenzy, release the cool, salty sea and oceanic flesh. They are gone in an instant. And I, intoxicated, am in bliss.

Abe's and Son Deli, off Bustleton Avenue in Northeast Philadelphia. Bagels as large as hubcaps. Corned beef the way it ought to be: sliced thin, moist, meaty. Memories of Grandma Green's Sunday brunch on "D" Street. A table replete with three different kinds of lox, sable, smoked whitefish, herring, slices of fresh tomato, chopped onion, cucumbers, and capers. Lou Rawls on her stereo console, with his soulful, mellifluous voice wafting in the background. It was one of the few times I remember grandma dancing. She was so happy, feeding us and listening to "Lady Love," dancing her Grandma cha-cha dance to the disco groove. Ethel Green, raised in Laurel, Delaware, was a school teacher and nurse. She was a short, feisty woman, with a healthy dose of Jewish guilt to be slathered on when she deemed necessary. Grandma Ethel was a cross between Clara Peller, of Wendy's "Where's the Beef " fame, and the mother in Woody Allen's "Oedipus Wrecks," from the film *New York Stories*, who dogs her beleaguered son Sheldon even in the afterlife by appearing in the Manhattan sky. And she loved food. She was learned and took classes in various subjects right until she could no longer leave her apartment. Before her decline, dining out was a delight for her, and dining with her, be it at Fisher's or the Melrose Diner, was always a treat.

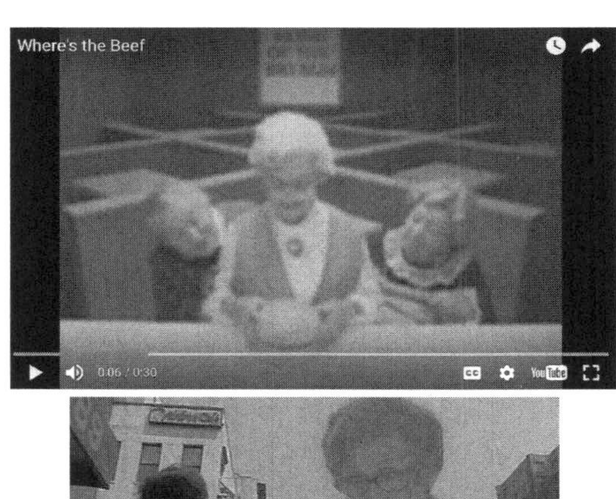

While I could argue that coming of age in the '70s and '80s didn't afford nearly the number of culinary options, either market or restaurant, that my children have now, I was not particularly sheltered.

Yes, Hannah and Libby have grown up, practically from the time they were able to digest solid food, eating Korean, Japanese, Indian, Ethiopian, Chinese, Italian, authentic Mexican (just say NO to Chimichangas and say YES to ceviche, tamales, carnitas de michoacan and mole!), Middle Eastern, and Thai, to name a few, but I also have plenty of joyful memories revolving around gastronomic delights.

There were the rare but exciting ventures to the famed Georges Perrier creation Le Bec-Fin, reserved for special occasions. Equally as thrilling were the family-style Italian restaurants in South Philadelphia. To this day, I recall my father taking us to a local favorite of his, in the spring of 1980. I was thirteen. It was a few weeks after a brutal Mob hit left Angelo Bruno ("The Gentle Don") dead, his bloodied head thrown back, splatter everywhere, as he sat in his car outside the very restaurant in which we were about to enjoy the best homemade meatballs and pasta anyone could fathom.

The local rag, *The Philadelphia Daily News* (the equivalent of the *New York Post*), had no problem publishing the horrific image on the front page. That photo that would give me nightmares for years. It was a very painful time for cities like Philadelphia: the years of Frank Rizzo, a mean, corrupt, paranoid mayor. Police brutality. The radical and suicidal group MOVE. The Mob. Ahh, but the cannolis!

As I walk down the food-laden memory lane of the City of Brotherly Love, let me not forget the cheesesteaks for which Philadelphia holds the title of largest consumption per capita: Pat's, please, with mushrooms and the faux-cheese Cheez Whiz, with its highly unnatural yellow hue, The soot-laden, empty-calorie but temporarily delicious soft pretzels. Reading Terminal, with bonneted, soft-spoken Amish ladies serving up baked goods while the bearded men presented artful cuts of meat and sumptuous sausages. Scrapple, anyone? It's a brick of meat containing whatever they don't put in sausage. The Korean groceries that popped up like so many dandelions as the immigrant population swelled. Sadly, that was about it. The rest included such regular horrors (sorry, Ma) as tuna casserole, Hamburger Helper, and Howard Johnson's fried clams, which to this day I believe were really defective rubber bands, deep-fried and masquerading as food. Thick-cut, nitrate-free applewood smoked bacon? Not a chance. Cheap, fatty, chemical-laden bacon that when cooked left a stringy pile of fatty, oversalted, and crispy meat not worthy of Bacon-Bits. Kale? No, Iceberg lettuce was the only choice. Oven-roasted, honey-brined chicken? Nope. Instead, a bucket of Kentucky Fried Chicken (now, not so cleverly, re-titled KFC, as if we somehow forgot what the acronym's roots were). We had miles to go before we ever learned to eat with a modicum of health in mind. Localvore? Huh?

Growing up in a largely Jewish region, the irony of the popularity of local Chinese restaurants was not lost on any of us. *Trayfe* still tasted good, be it the glutinous, insulting "shrimp with lobster sauce" or fried pork won-tons and egg rolls. The eating of bottom-feeding crustaceans or swine rolling in their own feces was given a pass when it came to dining out at Chinese restaurants.

I pine for the days my mother would take us to watch Dad play in his softball league. This was a passionate group of dads, playing with a fever stored up after a stressful week at the office. Tempers flared from time to time, but in the end it was a fraternity of fun. And Mom would bring hamburgers she had cooked at home. Wrapped in tinfoil, by the time we reached the ball field they would have a certain twice-cooked taste. They had steamed themselves, so that the flavor of the meat permeated the bun itself. They were divine, and to this day I can't seem to recreate this comfort food.

One particularly fateful Sunday, Dad slid into home plate on the fields of Haverford College, slamming into the unsuspecting catcher, soaring, twirling in the air only to land awkwardly, with a loud cracking of his leg that could be heard in the outfield (he also broke the catcher's shoulder). I remember the fear in my mother's eyes. I recall the green wool army blanket they threw over him and the ambulance driving onto the field. But most of all, I remember how good those burgers tasted just before Dad's valiant effort. Oh, and by the way, his slide was declared safe, and the run was counted. Dad would later take refuge with his full-length cast in the basement, having a beer, listening to Paul McCartney and Wings or Cal Tjader.

Today, most of us have friends who are vegetarian, macrobiotic, vegan, lactose-intolerant, gluten-free, low-carb, no carb, raw food, and so on. We're inundated daily with information about how to eat, how much to eat, what to eat, and where to eat. The diet industry is a corrupt multibillion-dollar scam, for the most part. Want a great diet without the pills and the gimmicks? It's rather simple: Eat less junk. Eat more fruits and veggies and exercise daily. Ta da! Done! (Of course, sometimes I subscribe to this and sometimes I don't.)

We are indeed living in a strange world, where on the one hand many of us can enjoy heirloom tomatoes, heritage turkeys, organic everything, grass-fed beef, free-range chickens, and world-class cheeses, and on the other hand we have one of the most unhealthy societies in the world, with statistics for diabetes, obesity, and heart disease very grim indeed.I deeply admire those who eat with conviction especially if they believe that their choice will lead them to a better state of mind or conscience. I remain torn between pursuing a diet that I know will take me and my body to a "purer" or at least healthier path, and simply enjoying the art and beauty of all that tremendously good food.

We're all on a learning curve. For some, that curve remains flatlined; for others, there are peaks and valleys. But it is indeed a fact, not myth or legend, that the best outcome and indication for survival from cancer is based upon numerous factors including the aggressiveness of the disease, how much of the tumor has been removed, and one's mental and physical health. A healthy diet is critical in so many ways.

Even before the "event" (or "The Big Surprise," one of my favorite Felice Brothers songs of late), I was trimming my intake of red meat. Given that I'm also prone to colorectal cancer, having tested positive for the inherited APC gene, that makes sense. Am I willing to give up entirely the exhilaration of a 100 percent organic, grass-fed, free-range local beef burger, served on a grilled English muffin with Grafton cheddar? No. But no more than once a month. I love pretzels: my downfall. Carbs are generally bad. White flour is toxic. Whole grains all the way home. Will I stop ordering the six-pack box of the most amazing pretzels in all the land, Martin's of Akron, Pennsylvania? No. But I will limit my snacking. I bike, I ski, I walk, I hike. I love, I laugh, I love. The battle is already halfway won. I will live to eat, not eat to live. Life is indeed too short to not enjoy the art and beauty of food.

Among my other savory experiences: salmon cooked for hours by wood fire in Eric Aho's Finnish fish smoker, which he had custom made in Finland and then dragged home through the Helsinki airport.

Made of submarine-grade steel and quite heavy, the *savustus pönty* is an exquisite invention. Using wood chips of hickory or applewood, the results are mouth-watering. Add to this his homemade *graavilohi* (gravlax) and a shot of chilled vodka followed by a slice of onion and smothering your face in pumpernickel, and you are in Finnish heaven. (Then off to the sauna!)

Then there's dining at The Russian Tea Room, with its upscale peasant food, glittery crystal, and fine vodka.

Or Sammy's Roumainian Steakhouse (with a discount coupon for an angioplasty). Other delights include Yonah Schimmel Knish Bakery, Katz's Deli, or Doug Last's expertly smoked turkey, painstakingly cared for during thirty hours over soaked applewood chips. Never have I had turkey like that, melting off the bone and melting in your mouth. Or Tim and Charlie's hand-crafted Paella cooked in an authentic paella pan over an open fire, the saffron threads imparting a distinct and heavenly flavor throughout the chicken, chorizo, shellfish, and short-grain rice. Lord, I'm hungry again...

Other memorable moments: snake brandy in rural China, fresh dim sum in Hong Kong, fried goat brains in Puerto Rico, bulgogi in Korea, and street-cart falafel in Cairo. If a producer would listen, I'd propose a reality show with simple rules: it's your birthday and you have, at the start of your big day, exactly twenty-four hours to travel the globe and indulge in culinary delights from around the world. Indulgent and gluttonous? Yes. But fun, for sure.

A final food memory. In summer, 1991, I was a resident member of Bread and Puppet Theater, in Glover, Vermont, which boasts several large clay ovens in which founder Peter Schumann's famous hearty, old-world sourdough rye is baked. At the end of the summer, before the international cast and crew said their goodbyes, there was a feast. The wine flowed freely, and in the clay ovens were several suckling pigs cooked divinely and served in a most elegant fashion. Forget the flowery language. Yum. Words fail. Oh, to relive those days of Bread and Puppet, of roast pig and fine wine. Of aioli and rye bread. Days of preparing aioli for the masses left my entire body reeking of the sweet, pungent aroma of fresh garlic (which, I might add, is an excellent cancer-fighter).

As you may have noticed (and sincere apologies for the indulgent writing), I could go on and on, prattling and pontificating about the joy of food. Let us not forget the great food films: *The Cook, The Thief, His Wife and Her Lover, Tampopo, Fried Green Tomatoes, Delicatessen, Babette's Feast*, and *Ratatouille*, to name a few. The books: *Down and Out in Paris and London* by Orwell, Mark Kurlansky's forays into *Salt* and *Cod, Larousse Gastronomique*, Pollan's *In Defense of Food*, and *Omnivore's Dilemma*, anything by Ruth Reichl or Bourdain. The real dilemma is reading about eating leads to...more eating!

But for now, I'm off to sleep, wondering what adventure awaits tomorrow. I leave you with a favorite food-related video clip.

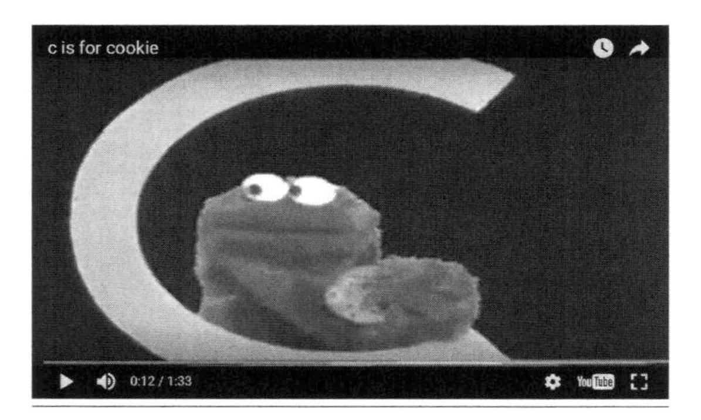

Thank you for reading. And no midnight snacks! Not for the faint of heart, with all due respect and love for the late, great Julia Child:

Bonne nuit and bon appétit!

'Tis very certain the desire of life prolongs it."
—Lord Byron

Monday, September 12, 2011

"Life is better than death, I believe, if only because it is less boring, and because it has fresh peaches in it."
—Alice Walker

The pearlescent, azure-hued, soft fullness of a gently embraced blueberry, pulled with two or three delicate fingers, dropped in the mouth, followed by the warm rush of deep sweetness. Or perhaps a raspberry, even more delicate, necessitating even more care and love. The visceral reward defies description.

The first hint of an autumn breeze brushing against cheeks after a long, humid, rainsoaked summer, with perhaps just a hint of rustle among the dying leaves.

The brilliant hue of roadside wildflowers, reds, oranges, yellows, and blues, aching to be admired amid the weeds and brush.

"I don't wish to refer to cancer as a gift, as it begs explanation and is complicated," explained a dear friend, a survivor herself, as she sat in my darkened room in the Neuro-Surgical Ward at Dartmouth-Hitchcock Medical Center. "But there is no question such an experience by its very nature allows you to see the world through a different lens."

When I held my dying grandmother's hand many years ago, as she lay twisting and writhing in discomfort, spending her last moments with her body pulverized with the effects of emphysema, I finally said, "Grandma, it's okay. You don't have to fight. You can let go. I love you very much and I always will." She moved on, an hour later, as she slowly let herself go, into the slipstream. Where she went I have no idea. But at least her body was no longer fighting itself.

There's a phrase assigned, correctly or not, to the Lakota Sioux leader Crazy Horse, Tasunka Witko: "Hóka-héy. Today is a good day to die!" While the origins are debatable, and the phrase has been "Hollywoodized," I've often thought deeply on this, whether used as a warrior call or to illuminate the reward of living a full life. While I have no intention of going anywhere at the moment, the stealthy brain cancer part of me forces my hand and heart a little deeper into a journey I had not anticipated taking.

What it boils down to for me, until there is nothing left but steam in the pot, is this fundamental question: do I want to leave this earth as happy as possible or as miserable as possible? Do I want to drink the juice from those blueberries and raspberries or let them wither on the vine? Do I never, ever stop to truly crane my head into the wind and feel that breeze on my face, or do I pause, even once a day, to take it all in.

There is much to be unhappy about. As we struggle past the numerical landmark of one of the most tragic days in recent US history, with so many lives lost and damaged forever, other human and natural disasters, large and small, are invoked. Countless wars, both geopolitical and religious. Nagasaki, Hiroshima, the Holocaust, Korea, Vietnam, Iraq, Afghanistan, Chernobyl, Rwanda, Bhopal, crime, poverty, starvation...where could the list possibly end? Where does it begin? To this day, reports I wrote in middle school on the Kent State massacre and the People's Temple in Guyana chill me to the bone, two examples of evil embodied. I'm grateful I attended a school that didn't hide me from the harshness or the beauty of the world, within and around.

And, no surprise to many, there are now 9/11 survivors, most of them rescue workers, who were misled or blatantly lied to by our own government, who have died or are dying of causes directly related to the billions of pounds of toxic dust inhaled after the attacks. Those who told the heroes that the air quality was fine to breathe included then EPA chief, Christine Todd Whitman, and then mayor, Rudy Giuliani. A disgrace. And I do believe anger has a place, especially if it forces us to question and challenge. No lemmings should we become.

But there is indeed a balance. Not for a single moment have I asked myself "Why me?" or "Why now?" A friend, who incidentally is quite a good card player, shared that we are "all dealt a deck of cards" and we have little impact on which cards will be chosen.

Are our glasses half full or half empty? I prefer mine spilling over whenever possible. There is no other choice lest we wind up curled in the corner in a fetal position, driven mad by the fear, pain, and hatred around us. I recognize that for some, coping with this madness results in just that: madness. But I have little time to cry in my oatmeal, at least for too long. I tell myself it's okay to cry, to get mad, irritable, frustrated, even sink into the lows of depression. All of which I have been feeling, for obvious reasons, more frequently.

But I will not allow these emotions to consume my days. We have but one chance to enjoy the blueberries, the raspberries, the wind, the rain, and the flowers.

\k -'myü-n -t \

Monday, September 12, 2011

The shaman on the NYC subway I mentioned previously continues to whisper in my head: "I'm a lucky man." Yes, I have brain cancer. Yes, it is extremely rare. Yes, there is no cure. There is little data. Yes, I have had two craniotomies in one month. "Ah, but a mere flesh wound!" I am home again and forcing myself to rest. My head hurts, the medicine is a bear—or, rather, makes me feel bearish—and I feel like my skull, brain, and dura have been manipulated, sliced, and cauterized, scoped and scooped one too many times. But it's also, quite simply, a miracle. Or merely incredible. I have bought much time. I'm embracing the unknown, slowly. With the expert craftsmanship of Dr. Erkmen and his team, the ensuing and superior oncology treatment with six weeks of radiation from Dr. Fadul and Dr. Jarvis and their team, and personal support from dear friends and family, I have climbed another mountain and am ready for the next. Huff, huff, pant, pant. I think I can, I think I can. I *know* I can, I *know* I can.

It is also, the last time I checked, 2011. (I have, for the need of assessing mental function, been asked the date, where I am, what my name is, and so on, too many times to mention.) It is not 1200 BCE, 600 CE, 1860, or 1950. Or even 2008. The world of medicine continues to advance in incredible ways, and many of us have benefited from these advancements.

Walking in any old New England cemetery, as I often do when given the chance, offers a very poignant, sadly poetic portrait of a world not long ago, when life expectancies were significantly shorter and parents seemed to outlast multiple children. There are so many child graves in these plots, with beautifully carved slate or cast iron lambs (a symbol of innocence) resting atop stone. The stories these children and parents suffered leave much to the imagination. Death, even more so then than today, was as much as part of life as the reverse. Yet I feel strong, eager, healthy, and full of vim and vigor, among other things, I am told.

My temporary life in the hospital was not even remotely close to that of the scene above, from *Monty Python's Meaning of Life,* (certainly not at DHMC) although I think we are well aware that the health care system is, in this country and around the world, in dire need of radical change. There are too many without adequate, even basic, health care. As the Vermont governor and so many others continue to chant, health care is a right, not a privilege (sadly, not everyone believes this). In fact, Dartmouth College's outstanding President Kim, co-founder of Partners in Health, recently initiated a landmark effort: the Dartmouth Center for Health Care Delivery Science is a remarkable, collaborative, cross-disciplinary achievement to help improve upon and advance health care delivery, much the same way the Dartmouth Atlas has become the standard for measuring the efficiency and effectiveness of health care across the United States.

In no way did I ever feel like the pregnant woman in the clip, being barreled down the hospital corridor, at least not that I recall. One can indeed say, do, and feel very strange things under anesthesia. According to the "download" with the head anesthesiologist, I was highly emotional coming out of the operation, sobbing and yet still cognizant that my emotional outpouring was catalyzed by the medicine: a cork unpopped, letting loose the geyser of emotion I continue to hold within. The Monty Python clip certainly captures the medically induced haze and frenzy of how fast things seem to fly when being wheeled (albeit *much* more gently) into the operating room with lots of machines that go "bing."

There was a woman with whom I shared a room the first night during my second round in the Neuro Special Care ward. She was a sweet, gentle woman, with buzz-cut hair. I don't know why she was there, but in addition to her immediate needs, she was deaf and appeared to have no family members or friends to care for her.

She had none of her own clothes and desperately needed what I gathered to be a translating device left at her home in southern Vermont. It appeared she'd been there for at least a week, if not longer. The nurses, doctors, and social workers were doing everything in their power to help her, and she had a personally assigned social worker/translator with her for a few hours, but it was also clear that exasperation was in the air. One of the nurses lent the woman her own computer so she could Skype with someone, presumably in California. It appeared that even in these technologically superior times the best institutions with the most outstanding resources could still become hamstrung by red tape, HIPAA rules, protections, and limitations. And I'm sure I have only a small fraction of the story.

I am, by nature, claustrophobic. To imagine myself in her world, in the hospital, far from home, trapped by a profound inability to communicate, left me very sad and feeling for her deeply.

In the ward, where privacy more or less disappears, going to the bathroom became a shared experience, as the need to measure liquid waste output and maintain dignity with a simple washing of the face or brushing of the teeth is vital. When I walked past her bed, I'd give her a smile, and finally, at one point, I came over to her and held her hand. We were communicating with our eyes, our hearts, and our palms. Nothing had to be said. It was all either of us needed at that moment.

"Community" is one of those catch-all phrases that can be used so frequently, so casually, it often seems to lack meaning. And yet, the need for community is what makes us human. We are by nature social creatures, and whether we reside in a tribal village, a high-rise apartment building, a small New England town, or a sparsely populated desert plain, no matter how ascetic we wish our existence to be at times, in the end our desire for human contact trumps all other needs. I think of Tom Hanks befriending Wilson the volleyball in *Castaway*, or the old codger Felix Bush, played by Robert Duvall in *Get Low*, as he attempts to draw back the community he divorced himself from so many years ago by inviting everyone to his funeral (for which he is present). Through sad experiments, we know that chimpanzees will bond with any object if kept in isolation. In the end, we are never really, truly alone. At least, we don't wish to be.

I studied in the UK in college, and in addition to learning to appreciate warm beer, Pinter, Beckett, Albee, and Stoppard, I benefited from joining the Fell and Cave, a mountaineering club at the University of East Anglia. We hiked fells, otherwise known as "an open stretch of country or moor," and did a lot caving, also known as spelunking, mostly in Wales. The hiking came naturally, but the caving was another matter entirely.

I'm don't think I overcame any bigger mental obstacle during those times than lowering myself, with helmet, climbing gear, and lantern, into a hole in the ground flowing with water, roped together with my caving mates and descending into the deepest depths of the earth. It's nearly impossible to simply change your mind once you go in, as the effort to squeeze, twist, corkscrew, and manipulate a body through narrow, wet passages allow no room to simply turn or go anywhere but forward. It was, at its essence, mind over matter: matter had to be ignored or embraced but not fought, lest one panic and become physically stuck, and ultimately entombed to die, as sometimes happens.

I thank this community of cavers every time I have to insert myself into yet another MRI tube. It all connects, all of our communal experiences.

❧

"Mark, what are you doing outside? You need to be careful of the light!" Professor Hartov exclaimed as a I waddled along the path outside the hospital after the surgery. Beaming a hearty smile, Alex, who I knew when I worked in development at Dartmouth's Thayer School of Engineering, is a professor of note and was directly involved in the clinical trial, called 5-ALA fluorescence, in which I partook. There's a film not for the faint of heart but fascinating if you're able to watch: a medical outtake of a similar tumor resection (different diagnosis) using 5-ALA fluorescence, presumably in Germany, where the initial studies were launched (the black light effects should be set to trance or house music). For some this may be graphic, but the purpose is educational. I found it fascinating.

Here I am in the sculpture garden with artist Barbara Kaufman's gift to DHMC: my new friend. DHMC is blessed by the art of many, including friends Eric Aho, Jonathan Clowes, Henry Isaacs, and Doug Trump. Art truly does heal all.

Another friend, and fellow skier, Professor Brian Pogue, was also part of the study. Knowing some of the players in this trial study was reassuring. I drank the "potion," a dye the would, in three hours, help illuminate residual cancerous tissue under black light. Dr. Erkmen said he was pleased with the results of the disco party that was happening inside my head (my words, not his). I had some mild nausea and had to be kept in a darkened room for a few days; any venturing out had to be done under cover and with sunglasses. Post-op, I looked like a Beduoin bluesman. Wandering around DHMC at 3:00 am, amped from steroids, I felt like a lost soldier in a deserted airport terminal. In a strange way, it was comforting.

Everywhere I turn, examples of the communities in which we exist remind me what gives us our lifeblood, in some cases literally. While visiting Norris Cotton Cancer Center, I was pulled toward the reams of literature. One pamphlet outlined why giving platelets for blood donations was essential to cancer care and research. I beamed and winced simultaneously. I always loved giving blood. Some argue it was for the free sandwiches and snacks, which it may very well be, but now here I was, benefiting from the generosity of others via a gift I myself had enjoyed giving. The wincing came from the fact that I'm unsure whether I can give blood again. And that I will miss the free sandwiches.

I've spoken before of the community of cancer. When my event came to light, stories of those who'd been afflicted or had family and friends who'd been touched came pouring from every seam. There's no question that there is an immediate survivor bond—an "oh, you as well" connectivity. There are warm hugs, deep eye contact, and sometimes tears. It's extremely powerful and often overwhelming. Some are exceptionally private, others share freely. No judgement is passed. I have friends I haven't connected with in years, and suddenly, with the facilitation of social media, I find that they're survivors as well, and the bonds we had weren't lost after all but in fact strengthened. With others there is simply the *knowing*, and that's all there needs to be. Endometrial, neck, colon, lung, ovarian, bone marrow, prostate, breast, and tongue cancers, radical hysterectomies, leukemia, brain tumors benign and malignant: the list is almost too much to bear. This community, combined with that of DHMC, its own little city, gives me great comfort. Where we live, how we live, with whom we live fills my heart.

And while toes are stepped on and mistakes made from time to time, the very nature of our community helps it heal. I remember around twenty years ago, during a particularly nasty battle over whether Rockingham should allow a prison to be built, a dear friend/multigenerational Vermonter/father/farmer/neighbor extraordinaire, Pete Stickney, shared some candid feedback on something I had said or perhaps written in the local paper: "Green, you're awesome, but you are gonna get yourself killed" (or something to that effect). He wasn't serious, but his warning was clear. Loving thy neighbor is a pretty good idea, and living in a small community requires a different degree of patience, care, and feeding, especially when there are differences. This beauty and this challenge makes me love where I live. The community efforts in the aftermath of Vermont's recent flood damage was a perfect example of the *why* and the *who* and the *how*.

As an aside and mea culpa: I learned a long time ago that tailgating on Westminster West road is very unwise, because it's more than likely you'll know the driver you're dogging. I've been scolded enough times by friend and neighbor to know this to be true. I, Mark R. Green, hereby apologize for all previous driving mayhem and plead no harm intended, just sheer head-in-the-clouds daydreaming combined with loud music and an irrational need-for- speed. I would like to think I am faring better lately, as it's more than a year since I've been pulled over. (Friend and former neighbor Detective Ruse, can you please confirm this?)

To close this post, I'd like to share a seminal moment in cinema: the final scene in *One Flew Over the Cuckoo's Nest*, a 1976 film directed by Milos Forman, based on the book by Ken Kesey. This is in no way a reflection on my exceptional experience at DHMC. There was no Nurse Ratched, I didn't feel controlled, and I believe I had the very best care. While I do identify somewhat with JP McMurphy's rapscallion demeanor, I received no involuntary electroshock therapy. Rather, Chief 's self-release is a metaphor for my own release. With the love and support of the many communities in which I dwell, we are all lifting the heavy sink of disease and illness, heaving it through the walls of our imprisoned bodies, and letting ourselves loose in the fields to be free and live. And love.

The weight... the wait... the hourglass

Monday, September 19, 2011

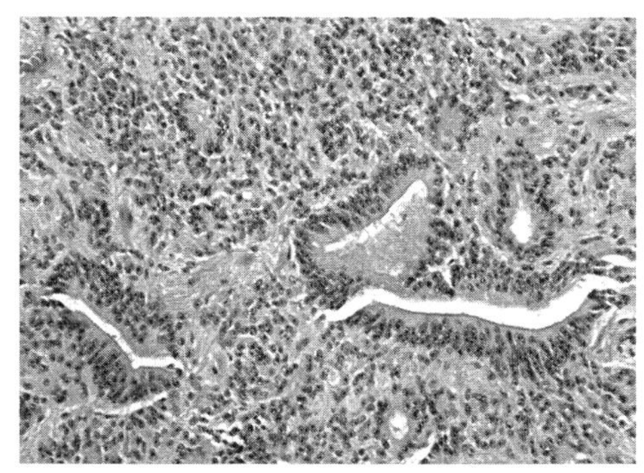

Anaplastic Ependymomas are characterized by a brisk mitotic rate and microvascular proliferation.

Dreamscapes of late include rushing water, deep crevasses, and sliding, curiously, down mountains of shattered safety glass. I find myself swimming in a vivid sea of color, and it takes little time to realize that I am completely out of my body, drifting, swirling inside fountains of brilliant light. I am ensconced within the color. I hear Hannah's voice. I am bodiless. I am the color.

I've slid down into a valley, and she's above me looking down, her face silhouetted by a bright blue sky. There's bewilderment, but, strangely, a peculiar calm. She's worried. I'm afraid. But we both know we're okay. I've cut my arms and hands sliding down the glaciers of glass—all the same small cubes of crystal blue. And the dream ends. That's all.

Have you ever been in a car accident? Time seizes up completely. Things move in slow motion. Sound compresses. Centrifugal force wreaks havoc on the brain's ability to process speed, motion, sound, sight, sensation, and smell as g-forces push the brain to and fro in nanoseconds. And then the car stops. Broken glass. Twisted metal. If you're lucky, you might walk away with cuts and scrapes.

The wheels might still be spinning. The radio might even be on. But as you come to, you realize that nothing is what it was. Things come to a rest.

In 1993, I was driving a rented convertible beneath the stars through the winding back roads of Lompoc, California, north of Santa Barbara, heading back to my hotel after a day's work. Top down, of course. I was exhilarated. I believe the Cranberries were on the radio, the Celtic-infused washes of sound filling my heart. Delores O'Riordan. *Ode to My Family.*

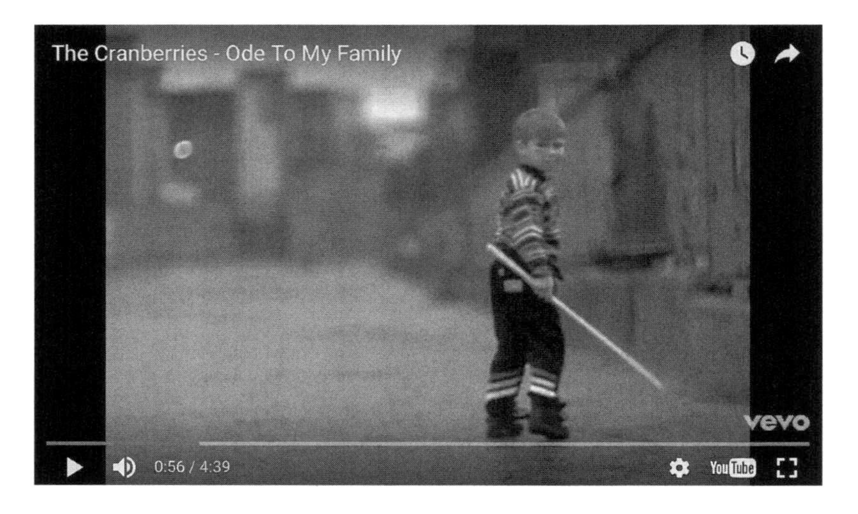

Rounding a corner, caressing the rock boundaries and brush, a deer stood broadside, head cocked in my direction and eyes aglow. I struck it in an instant, sending it soaring over my head and the open-topped car. The airbag deployed, choking me with the talc powder used to release the device. I was able to swerve off to the side of the road, sliding along the gravel shoulder, and turn off the engine before drifting into the canyon ahead. The headlights pierced through the settling dust.

There were no cars. It was dark and quiet. I had no idea where the deer went, what shape it was in, or even what shape I was in. Pushing aside the airbag, I stepped out and began walking around the car. The front end was battered, but the car was drivable. Eventually, and

I don't recall how, as this was before cellphones, a police officer came to assess the damage. He found the deer and dragged it by its hind quarters, heaving the animal over an embankment. After checking to see that I was safe, he determined that no laws had been broken and told me I was welcome to drive home with no penalty. Enough damage had been done. Numb from crushing the life out of the deer, sore from the accident itself, and feeling as if time has been temporarily suspended, I limped home.

Another time, when I was about ten, my mother, grandmother, sister, and I were heading along the Schuykill River to Philadelphia. It was dusk and raining heavily. Coming quickly upon a particularly nasty curve, the car, a Ford Grenada of the most ugly demeanor, hydroplaned and continued forward despite mom's efforts to follow the road. We seemed to fly through the air, soaring, until the guardrail cables managed to grab the car, slowing our speed and tearing off the rear bumper. We were temporarily suspended, facing the river. The car abruptly pulled back, and everything stopped moving save for the torrent of rain raging against the glass. Again, time seemed to stop. Frozen. Suspended.

Time continues to be temporarily suspended. Some days I sing with happiness, others I feel as if I've just walked away from yet another car crash occurring in a fifth dimension of time. There are "out of body" days. My sleep patterns are completely off, and taking medications is nothing more than a band-aid that often leaves a sticky residue. Not being particularly fond of taking any medications unless absolutely necessary (not by any moral or political impulse, but because I don't like to feel robbed of my true self, much as that true self sometimes needs a rest), I've found that the cocktail of steroids (for post-op swelling), anti-seizure meds, pain killers, and sleeping aids are of little use. My entire body chemistry is seeking a new normal, whatever that will be. Such medication seems to have minimal effect; I do not consider this to be a detriment.

For someone who wants to know what he's going to eat for breakfast the night before, I've had to let go of a lot of my compulsions for law and order and try to accept a life of unknown. "Embrace the unknown," a friend and cancer survivor shared. I'm trying.

What I tell close friends who wish to know more is that some force, uninvited and unexpected, has come into my life and decided to turn my hourglass over prematurely, and that there's no way to upright this wrong. We have no idea how much sand is really left. In many ways, none of us do, being mortal beings and quite vulnerable. It drives my engine. I have so much to do, and now even less time for the irritants that can seem such a waste. Each grain of sand seems so large and significant now.

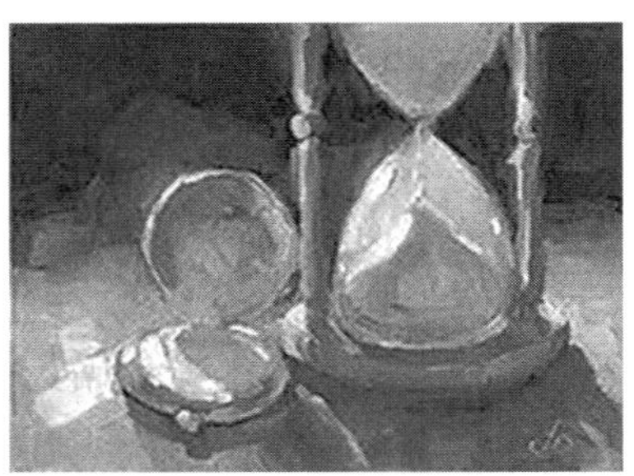

I feel there's anger percolating, simmering beneath the surface. Elisabeth Kübler-Ross's stages of grief has been a guide for so many, a road map for the yet-to-be-traveled emotional highway. Of course, many victims of trauma and tragedy will go through, and back through, various of these stages. But she set the stage and deserves credit for helping people understand that grief, loss, and suffering are a plastic, ever-changing evolution of the mind, body, and soul.

Funny thing is, I'm not quite sure what I am mad *at*. I don't wish to unleash my frustration toward anything or anyone, and know that physical exercise and music are beneficial salves. But I'm also *trying* to seek a path toward acceptance of this anger and to channel it. Name it, own it, and let it burn off like a lit fuse. I find myself reflecting on unfinished business. Scarred friendships. Actions or inactions regretted. Things I wish I'd said or not said. It's enough to drive one mad. I also know, deep within, I have to let it (whatever "it" is) go. But where, when, and how?

Today I finally cursed this rare, deadly cancer's name. I was screaming as I walked into the forest behind my house. I wanted to smash windows, throw rocks, break things. But I didn't want to hurt anyone or anything. I just needed a release from the mounting pressure of living with a disease I neither invited nor prepared for. I resent the time away from friends and family, from my physical pursuits. I have a deep desire to get back to work and raise millions of dollars for a school I dearly love and believe in. But being mad at something that won't respond is in itself an exercise in futility. It's been helpful to speak with friends who've experienced similar trauma, to know that these waves of frenzied emotion are all natural, normal, and I dare say predictable.

In addition, there's the weight of the wait—that's the worst part of all. It amounts to a form of permanent torture, really. A spiritual waterboarding. The need to know, but not knowing.

Anger is a funny thing because it's a deceptive emotion. Actually all emotions can be guilty of deceit. Being heartbroken by someone you love may very well be about being hurt, but the tendrils of despair are long and intertwined within our past relationships, our current situation and our fear or worry of the future. I truly and fundamentally believe that if the following equation for emotion was analyzed, dissected and somehow implemented in domestic relationships, foreign policy, etc, the world would be a better place:

> If one understands, at its core, that ignorance breeds fear and fear breeds hate and hate brings violence and violence brings death physical, emotional and spiritual, there would be less fear, hate, violence and death if we can launch an all-out assault against ignorance.

I don't accept, on any level, racist, sexist, homophobic, classist, xenophobic, antihuman attitudes. But I understand their existence, because at the root they're predicated on ignorance and fear. Certain political parties are quite deft at fomenting and fermenting this fear. It wins votes, but at great cost. We're no doubt facing another interesting, maddening, and sad political season. It's already started, or rather, it never seems to end.

So how do I both embrace and fight this cancerous invasion of my most sacred space, my brain? After all, the brain is us. It's who we are. I'm trying to understand as much as I can about this illness and use that information as a tool, even a weapon. Knowledge truly is power.

> "Anaplastic ependymoma (WHO grade III) is a malignant glioma of ependymal origin with accelerated growth and an unfavorable outcome, particularly in children. Incidence data vary considerably. No specific genetic alterations for this

tumor are known. Prognostic correlations between histology and clinical outcome have been inconsistent. In a large series, no correlation between survival times and classic histopathological findings of malignancy were observed."

"WHO Grade III tumors are also known as anaplastic ependymomas. Incidence data varies based on reports, with only relatively small series of patients included in each of the publications. The definition of the microscopic characteristics that distinguish a Grade II from a Grade III tumor are currently being refined. Evidence of active cell division (mitoses) and formation of new tumor blood vessels (neovascularization, a component of angiogenesis) are typical findings in the Grade III tumors."

"Overall, in surveys of adults with ependymomas, 10-year survival rates of 45 percent were reported."

What I don't understand I fear, and what I fear I loathe. With this brain cancer, I'm trying to understand, trying to harness and channel the fear and push the loathing to the side, or into the abyss. And I do this as I wander, endlessly, into the unknown...armed with knowledge, hope, twenty-first-century medicine, and most critically, most essentially, love from friends, family, and community.

I'm a lucky man.

"Trilogy – Power. Precision. Versatility"

Tuesday, September 20, 2011

"Life is not measured by the number of breaths we take,
but by the moments that take our breath away."
—Maya Angelou

Imagine a small airport terminal at 3:00 a.m. There was a silent, somewhat eerie calm to the radiation area today as I explored where I will go over the next six weeks to receive a daily dose of radiation therapy to my brain. A machine called the "Trilogy," which sounded and looked like something from *The Matrix*, will be the delivery device. I will lie down, be locked in place, and covered with what I call my "Nacho Libre" mesh wrestler mask (well, that's better than Hannibal Lecter, who also came to mind).

It was a long, wearisome day, made all the better by the fact that I continue to marvel at, and am grateful for, the care and kindness received from *every* individual I encounter at Dartmouth-Hitchcock and the Norris Cotton Cancer Center. I don't know what President Weinstein is putting in the employee water coolers, but the people of DHMC seem to be well aware that they're in an industry where people matter and need to be treated humanely, in an environment that by its very nature can often feel inhumane.

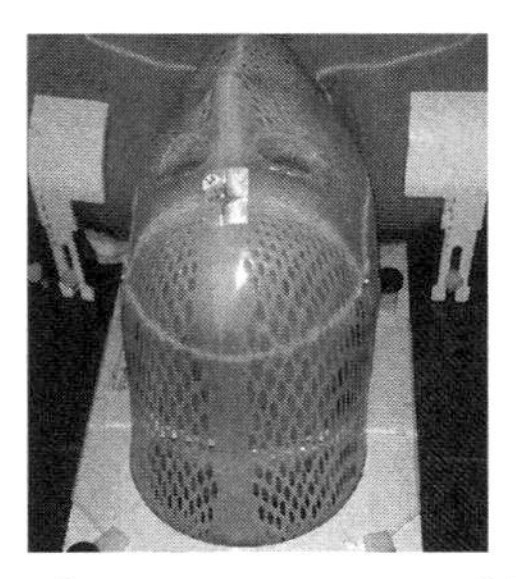

Blood drawn to check CBC counts and liver function per protocol after participating in the 5-ALA clinical trial. Rechecking the setup for ensuing radiation therapy. Stitches out. Review of situation, recommendation of continued use of antiseizure meds until EEG is conducted to ascertain any seizure activity (yes, the damned cancer is still serious and rare and data sparse, but my immediate outcome post-op is quite strong), confirmation of pathology report, agreement to participate in another trial, this time a randomized, double-blind, placebo-controlled clinical trial using the drug Nuvigil.

> "The purpose of this study is to determine if Nuvigil® improves fatigue experienced by people receiving external beam radiation therapy for the treatment of malignant gliomas. It is also being done to determine if Nuvigil® improves cognitive function (perception, thinking, reasoning, and remembering) and overall quality of life in people receiving external beam radiation therapy for the treatment of malignant gliomas. Another purpose of this study is to see if people who receive Nuvigil® have more or less side effects than people who receive placebo. Placebo is a substance that looks like an active drug but has no active ingredient."

We shall see…I'm a placebo junkie, as long as they're locally grown, organic, healthy, free-range, grass-fed, and gluten-free.

"Some say the glass is half full, some say the glass is half empty. I say "Are you gonna drink that?"

Family Perspectives: "Prostrated"

Monday, September 26, 2011

My mother published a piece on the NCCN website (National Comprehensive Cancer Center)

The Big "CA"

by Beverly Green

That day I opened my husband's mail—something I had never done before. The return address was from the urology department at a local hospital, and I knew the contents were the results of his annual prostate test.

"CA" leaped from the page. It could not be. How could I be reading that my husband had prostate cancer? With test results in hand, including something called a Gleason score, I spent the next few hours at the computer trying to learn what I hoped was not true: that he did indeed have prostate cancer and that the Gleason score was high—not a good sign.

The challenge began in determining the best treatment. That was the beginning of a long education and a process which I labeled "Dueling Doctors." The surgeons said "operate," the radiologists said "radiate."

IMRT, IRT: the letters sounded more like stops on the New York subway than anything medical. Each choice had pros and cons of its own. A decision had to be made.

I also read reports that there was no definitive treatment. There was research that said that doing nothing at all if the patient was in his 60s was an option. The "wait and pray" approach. There were friendly reassurances: "but you caught it early" and "no one dies from prostate cancer." That was heartening until I read the obituary of a movie star who had died of prostate cancer.

After weighing the pros and cons of surgery and radiation treatment, my husband decided on radiation treatment followed by a two-year series of injections to halt the production of testosterone because testosterone is a breeding ground for cancer cells.

Cancer Happens to the Spouse, Too

It is a tense and confusing time for both patient and partner. Although it was his cancer and his body, the treatment and its results (one such result is usually a deep depression) became a very real part of my life. A prostate cancer diagnosis brings with it both emotional and physical changes, and both are difficult for most men—and their partners—to handle.

Our job as the partner, the caregiver, the one *without* the cancer, is to support and comfort, stand back and accommodate, help and accept. But sometimes we are left uninformed about how these changes will affect our partner, us, and our emotional and physical life together. I quickly realized that I had questions, concerns, and needs that I could not easily share because there was no one to share them with. Although I found support groups for men with prostate cancer, I was not able to find any such groups for their partners.

I will try to shed some light on what these changes may be—for your partner, for you, and for your life together. There was no one to do this for me.

First, some advice.

Find the hospital nearest you that specializes in treating prostate cancer. This is not a time for your local hospital or family doctor. Get an opinion from at least two specialists (usually one surgeon and one radiation oncologist) so you can discuss the options for different treatments.

Go with your partner to the visits, even if you have to insist. Ask questions. Write down the answers. Make sure you are satisfied that your concerns have been addressed. If the doctor does not respect your need for information, find another doctor.

Most of all, become familiar with the emotional and physical changes that will affect you, your partner, and your relationship.

Cancer Often Changes Things...

We have all heard about testosterone. It is the stuff that makes men, men. The injections given as part of my husband's treatment halt production of testosterone, and the effects vary. There can be body changes, which are somewhat akin to what women go through during menopause: muscles soften, breasts enlarge, and waistlines expand. One of the more difficult and least talked about changes is that there will an absence of sexual urges and ability. Or as the doctor said to my husband, "You won't even think about sex for at least two years and maybe more."

Needless to say, this is emotionally charged and relationship-changing information. I remember hearing those words and thinking, well, sex isn't all about intercourse anyway. But what the doctor did not mention was that with the lack of ability comes lack of interest in anything remotely sexual. True, we could kiss and cuddle, but something happens to the intensity when both of you know there is no chance that it will lead to anything else. So the kisses became "friendly" and the cuddling more like comfort hugs. For the next few years the relationship settled into a friendship much like that of college roommates.

Despite the fact that I was glad that there is treatment for prostate cancer, and that it's one of the more "curable" or at least manageable cancers, it can be a lonely few years. It is a hard subject to talk to friends about, and often difficult to discuss with your partner. I felt selfish for thinking about my own needs when we were both going through the trauma of dealing with cancer. Both you and your partner will need to find a way to navigate through these changes together; we still are.

But there is a bright side. With early and proper treatment, you have a partner who will be cancer-free. It can also be an opportunity to explore other aspects of your relationship, and a time to look forward to rekindling the romance you have missed.

In our case, we have become good friends who have been there to support each other through this scary time. There is a tacit understanding between us that our relationship may never be the same, but as I look across the bed, I am glad he is cancer-free and there next to me.

"home, is where I want to be, but I guess I'm already there..."

Monday, September 26, 2011

"It's a shame to be caught up in something that doesn't make you absolutely tremble with joy."
—Julia Child

Perhaps one of my favorite celebrities and most beloved of all quotes. Thank you Julia. And by golly, radiation and brain surgery is no joy but I will carry her words with me to push past this and find the tremble...the good tremble...

Two days to the start of radiation therapy to my brain. Six weeks, five days a week. Barb, who works as a physical therapist at a remarkably loving place, Sojourns Community Health Clinic in Westminster, Vermont, now has a second job, unpaid, in addition to being a mom of two of her own children and trying to tend to her own needs and challenges. She has scheduled all appointments, kept track of the meds to ensure I'm taking the right dosage ("two or three blue ones?!"), arranged transport, and is with me on every doctor visit. I'm a lucky man. I wonder and worry every day about those with nothing. With nobody. I think about the fact that three out of every ten Texans have no health care, that the state has one of the highest rates of uninsured children, and is one of the few with rising infant mortality. (*Who in the world is voting for Rick Perry?!* The politics of mean are alive and well.)

But this is where the guilt comes in. Barb didn't ask for a partner with an incurable illness. I used to joke, "I promise not to be a burden to you...." I know I'm enough of a handful as it is. A PITA (nod to my friend Tammy W. for the acronym for "Pain in the Ass!"). So much for promises. I've promised her I won't become even more of a burden, and if I do, to toss me in a boat without a paddle and send me downstream.

While I am a tinkerer, I have yet to figure out a way to jury-rig the microwave to self-administer radiation. That might save a lot of time, no? Not quite sure how to direct those beams...popcorn is one thing, but my brain? Hmm.

Today I had an EEG (electroencephalogram, more hair ripped off my chest) to analyze brain activity (very little, the nurse and I joked) and determine if I can taper off the 1,000 mg daily dose of Keppra, my antiseizure meds, which would be welcome. Keppra, by the way, sounds like a yiddish word, kepele, which means head. As in "a leben ahf dein kepele," which translates into "a long life upon your head!"

I'm told that fatigue and nausea are likely within the first few weeks of radiation, with hair loss (not much to lose) and redness as well for a few weeks following. Given my proclivity for physical and mental hypestimulation, slowing down a bit might not be so bad. We shall see. I will work in the morning and leave midday.

Soon I'll be seeing somebody professional to help me process the avalanche of emotion I experience daily. It's nice to live in age when seeking help has less stigma than it once had. Even the military is making great strides to embrace the notion that trauma to soldiers happens to the heart and soul as much as to the body. I need some new tools in my toolbox to cope with the road ahead. I suppose we all do. For me, yoga, friends, breathing, exercise, music...more fruits and vegetables...

One of the most difficult things of late has been facing the reality that while some cancers are in fact "beatable," this is one you can only "beat back." There's no "winning" or "beating" this. It's incurable. So much is unknown. The best approach, in addition to filling the empty space in my head with love, humor, friendship, community, food, music, and journeys into the wild, is keeping it at bay and watching it like a hawk watches its prey, or a CIA operative watches a target. Perhaps a clinical trial will come along and offer hope. It's one of the reasons I went to MD Anderson (which is, ironically, in Texas!). Already, the 5-ALA trial, in which I participated with great success, is becoming international news.

There are unavoidable awkward moments when well-meaning friends and neighbors become tongue-tied. When I see them fumbling for words, I try to help by letting them know that there's really no easy language for any of this, and it is perfectly okay to not know what to say. Some offer love, kisses, healing, prayer, hugs, a bottle of scotch (!), and some offer their own experiences with cancer and disease.

The hard part is when they share, optimistically, "Oh, you'll beat this! If anyone can beat this, it's you!" While I agree that the battle for the spirit is at least half the battle, those are high and hopeful stakes. These words of encouragement are helpful and vitally important; they're the wind in my sails. But I believe that because we're generally so isolated from the realities of our own mortality and the fact that in the end we all wind up as stardust, or simply compost, we lack a common language. We let children play outrageously violent video games and watch unnecessarily horrific films, yet shield them from the realities of real death and dying, mistaking this for protection. I think it distorts reality and confuses us all.

One of my aims in putting everything on the table is to demystify some of the unknowns, in the hope that by charting a course for my disease I can help others heal, that I can help them understand the physical, mental, and spiritual toll this awful mess creates for all involved as well as the opportunities it presents. It's the end, it's a new beginning. I am *here*.

Words and sentiment are meant to help heal and support. But, depending who's offering those words, I might nod and smile and offer thanks, or I may bluntly share, "No, actually, this one doesn't get *beat*." There is no "win," only buying time. And it's in a currency I don't fully understand.

Thinking back on Aleksander Hemon's heartrending essay "The Aquarium" in *The New Yorker*, about losing his young daughter to brain cancer, I don't think I realized at the time how apt the aquarium metaphor is. I am indeed encased in a world where I can see and hear what's happening, but there sometimes remains a translucent wall between myself and the world around me. It's a bizarre, out-of-body experience, and I often feel a sensation of floating above the clouds. I think it's a protective mechanism.

Sometimes this affliction is emotionally debilitating. It's common for cancer patients (and others with life-threatening illness) to contemplate their own mortality in a new light. Experiencing the death of a friend, neighbor, loved one, or family member offers a similar opportunity to reflect and look forward, to ponder plans not yet made, dreams desired and unfulfilled.

The mere thought of leaving Hannah and Libby, my two empowered, intelligent, worldly daughters, brings me to my knees. I try not to dwell on this topic too often. But there are reminders. Even a Hyundai ad, Hope on Wheels, for support of children with cancer, brings me instantly to tears. Any thought of Barb, my parents, sister, family and friends, community...in this regard...it's just too hard... words fail and in this instance, don't have a place. To be frank, I think we are all still in shock.

Hannah, who was with me from the beginning, including being there when the doctor delivered the news of the cancer, continues on her own path of strength, pursuing her dreams and leadership. She recently and without my knowing, started a cancer support group at her school. There are over 50 members, students whose lives have been affected in some way by cancer. And just a few days ago she and a group of students initiated a group to help fund raise for a walk for breast cancer. She has already doubled her goal. Again, I knew nothing.

And Libby continues on her great path, her love of horses, of music, of cooking and of good friends. Libby is a joy with an infectious joie de vivre that knows no bounds. This has matured my daughters in a way no parent wishes, but I believe it has made us all stronger and closer.

Other times the diagnosis has been empowering. I feel emboldened. Speaking my mind, expressing myself, for some reason, feels easier now. This very blog has been in my heart forever but I have not had the bravery to jump in. My artist-musician-culinary-writer-political-entrepreneurial-leader friends I have only unparalleled respect for: putting your heart, body and soul on the table, exposed, for all to see, to be criticized and judged is the ultimate risk. It is a brave act and they are courageous.

Today my mother sent me an Elvis CD entitled "Gospel Favorites." Her favorite Elvis gospel song happens to be "How Great Thou Art." She lives in many worlds, my mother. She holds two master's degrees, was a dean, taught English and psychology at the high school and college level, has her nails manicured weekly, and plays classical piano on her most beloved object, her Baby Grand Steinway. In another world, she drives an old and much-loved Chevrolet Blazer with a vanity plate which reads "Meta-4s," speaking to her literary roots and teaching background, and on the front, an "I Love Elvis" plate. She is a country mouse living in a city nest.

I grew up listening to Elvis (as well as her true love, Joan Baez) and was moved by her gift. I remember clearly the day he died and yet I was two days away from becoming ten years old. My mother was sobbing as if she had lost a best friend as the crackling news came over WABC-AM radio at the cabin where we spent our summers. As complicated as I find organized religion to be, give me some great gospel any day and I'll sing to the sky: Sacred Harp, Mahalia Jackson, Blind Boys of Alabama, etc.

For you Momma.

Nsoromma

Sunday, October 02, 2011

Nsoromma, an Adinkra. One of the many West African Symbols for Guardianship —"Child of the Heavens"

Last week I went to New York City for my first post-diagnosis, post surgery, work-related visit. I absolutely love NYC and always approach the city with some mental and physical preparation much in the same way I prepare to hike a large mountain, paddle a long stretch of river or ski a 10 or 25K trail. I think of it as urban hiking. I love to get lost in NYC (actually I love being lost in general, scouring the remote regions of the world, knowing that, if prepared and not too foolish, I will always, eventually, find my way home). In many ways this completely earth-shattering event of two brain surgeries and stage III brain cancer diagnosis has offered a similar challenge. I am resolved to train myself for the road ahead, explore every aspect of the disease and arm myself with as much information as possible. I may get lost in this journey, but I know I will find my way home.

Among the many events we packed into a few days (including some very fine meals amidst some delicious conversation), Putney School colleagues Alison and Christie organized two moving and illuminating events for alumni. Friday evening, nearly one-hundred Putney alumni and their families gathered in the hallowed and humbling Cathedral Church of St. John the Divine in Morningside

Heights for a reception followed by a community sing. Putney School's sing, held weekly at the school, always gives me goosebumps. From shape-note songs to African spirituals, from old folk songs to English rounds, "Sing" is one of the more important traditions at the school. Putney was founded as the premier school of progressive education in 1935 by visionary Carmelita Hinton, with a focus on academics, ethics, labor, community, the arts, and stewardship of the land. It was also, among many firsts, the first coeducational boarding school in the US. Voice or no voice, tone-deaf or musically inclined, everyone sings. And we are all the more healthy both as a community and as individuals.

The following morning we were given a private tour of the African burial grounds at 290 Broadway, led by alumna Peggy King Jorde, a famed architect who has been a major force in efforts to reclaim, save, and honor the thousands of unnamed Africans buried beneath Manhattan. We gained insight into early American history that has sadly been deleted from our history books and classrooms. While it may come as no surprise to many, much of the city was built with slave labor, and many of the victims were buried on the Island of Manhattan. In this case, where the government had planned to simply build on top of the site, 419 human remains were recovered, given a proper resting place, and honored. The site is now one of the most popular historical museums in the country, revealing a hitherto untold aspect of our nation's past, and the effort has been called one of the most important historic urban archaeological projects undertaken in the United States.

Outside, along with several burial mounds that were left unmoved, is a moving tribute, set in polished granite, to those of West African descent who were brought here as slaves and died the same. A rotunda contains etchings of spiritual symbols from Native American, Christian, and West African faiths, among many others. The experience led me to think about symbolism and how I wish to both honor and respect the powerful forces that, despite attempts to explain the unknown since humankind began, lie beyond our grasp. One that caught my eye was the Nsoromma, a symbol of guardianship. I've been seriously considering getting a small, discreet tattoo of this symbol, having been inspired by a brain cancer comrade who had an elaborate and striking octopus tattoo made to reflect her own journey. She shares her story on the Liz Army blog, an inspirational site written by, as she describes herself, "cool chick with brain cancer."

Tattoos leave me with many mixed emotions for a variety of reasons, many related to health, history, association, and what they'll look like down the road. But rather than delve into that abyss, I will try not to overthink or intellectualize. I have friends with tattoos I admire, and others that make me wince. It is purely a personal choice. Of course body modification has been with us since we discovered fire, so who am I to judge? Is there really any difference between ear-piercing, piercing in other places, tattoos and the wearing of perfume, makeup or jewelry? Anyone familiar with the stunning beauty of ancient Egyptian hieroglyphics can appreciate the fact that such art did not always have negative connotations. This notion of a tattoo, embracing a symbol that has deep meaning to me, is just another stone in the foundation I'm building for a house in which I hope to live as long and as happily as I can. Tattoo or not, I'm moved and remain intrigued by what I saw in New York..

Part II- Update

Three radiation treatments down, thirty to go. I show up at Norris Cotton each afternoon, scan my "radiation card" with a laser pen to sign in, and wait for the staff to call me back to the machines: HAL 1, 2, and 3, as well as a back-up (my names, not theirs).

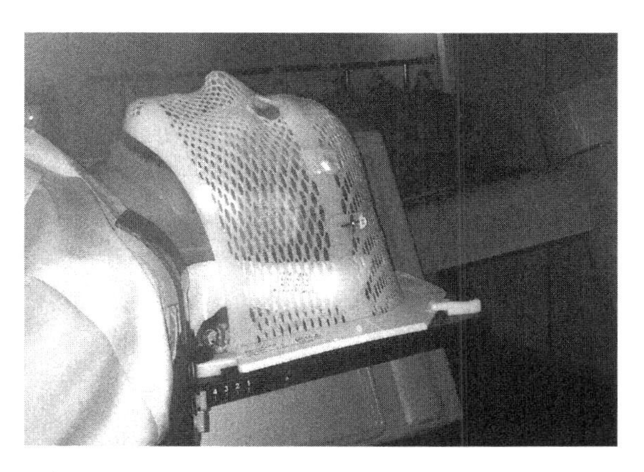

Again, I'm amazed at the high level of care at Dartmouth Hitchcock throughout this experience. Everyone seems to approach their role with kindness and professionalism. I'm whisked into the radiation center and immediately lie down on the table. My feet are bound together with a large rubber band to help prevent movement, and the mask, custom-made to my facial contours and features, is tightly affixed and locked down.

The technicians talk me through each step and go into the next room to avoid unnecessary radiation exposure (each treatment consists of 180 units of radiation) The treatments themselves take no more than ten minutes. While they're painless, I'm told that in a week or so I will probably begin to experience fatigue and, despite the medication I take one hour prior to treatment, nausea as well. Effects like these, as well as steady headaches and completely shattered sleep patterns, have been with me from the beginning of this mess, but I fight them with the knowledge that it indeed could always be worse. My face is already starting to blister and become red. Some days are worse than others, but in general I feel strong. Indeed, I'm trying to locate that center and not allow myself to be short-tempered. I do find myself less willing to put up with anything that seems a waste of time or that projects negative energy. I do have a protective, subcutaneous weapon buried deep within me that makes me able to say to anyone who hassles me or my family, "Don't mess with me, I have brain cancer." I find it empowering, but like all weapons, I realize I need to be cautious about how and when to use it. No superhero I, nor Clint Eastwood, nor Incredible Hulk.

That hourglass is still full of sand, but I want to make every grain slipping through to the bottom count. I have no time to waste. I'm also striving to live more in the moment. A friend who's a practicing Buddhist and deeply familiar with healing and all things spiritual is going to help me learn how to meditate. As I told her, this act alone may be as hard as dealing with the surgeries, treatment, and cancer. My form of therapy has always been cycling, skiing, hiking, enjoying fine food, and friends. I look forward to the next phase of this trek… and I will continue to dance…

"When the music changes, so does the dance"
—West African Proverb

to live is to fly

Wednesday, October 12, 2011

My father gave me the greatest gift anyone could give another person: he believed in me.
—Jim Valvano

When I was a boy of fourteen, my father was so ignorant I could hardly stand to have the old man around. But when I got to be twenty-one, I was astonished at how much he had learned in seven years.
—Mark Twain

We walked slowly along the shores of Lake Champlain, my father and I. The warmth and light of the autumn sun burned off the morning haze, unveiling the splendor of the Adirondack mountains across the water. This was the first time since 1998 we'd spent more than an afternoon together, alone. Not because of any rift, but simply because, while we had spoken many times of doing so, getting together hadn't pushed its way to the front of the jukebox.

Other selections seemed to always interrupt our desired family soundtrack.

This past weekend was a revelation of sorts, and on many levels. Looking through the lens of family, I was able to capture a portrait framed by love, admiration and, an appreciation for being "in the moment" with my father. Ah, that "being in the moment" thing. I think I'm beginning to get it. Lately I've been working with a close friend, mentor, cancer survivor, and Buddhist to learn the practice of meditation. As she said, it's called a "practice" for a reason. My K-12 Quaker education, attending weekly Meeting for Worship for thirteen years, proved to me that we can all find our centers if given the opportunity. Sitting in silence for thirty to forty minutes is entirely possible, even for me. I know this.

As I've mentioned, and as I shared with my friend, with Barb, and with my doctors, learning the art of meditation and calming my brain would be in many ways more challenging than overcoming two surgeries and radiation treatments. The trauma of an incurable cancer diagnosis, on the other hand, is permanent. One learns, over time, to manage this immobile storm cloud rather than declare victory or assume it will just disappear. Neither is post-traumatic stress disorder or losing a limb, sight, hearing, or other functionality always going to be fixable or curable. One simply adapts, manages, learns, and tries to accept. New tools are acquired, coping mechanisms are embraced, medication might be prescribed, alternative therapies practiced, prosthetic devices made. Giving up or surrendering is not an option. Down the road at some point, I suppose we all "let go"—but that, I believe, is very different.

"You're the first patient we've had to tell *please slow down*. Usually we're trying to get patients going," my radiation oncologist told me.

I agreed that perhaps I've been pushing too hard, but that's just how I've responded to this mess. Everyone has a different threshold and responds according to their own psychological-physical-spiritual makeup. But I'm beginning to recognize my limits, which is very humbling, and sometimes frustrating. In the past, all too often I'd forge ahead, ignoring what my body was telling me. I'm trying to be a better listener.

Back to my time with Dad: Let me first offer some simple, practical advice. I believe I have only done so once before in this blog, when I shared, as I will again, that if you do not have life insurance, and you have children and/or a partner or spouse, stop reading this blog, pick up the phone and get as much as you can afford. Check with your employer if you can increase what they already offer, if they offer anything. Do not wait for "something to happen." If you are diagnosed with an illness such as cancer, or experience a life-altering accident, insurance agencies will quite literally laugh at you (at least one did) if you ask them about life insurance after the fact. And if they do offer a policy, the premiums will be astronomically high. You are quite simply not worth their risk. If you believe you have enough resources and assume that if anything happens your family will be cared for financially, get some insurance anyway. There are no guarantees that your investments or nest egg will be there tomorrow, next week or in a year. I wish I'd pushed harder and sooner for that to happen. We spoke of it for a long time but life always seemed to get in the way of *living*. Something always came up or intervened. Eventually, I demanded it.

While our once or twice a year golf outings, summertime breakfasts at the diner or occasional lunches if I happen to be in Philadelphia remain important, we wanted to get away this time.

We're both deeply grateful for the time we had, and look forward to more. I've promised my mother, with whom I speak more frequently, that we'll do something similar soon. She'd "threatened" to come along, but I emphatically requested that this be father-son time and that there will be mother-son time as well.

There's no time like the present to fulfill any and all desires to spend quality time with loved ones, be they friends, family or partners, whether a nice long chat on the phone, an hour over coffee, a weekend away, or more. In the end, as Lincoln said, "It's not the years in your life that count. It's the life in your years."

Dad and I spent most of that time eating or sitting on a park bench looking out at the lake. Sometimes we spoke, other times we read the paper or just sat in silence. My father is a quiet, loving, soulful man whose reticence can sometimes be mistaken for a brooding withdrawal. It's not. And while getting around has been difficult of late, as his ankles have been a source of chronic arthritic pain, we forged ahead, albeit at a slower pace than either of us were used to. We did the requisite stop at Ben and Jerry's, took a Lake Champlain scenic cruise, visited a few art galleries, snacked at the farmer's market, and one evening went to some hipster joint where we listened to live Bohemian jazz. That we were the only ones there over thirty and had no (visible) tattoos or piercings was of no consequence.

The last time we'd spent that much time together was when he accompanied me on my move to Sedona, Arizona, where I'd taken a position as director of admissions at the Verde Valley School. Towing the car on a flatbed behind us, we filled up the twenty-four-foot U-Haul to the roof and headed west. Despite a few disagreements over driving, and one lengthy dispute over my desire to make a stop in Memphis, we had an extraordinary time: chicken-fried steak with sausage gravy at the Loretta Lynn Truckstop, double-decker freight trains ambling across the Texas Panhandle, feedlots seemingly larger than the state of Vermont, truck stops as large as small New England villages, and one comically touching weepfest when Harry Chapin's "Cat's in the Cradle" came over the radio—the ultimate father-and-son tale of waiting until it's too late to connect.

To celebrate our journey, Dad had customized t-shirts made up, white with green lettering and festooned with cacti, that documented the highlights and some of the towns we passed through.

One one side:

- *Road Trip '98*
- *No Refunds After 15 Minutes (sign at front desk at cheap hotel)*
- *Hitchhikers May Be Escaping Inmates*
- *Sparkling Tile Rest Rooms*
- *HO-Made Pies (curious sign at local bakery)*
- *Speed Limit 52 MPH*

And on the other side:

- *Saxtons River, VT: Elkins Park, PA: Woodstock, VA: Bristol, VA/TN: Bulls Gap, TN: Crab Orchard, TN: Buffalo, TN: Toad Suck, AR: Conway, AR: Cherokee, OK: Clinton Lane, OK: Vega, TX: Milagro, NM: Grants, NM: Flagstaff, AZ: Sedona, AZ, Oak Creek Canyon, AZ.*

The revelation I experienced over the weekend was this: it's been about two and a half months since the landslide. It's been a harrowing, confusing, frightening-to-the-core experience for all of us. The cancer has invaded our lives metaphorically and literally. We've learned much, and continue to do so. We've climbed many mountains, my family, friends, and I, and will do so forever. But the contours of this journey will eventually flatten out as we find sure footing and become as comfortable as one can be with our new reality, knowing that at any time we may find there are more mountains to summit.

There will be times of stress, fatigue, sadness, fear, anger, emotional and physical pain, but alas, such is life itself. I have dreams, hopes, goals, and wishes yet unfulfilled for my family and friends, for my career and passions. None of these desires has been checked at the gate. If anything, this event has only bolstered my resolve: to strengthen existing bonds, to be a better father, son, partner, friend, neighbor, worker, human. To live to see my children continue to evolve. Perhaps witness the birth of grandchildren. To bicycle across the US, travel to faraway places, write that book...the list is long, and I have miles to go...

I can no longer focus on grim statistics. I'm not a statistic. We are not statistics. We are sentient beings. I'm learning to filter this new library of cancer that has appeared, like some frozen chunk of blue effluent dropped from an airplane, crashing through the roof and landing in my living room.

Steve Jobs—wise, brilliant, and perhaps one of the most influential people in recent memory—lost his life to pancreatic cancer. His Stanford commencement address, among his many speeches and lectures, continues to receive enormous attention. In one of his many moving passages, he speaks of facing the realities of death:

> "Remembering that I'll be dead soon is the most important tool I've ever encountered to help me make the big choices in life. Because almost everything—all external expectations, all pride, all fear of embarrassment or failure—these things just fall away in the face of death, leaving only what is truly important. Remembering that you are going to die is the best way I know to avoid the trap of thinking you have something to lose. You are already naked. There is no reason not to follow your heart."

The revelation from this weekend, as I move through whatever stage I'm going through, is that I am stronger than ever. I'm tended to by a phalanx of supremely gifted doctors, nurses, technicians, and other medical staff, and living in a time when the marvels of modern medicine continue to unfold. I have a great job at a great institution and work with great people. My aspirations are clear, and I am driven to achieve them. Most importantly, I am lifted up by loving family, friends, community, colleagues past and present...and that has made all the difference.

"To live is to fly
Low and high,so shake the dust off of your wings
and the sleep out of your eyes." —Townes Van Zandt

LIVEVIL

Friday, October 21, 2011

If you're going through hell, keep going.
—Winston Churchill

Feed your faith and your fears will starve to death.
—Author Unknown

In college, being creative, madcap students, we created some legendary events to activate what wasn't being stimulated in the classroom: art happenings, art festivals, art-attacks, avant-garde poetry gatherings, guerilla theater, protest theater, musical events. These were often within the subtext of a good old down-home party, albeit with a higher calling. Or so we thought.

What else does one do in upstate New York when the sun hasn't shown for weeks and the bone-chilling, damp, gray cold air has permeated even the warmest of down jackets. When you feel as if you've unknowingly marooned yourself on a distant planet where the nearest large town is Utica, a place that's been desperately trying to scrape the barnacles off its rust-belt past? (To be fair, the Munson-Williams-Proctor Art is a gem, the region is a photographer's paradise with everything truly frozen in time, and while the city is still clinically and economically depressed, efforts are clearly afoot for revitalization.)

Café Stupide. The Fuzzy Suite. The "I'm Gonna Be Hypno-Tised" gala. Parties where we festooned ourselves with aluminum foil and mockingly-lovingly embraced heavy-metal heads. The quite astounding gatherings of exceptional musicians who formed such bands as PIE, ripping through Stevie Ray catalogs, Dead covers, and originals. The jazzy, martini-soaked speakeasy re-creations, cocktail parties serenaded by Django Reinhardt, and late-night forays into the musical wilderness with Jandek, the Cocteau Twins, Tom Waits, or Eugene Chadbourne. And let us not forget the masterful (and co-educational) midnight construction a twelve-foot-high snow penis, a nod to the domination of the phallus in icy snow (or just a large, shocking object to greet people when the sun rose the next morning).

Some events remain suspended in a cloud of mental debris. I think the dust, along with the chicken-wing bones, empty beer cans, and smashed cigarettes may still reside on the sills and ceiling tiles of those dorm-room suites.

One themed party, though, seemed to be recurrent. It was focused primarily on living up to its palindromatic name: LIVEVIL. No, participants were not, save for eardrums, livers, lungs, and in one instance, a shredded buttock resulting from an icy sled run in the woods when the borrowed lunch tray cracked in the cold. But the goal was to simultaneously celebrate the darkness and combat evil in all its forms.

Now, for some reason, when I think of cancer, I think of that title. LIVEVIL. Evil is alive and well. Many images come to mind when trying to comprehend the embodiment of this disease, for there is nothing un-evil about it.

In one of my favorite films, *Spirited Away*, by the acclaimed Hayao Miyazaki, features a stunning array of mystical beings. In one scene, "No Face" (shown below with protagonist Chihiro) swallows a servant in order to speak and gives gold to the staff in return for food. "No Face" eats voraciously, devouring everything in its path and causing it to grow to immense size as it swallows others. It's unstoppable. "No Face" is cancer.

Other Hollywood demons, many based on centuries-old embodiments of evil, can be linked to how I feel about this cancer and why, as one friend who's a cancer survivor shared, I have to be mindful now that I'm on the "inside" not to forget that the mere utterance of having cancer "freaks people out." I'm learning to temper how, when, and with whom I share the details, often referring them to this blog for further investigation if I'm too drained or too busy to delve.

Visual Musings on Evil Embodied

Ripley: How do we kill it, Ash? There's gotta be a way of killing it.
How? How do we do it?
Ash: You can't.
Parker: That's bullshit.
Ash: You still don't understand what you're dealing with, do you?
Perfect organism. Its structural perfection is matched only by its hostility. — from *Alien*

"Little pigs, little pigs, let me come in. Not by the hair of your chinny-chin-chin? Well then I'll huff and I'll puff, and I'll blow your house in." —Jack Torrence, *The Shining*

What's the most you ever lost on a coin toss?
—Anton Chigurh, *No Country for Old Men*

"This shark, swallow you whole."
—Quint, *Jaws*

"I felt them. Everything went cold [...] And I felt … as though all happiness had gone from the world … and I remembered … dreadful things …" —Mrs. Figg, *Harry Potter, Order of the Phoenix*

Captain Bligh, *Mutiny on the Bounty*
Amon Goeth, *Schindler's List*

Of course the list for non-fictitious characters in history who could easily feed the flame of cancer would be endless. Stalin, Idi Amin, Pol-Pot, Queen Mary I, Hitler, Saddam, Ghadafi, Bin Laden, Hirohito, Attila the Hun, etc. as well as those within the literary realm including Grendel, Beowulf 's mother, Bill Sikes from Oliver Twist, The Devil himself, Dracula, Lady MacBeth, Claudius, Aaron the Moor and so on. They are all apt and all remind us of the nature of evil in our nature.

So what is this "live-evil"lurking within?

A few videos help illuminate the very basics: one from the Mayo Clinic and another on the role of nanotechnology in cancer research. Truly mind-blowing science.

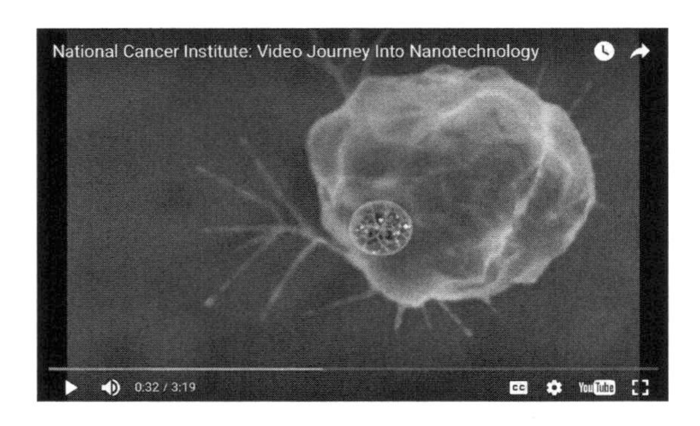

A basic cancer video introduction from MD Anderson: Brain cancer and this anaplastic ependymoma lurking within creates a complex synergy of emotion: hope and despair, courage and weakness. Love and hate.

Love will win either way. It always does. And always will.

An old Cherokee chief was teaching his grandson about life...

> "A fight is going on inside me," he said to the boy. "It is a terrible fight and it is between two wolves.
>
> "One is evil—he is anger, envy, sorrow, regret, greed, arrogance, self-pity, guilt, resentment, inferiority, lies, false pride, superiority, self-doubt, and ego.
>
> "The other is good—he is joy, peace, love, hope, serenity, humility, kindness, benevolence, empathy, generosity, truth, compassion, and faith.
>
> "This same fight is going on inside you—and inside every other person, too." The grandson thought about it for a minute and then asked his grandfather,
>
> "Which wolf will win?"
>
> The old chief simply replied, "The one you feed."

While Jakob Dylan does in fact have a terrific song, "Evil is Alive and Well," I will leave you with this...one of the best road songs on the planet. Turn it up. LOUD. Time to get in the car and drive...with one headlight...

Wonder...

Thursday, October 27, 2011

"There are only two ways to live your life. One is as though nothing is a miracle. The other is as though everything is a miracle."
—Albert Einstein

1 year. Narrowsburg, New York, 1968, with Grandma Bertha Bennett

I lost my hair last Friday. I'd been told that somewhere along the radiation highway, the hair-loss checkpoint would be encountered. My dear friend Charlie and I were flying south on Interstate 91 from radiation number fifteen (out of thirty-three) in his celestial blue Z3 roadster convertible. Top down, with the cooling autumn Vermont air filling our lungs, we smiled knowingly. Words needn't be spoken when you're in a convertible. If you'd told me we were soaring above the clouds, I would have believed you.

My scalp, feeling a little tight since the surgeries, was itchy. I unconsciously pulled on what little stretches of hair I had left on my prematurely balding pate. To my awkward surprise, I grabbed a sizable clump of hair. I reached back again. Another clump. "Charlie! Check it out! My hair! Wow!" I exclaimed. He turned, amused by my own bemusement, and we laughed. While I had little hair to lose to begin with, the sight itself was surreal. I felt like a sad, tired taxidermied possum, sitting on the windowsill of some barbershop, with its faded, dried-out, shedding hair and patchy spots. Despite the oddly comic nature of it all, for both of us, and later for Barb and the children, there was pause. Barb later shared that on the morning of that day, she'd found the keyboard of the computer covered with hair, which she quickly identified as coming from my scalp. (Insert joke here, go ahead.) A reality check. A small wave of sad.

For the past week I've been wondering if the radiation was a placebo. I joked with the staff, "Are you sure that thing is turned on?"—because I feel that I have yet to experience the full, cumulative physical effects of the radiation. Yes, I get tired, slightly nauseated, irritable, and have some fairly intense headaches, but how much has been from the radiation is hard to tell. These uncomfortable symptoms may just be the result of watching the Republican "debate."

My appetite hasn't waned. When I asked if I would lose weight, Barb smiled and said, "Yeah, if you stop eating." My internal motor tends toward overdrive anyway, so maybe I'll slide through this with little trauma. But indeed, the daily dose of 180 cGy (centigray), for a total of 5940 cGy, is very real.

Ah, Trilogy, you fine, sleek linear accelerator, I know ye too well! You, with your oh-so-powerful "advanced motion management capabilities" and your sexy "Gated RapidArc open motion management interface." I am indeed grateful that "treatment times are shorter" and am even more thankful that "the precision of Trilogy allows you to spare healthy tissues to an extent that was unimaginable only a few years ago"—because, well, this being *my brain and all*, I'd like to preserve what little healthy tissue I had to begin with.

The reality of losing hair due to the effects of radiation therapy offers a very visual reminder of what is often a very hidden disease. Weight loss, skin changes, and other signs may exist, but the loss of hair is jarring for many. So while it was expected, it was a bit of a startle to see that I now have patches of hair missing where the beams were targeted to penetrate my skull and, we hope, kill off the residual cancerous tissue. There are very thin margins when using radiation to get at brain cancer. There's little room for error. But some healthy tissue must be sacrificed to ensure maximum coverage and the best outcome. I'm told that much of the damage will, over time, repair itself, but what of the once-healthy tissue that doesn't repair? We shall see. After all, recent research has disproven the notion that the brain is a fixed object. We actually have an incredibly plastic organ, capable of adapting and compensating in ways never before believed. (A must read: *The Brain that Changes Itself*, by Norman Doidge.)

Unfortunate 3-Piece wool suit, Age 11?

As this rare form of cancer is incurable and known to recur, the ependymal cells which claim themselves are truly sinister, like billions of ticks who have burrowed their heads too deeply to be completely removed. So they are radiating as much as they can. As this is a one-time form of treatment, the next line of attack, barring another surgery, will most likely be in the form of clinical trials for which I will be eligible and am already enrolled in a national registry.

My initial surprise about losing my hair was followed immediately by guilt and profound sadness as my thoughts turned to a coworker currently undergoing radiation treatment for breast cancer. She, with a beautiful, cared-for mane of hair, was losing all of hers. Devastating.

Without question, hair loss has nowhere near the emotional weight for men that it does for women. Additionally, breast cancer—the most prevalent cancer in women, which will result in 230,480 new cases and 40,000 deaths this year alone—attacks yet another visible body part that holds much power, both symbolic and real.

I don't mean to say that men have it easier with cancer. That would be absurd, demeaning, and offensive. Cancer in all of its forms and stages is a rotten cockroach of a disease. But surely the emotional impact for women when it comes to these two harsh realities, hair and breast loss and change, adds yet another potent mess to deal with

15 yrs. Delaware River, PA.
Note air-guitar use of paddle, F-chord

when the freight train of this disease has crashed through your home. My heart sinks, and I can't even fathom, try as I may, this additional trauma.

So the hair for me. No big deal. It was already wisping away anyhow. There's no mourning to be had here, except to say that at one time I had a nice mane of hair and I'm sure it meant something. And now it's just patchy and thinning. The towheaded baby. The Prince Valiant look. The '80s feather. The '90s… whatever.

This is dedicated to those for whom hair is not a "whatever." At the Norris Cotton Cancer Center, there's a whole section dedicated to helping people cope with hair loss. Hats, sometimes donated, many handmade, are for sale. There's a wig bank, where patients can get a wig for free, and get advice on how to wear wig or tie a scarf. There's even a "Look Good…Feel Better" class to help women cope with such side-effects as hair loss and skin changes.

This is for the grandmothers, the mothers, the sisters, the daughters, the granddaughters. To women with hair of all lengths, colors, and qualities, who have to mourn yet another loss within a loss. For some, the hair will return. For others not. The flaxen, the cornrow, the silken, the dreadlocks, the curly, the wavy, the frizzy, the beauty of the scalp all by itself. My deepest respects and love. We will all make our way.

Back of barn with friends after rehearsal.
Bread and Puppet, Glover, VT, Summer 1991.

"Wonder"
—Natalie Merchant

O, I believe
Fate smiled and destiny
Laughed as she came to my cradle
Know this child will be able
Laughed as she came to my mother
Know this child will not suffer
Laughed as my body she lifted
Know this child will be gifted
With love, with patience and with faith
She'll make her way

Heavy Metal Thunder

Wednesday, November 02, 2011

It's a complete catastrophe!
—Nigel Tufnel, *Spinal Tap*

There are those who look at things the way they are, and ask why…
I dream of things that never were, and ask why not?
—Robert F. Kennedy

By one United Nations estimate, about 40 percent of the world's population — 2.6 billion people — does not have access to a toilet. Open defecation leads to contaminated water and diarrhea. About 1.5 million children die of diarrhea every year.
—*New York Times*, September 26, 2011

Talking over dinner recently at Putney School with a few colleagues, I shared that "sometimes I feel guilty about having cancer. There are so many with so little, living under such duress. Rape, poverty, hunger, war, crime, drugs, disease, environmental devastation both natural and manmade. *I'm alive. Shouldn't I simply be forever grateful for that?*"

Ken's response surprised me. Being a mindful, inquisitive soul, he immediately replied, "Yes, Mark, but you're thinking on the macro. We can't always live our lives on the macro and ignore the micro-level realities of our own struggles." I suppose it's what you do with those struggles, how you let them manifest. The struggle

between the body, mind, and spirit can wear you down if they're all at war. Alas, I suppose that's one of the ultimate quests, to find that balance, that center. And now I carry a permanent backpack filled with heavy metal. (Ironically, plutonium, which is radioactive, is the world's heaviest metal, with an atomic weight of 244 Ar.)

It's been three months since the landslide. On August 1, I was hospitalized. On August 2, I had my first surgery to remove the tumor. On September 6, a second craniotomy to remove residual tumor. And as of next Friday, 11/11/11, which happens to be National Heavy Metal Day, I will complete my six-week course of radiation. I'm enjoying the heavy metal connection. (For a great portal into this musical phenomenon, check out Penelope Spheeris' *The Decline of Western Civilization, Part II: The Metal Years.*)

My head is now shaved, as it was beginning to look as if my hair had been gnawed by rats in my sleep (this happens all the time). I feel like Walter White from *Breaking Bad*, or a nephew of Shel Silverstein.

My headaches have worsened and fatigue has kicked in, but it really hasn't been as awful as I'd been warned. I look forward to tapering off the pain medication and steroids, which help reduce the swelling of my brain as it absorbs the radiation. Generally speaking, my emotions at this three-month juncture range from empowered, at peace, emboldened, supercharged, terrified, deeply sad, very rarely angry (what's the point?), deeply happy, and deeply blessed by the love of friends, family, and community. Most of all, my hunger for life feels insatiable.

Daughter Hannah and M.

In December I will have my first post-surgery, post-radiation MRI, which will help determine if there is visible tumor left. I will receive an MRI every three months as we keep a close watch on additional tumor/cancer cell growth. Brain cancer is tricky. Chemotherapy normally doesn't work because of the legendary blood-brain barrier, a brilliant construction to help protect the sensitive brain from foreign substances. Options are extremely limited. I could endure more surgeries if necessary, but of course that's not ideal. I've communicated with brain cancer survivors who log the dates of their multiple brain surgeries like hashmarks on a fighter plane, symbols of courage in the war against this cancer. But those surgeries also equal more trauma, more digging and more side-effects.

Brain cancer, when it starts in the brain, stays in the brain (like Vegas), sometimes moving to the spinal cord. Other cancers can be "cured" by removing the entire organ, or at least the part that's cancerous. Removing my brain, or parts of it, is not an option at this point (although friends and family might not notice the difference). This aggressive cancer will lurk. Cue up the *Jaws* music.

The landslide includes not only physical and emotional debris but also the additional challenge of absorbing and synthesizing the storm of information, both solicited and unsolicited. I welcome any and all input, because in the end I believe all dialogue is good. Communication, even when clumsy, is better than nothing at all.

Some musings on this. There have been many powerfully emotive moments when someone shares, heartfelt, in the abject sadness and fear we're experiencing. This is a deadly disease. There are mutant cells running amok in my head, and we're trying to kill as many as we can before they kill me. Nasty buggers, they.

Some respond to this awkward reality by expressing the very real notion that in fact we're *all* dying. But time and time again, I tend to believe the opposite. "No, actually, I'm *living*." Some days I feel more alive than I've ever felt in my forty-four years. I breathe deeper, my vision seems more acute. Frankly, it's a very bizarre sensation.

When I really dig down into the stark reality of facing death, I'm stopped in my tracks. My stomach drops like a stone. The air leaves my body, and I feel like melting into the ground. Flashes of my daughters, my loved ones, friends, family, and places all scroll at high speed before me. It can be a harsh reality check. But while, yes,

I might be dying at the cancerous, cellular level, I am living as never before. I've chosen to toss statistics out the window. It's been some of the best advice I've had. One of my favorite quotes from Dylan's *It's Alright Ma, I'm only Bleeding:* "He not busy being born is busy dying."

One of the two well-intentioned, innocent, oft-repeated but seemingly flip comments I hear most often (and which can feel like bamboo splints under my fingernails) is "Well, we're all dying. We'll all die of something eventually."

The other is "Well, we never know what will happen. We could be hit by a bus tomorrow." Of course at the most fundamental level this is true. But most of us, fortunately, aren't handed a decree so soon that our lives may be cut short by such a crappy, incurable disease. Indeed, while we could in fact be hit by a bus tomorrow, most of us aren't standing in heavy, bus-laden traffic 24/7.

I live in a remarkable community with literally hundreds of practitioners of health. Western, Eastern. Northern. Southern. Years ago I wrote an essay for our local food co-op, titled "Whole Lotta Healin' Goin' On," in which I catalogued the multitude of options available. A review of the local bulletin board reveals a plethora of medical alternatives. There's so much to learn and to try. And why not? I'll swim in any pond, and I believe in taking myself out of my comfort zone whenever possible. You never know what new light you might find. Nothing has ever been advanced without experimentation. And hell, if it works for you, who am I to judge?

That said, learning how to live with cancer can be bewildering, frustrating, confusing, aggravating, and irritating and can downright make you crazy. What do I do now? What do I eat? What do I drink? What should I do? What shouldn't I do? The books, the CDs, the podcasts, the healers, the spiritual meccas, workshops, compounds, retreats, and so forth, ad nauseam.

A dear friend and cancer survivor shared with me the same overwhelming experience. "I was trying to decide what form of treatment to undertake. I felt like I was in a coat room with each of the hooks a different therapy talking loudly about how I should hang my life on their hook. That their treatment was the most effective and hopeful for saving my life. I found it excruciating."

Her sage advice to me, as I find myself swimming in a sea of potions, elixirs, herbal remedies, tonics—new age therapies all promising to be "the cure"—was quite simple, profound, and poignant and has helped me immensely as I find myself annoyed by this aspect of the disease. I can't help but feel that this commingling of commerce and cure-all claims, this complete garbage with no basis in fact or reality, only creates science-fiction health that preys on the vulnerable, with an underlying and often sinister profit motive. Patent medicine is alive and well, it's just packaged differently and costs a lot more.

My friend's advice? "I believe that each of us needs to learn the fine and delicate art of really listening to our systems—our hearts, minds, and bodies. If something calls to your heart, I'd recommend that you give it a try, not expecting a cure but watching carefully for what, if anything, it might be doing to alleviate your experience. I don't know how else to walk these paths. I felt that one invaluable lesson I learned from cancer was to quiet and listen to my body and heart. Leave the mind's chatter aside. It's the body and heart that have important messages to which we need to learn to attend." Amen.

This week's Science section in the *New York Times* featured a beautifully written article by Denise Grady titled "A Tumor Is No Clearer in Hindsight." In it, she discusses Steve Jobs and his decision to put off surgery on his cancerous pancreas, start a vegan diet, and use juices, herbs, and alternative therapies. She writes:

> "...there is no way in this life to know what might have been—not in politics, baseball, romance or the stock market, and certainly not in sickness and health. Mr. Jobs's wish to avoid or delay surgery was not unusual. And given the type of tumor he had and the way it was found, his decision to wait may not have been as ill-considered as it seems at first blush."

Steve's decisions were personal and for him to make, and we the public know only a fraction of the truth. Who are we to judge? We all follow our own paths.

I will continue to eat well, exercise more, and listen deeply to my heart, mind, and body, and to follow paths that may or may not help fight my cancer. Some may work, some will fail. My meditation practice has already moved me forward in a way I've always desired but never stopped long enough to try. So for the first time since Quaker school, I'm finding my inner peace through silence and meditation. This is no mere elixir.

I leave you with a few additional items to consider if you have the desire and the time. (By the way, "If You Have the Time" is also the title of an excellent blog by fellow brain cancer survivor Matt Cotcher.)

> "To me, there are three things we all should do every day. We should do this every day of our lives. Number one is laugh. You should laugh every day. Number two is think. You should spend some time in thought. And number three is, you should have your emotions moved to tears, could be happiness or joy. But think about it. If you laugh, you think, and you cry, that's a full day. That's a heck of a day. You do that seven days a week, you're going to have something special." —Jim Valvano

The legendary basketball coach Jim Valvano's ESPY acceptance speech—11 mins long—delivered only months before succumbing to bone cancer, closed with:

> "Cancer can take away all of my physical abilities. It cannot touch my mind, it cannot touch my heart, and it cannot touch my soul. And those three things are going to carry on forever."

And in the music trivia department: the origin of the term "heavy metal" can be traced to many sources, including the great William S. Burroughs, but the first mention in song is attributed to a motorcycle reference in Steppenwolf's "Born to be Wild."

Heavy Metal Thunder…baby!

Run, Buck, Run. No Muggle He.

Tuesday, November 08, 2011

Buck, Brian Buckley McAllister III: A dear, dear friend, partner-in-crime, confidante, college roommate, New York city ambassador, stupendous father of two truly blessed children, loving husband to loving wife, number-one-son, brother, cousin, uncle, tugboat magnate, 9/11 volunteer, Tiki Brother musician extraordinaire, Park Slope community activist, Puerto Rico barnacle-scrubbing dockmate, Bread and Puppet tentmate, Grateful Dead "Dude, where's my car?" lost-soul mate, Okemo ski buddy, Farm and Wilderness devotee, a man with a deep roaring laugh, radiant eyes, and a lust for life…ran the NYC Marathon this weekend in under four hours: three hours and fifty minutes to be exact (3:50) while wearing a Harry Potter wizard costume, waving a wand, and sporting a t-shirt that read "Running for Moose." His account is nothing short of beautiful. He is a gift to all of us. Love You Buck…

"I don't know the exact nature of the wand I ran with, but it helped me. Sycamore, 15 inches, kind of crooked and heavily stained. But there is more to the story. As I think I mentioned, my buddy Moose is dealing with cancer. I wrote on my shirt that I was running for Moose. This unleashed spells that I don't fully understand, but may have been even more powerful than the Elder Wand. Don't get me wrong. The wand gave me amplified power, and increased my speed. There are bands all along the course, some official and some, like some of my friends in Park Slope, engaging in pirate performances. I waved the wand to the beat of the bands lining the course. I magically produced a lot of smiles that way. My friends in the Fifth Street Band played Gigantic, by the Pixies (by request), which I heard a block before I could see them. I remember the songs "War Pig", "Brooklyn" by JayZ, "Country Tonk" by the Stones, "Proud Mary," "Dreaming," "Please Tell

Me Why" by Lit (a particularly fitting song), "Beautiful Day" by U2, "Fireworks" by Katy Perry, etc. There was a lot of music I couldn't recognize by Latin bands, punk bands, Eastern European bands, marching bands, a Folkie woman singing originals along with her own keyboard, free jazz, funk, and a Hasidic rock band in Queens that might have been playing Green Day. My spells had extra effect on the heavy metal bands. I was able to send a charm to a wild-looking guy blowing into a plastic trumpet at a big street party in Fort Greene. And I got a great reaction waving the wand at about forty drunks at a balcony keg party in Greenpoint.

But the power of the wand was not nearly the power of Moose's name on my shirt. Perhaps 100,000 people yelled to me, "Go Moose." Many cried out "The Moose is loose." I felt a little bad for the other runners because my get-up drew a lot of attention. One thousand people cast words upon me like "You can do it, Moose" or "Don't give up, Moose" or"Keep up the fight, Moose." These spells had a curious effect on me. I gave high fives to hundreds of people who repeated the chant, including Russians in Bay Ridge, Latinos in Sunset Park, Park Slope kids, impeccably dressed Lubavitchers and hipsters in Williamsburg, a very loud firefighter in Greenpoint, auto mechanics in Queens, grandmothers with their grandkids outside the projects, yuppies on the Upper East Side, homeboys in the Bronx, a uniformed cop in Harlem, and foreign tourists in Central Park. I wish Moose could have been there in person to soak up the encouragement. They all repeated the same spell, and it had quite a power. When I could, I gave them all high fives, including hundreds of people.

The cloak was definitely not a cloak of concealment. A number of runners asked me what it meant that I was running for Moose. I got interviewed by a journalism student at the finish line who was confused about the combination of a large ruminant animal and magic. Maybe a hundred people said, "Yea, Harry Potter." About ten yelled, "Why is a witch running the marathon?" I yelled back at them that I was a wizard. Muggles!

But the best moment for me was somewhere near Bedford Stuyvesant. There was a DJ doing a live remix on a huge sound system of the hip hop standard "I Got The Power." You could hear it blocks away. When he saw me, he yelled into his mike, "Moose got the powah." I got so choked up, I had trouble breathing for a while, but after that I barely felt the miles.

I have sealed this magic outfit and the wand in a plastic bag. It should be treated as a biohazard. There may be a little blood around the nipples on the shirt. There may be substances on the cloak like vaseline or mucous, which may be something else entirely. The outfit was soaked through with sweat, tears, grime, grit, and every stripe of Big Apple humanity.

I am sending this package to Moose, unwashed. By the time it arrives, it will have fermented into a potent potion. I would give it the same name as the subtitle for the event. The Race for Life. Breathe it in, Moose. I hope it brings you a little magic.

—Buck

Buckley, you are my hero! YOU'VE GOT THE POWER!

Carpe Diem. Tempis Fugit. Gather Ye Rosebuds. . .

Thursday, November 10, 2011

SEIZE THE DAY. IF NOT NOW, WHEN? TIME FLIES.
GATHER YE ROSEBUDS WHILE YE MAY.

SILENCE like a cancer grows… and in this light, taking silence to task, my 15-year-old daughter, Hannah and I presented an assembly this week at her school, Northfield Mount Hermon, on "The Face of Cancer." It was Hannah's tale to be told. I followed her lead. Her idea. It was also the first time I really heard her full view of what she experienced during those initial calamitous days.

She's already launched the "NMH Cancer Team" for students whose lives have been affected by cancer or who simply want to become involved in providing resources and support. With her classmates she organized a walk for breast cancer, called Rays of Hope, that brought in nearly $4,550 for Baystate Health Center. The team now has over fifty members, and she's thinking of taking a similar initiative national. I'm sure she will. She was brave and courageous. Standing in the chapel, before the entire school population of nearly 700 students, faculty, and staff, she was proud and radiant.

We recognize that not everyone is comfortable with any of this. None of us really are. Many were moved. Some were a bit shaken.

Cancer, or any disease, illness, or trauma is a deeply personal, private matter. There are no "rules" for managing this sort of event. But we believe no good comes of silence when you're fighting something so deadly and devastating, and if by raising the awareness and consciousness of those around us we can help demystify and encourage understanding and the need for more resources, including research and support, then all the better.

> "Not everything that is faced can be changed.
> But nothing can be changed until it is faced."
> —James Baldwin

Hannah, who in first grade, we were told by loving teacher Ms. Gravel, "runs deep," has taken this proverbially insane cancer bull by the horns and thrashed it to the ground. Her younger sister, Libby, has also stared down this animal with bravery, courage and compassion. I am deeply proud. We are all holding on, together. Sometimes quite literally.

Gather Ye Rosebuds While Ye May, by John William Waterhouse.

Hannah Rose Green and Mark Richard Green

Morning Assembly, Northfield Mount Hermon School, MA

Hannah: Good morning NMH. I'm here today to introduce you to an amazing person, my dad. He's like me in a lot of ways; he's been my main role model since I can remember. He has a way of making friends with just a single sentence, maybe because he's always smiling, always optimistic, and constantly cracking jokes. He's also extremely active, and has more energy than any other middle-aged man I've ever met. But he's not just my role model, he's also my best friend. I could never ask for a better father and friend.

Mark: There are moments in life that are completely out of our control. Some are minor disasters, and others are of epic proportions. There's a particularly unstable glass shelf in our medicine cabinet, loaded with various items, which from time to time comes loose, sending everything sliding and crashing to the sink below, and you find yourself watching helplessly as the whole bathroom falls to pieces.

Hannah: This past summer, on a beautiful August day, the medicine cabinet fell. I came home from the pool to find my dad very sick. His eyes wouldn't focus, his speech was slurred and slow, and he couldn't walk straight. I knew something definitely was wrong when he didn't touch his dinner. He said he was having a migraine and went to his room to sleep. A few hours later, he came to tell me he had just thrown up and that my stepmom was going to take him to the hospital. "He just has heat exhaustion," my stepmom assured me. She said that there was no reason for me to come, because they would probably end up waiting in the ER all night for him to get an IV stuck in his arm and sent home. So I went to my mom's to get some sleep. But I didn't sleep at all that night, I was so worried about my dad. I waited all night for a text message from my stepmom to tell me that my dad was fine. That message never came.

Mark: Once I arrived at the emergency room, I was given a CT scan, and within twenty minutes the doctor delivered the news. I had a golf ball size tumor, and it was serious. What happened next was like being on an awful carnival ride. The feeling of shock and bewilderment we will never forget. Was the doctor kidding? Surely he was just kidding… I was immediately transported by ambulance an hour north to Dartmouth Hitchcock Medical Center. All I recall were the muffled sounds, the darkness, the *whirr* of the tires speeding up the highway.

Hannah: My mom delivered the news the next morning. She told me the doctors believed his illness could be attributed to something inside his head. I almost started laughing. Something in his head? I remembered a time when I was little, when my dad would stick pretzels in his nose to make me and my sister laugh. What'd he do, get pretzels lost in his brain? I thought. "Mom what are you talking about?" I asked.

She answered with a word that changed my life. A word I would hear a million times in the days to come, and a word I still think about every day, and will think about forever: "A tumor."

All I remember after that is uncontrollable crying, for hours, up until we drove to the hospital to visit my dad, when my mom told me I needed to be strong for him. I was so scared to see him. It meant that the tumor was real, and that I was not stuck in some crazy nightmare.

He was heavily medicated, because the tumor was putting pressure on his brain, causing him immense agony. He faded in and out of consciousness. When he was awake, he would vomit, cry, and ramble drunkenly about rainbows and unicorns. When he was asleep, he would curl into a crumpled ball, pale and weak.

Mark: I was stuck in a car crash that never seemed to end. I awoke, groggily, to a cacophonous riot of hospital machines, telephones, pagers, and people speaking softly and sometimes loudly, bright lights, a blur of sound and movement, and most painfully, the look of shock, fear, and worry washing over my family. All I could do was think of my two daughters. I didn't want to die. Not now. I'm not ready, I thought. The pressure on my brain was expanding. I was told later I had less than a week to live before the tumor, with no room left to expand, would have herniated into my brain stem, killing me instantly.

The tears welling up in Hannah's eyes as she looked on with confusion and fear were the most devastating. I thought of Libby, away at camp, not knowing any of this. "What was happening to my dad?" Hannah seemed to be saying without even speaking.

Hannah: In the ten hours I spent at the hospital that day, I watched my dad decline from bad to worse. He needed more medication every hour, woke up less, and became paler, more delirious, and more uncomfortable. The only part of his body that had any color was his neck, where the bleeding from his brain was pooling. I understood then that if that tumor was not removed as soon as possible, my dad would not be alive much longer. The surgery was moved to the next morning. Saying goodbye was the hardest. I begged to sleep at the hospital, but neither the doctors nor my family would allow it.

I was positive that if I left, it would be the last kiss goodnight I would ever share with my father.

Mark: But I did make it through the night, and at six the next morning my skull was opened up, the tumor removed, titanium screws and plates inserted, and sewn back up.

Hannah: His surgery finished with no complications, and I was rushed into the recovery room to visit him. My dad was awake and ready to party. He was cracking jokes to the staff and to the other patients, trying to make friends and have fun.

I remember this as one of the happiest moments of my life. The trials of the past day were over, and my dad and my life were both almost back to normal. Until, a few hours later, when the doctor returned with the diagnosis of the tumor.

Mark: Stage III Brain Cancer. Anaplastic ependymoma, to be specific. An already rare cancer, it occurs over 95 percent of the time in children. Not much information for the doctors to work with. What the doctors do know is that the cancer is incurable and is a lifelong diagnosis. They said despite all efforts to radiate it, the tumor will eventually grow back, and could be operated on again but not radiated again. There is no other treatment, save for experimental trials for which I will be eligible when the tumor returns. We don't know when the tumor will come back. It could be in a year, it could be in five, ten years, or more.

Hannah: The doctor hadn't even finished explaining before I was gone. I ran from the room, and cried on my mom's shoulder for a very long time. "He'll never see me graduate, never see me get a job, never walk me down the aisle, never meet his grandchildren." She didn't deny it like I wanted her to, but instead told me advice everyone should live by. "You can't live your life worrying about the future." It took me a long time to accept this, but it became easier when my dad returned home a few days later. He recovered quickly, and soon his illness was almost forgotten.

Mark: Until several weeks later, when I had a second brain surgery to remove the remnants of the tumor. At the end of this week, I will complete thirty-three treatments of radiation therapy to kill what they can of the cancerous tissue that remains. I will have to, for the rest of my life, monitor things with tests and MRIs. It's the emotional mountains that appear to be the steepest. Cancer is a sinister disease, and will now always be lurking within.

Hannah: I was already back at NMH when my dad had the second surgery, and I felt enormous guilt for not being at home to support him. But I quickly realized that I was not alone. My story is one in over 11.7 million. The story I just told happens every day to countless families around the globe every day. In the time I've been talking, four people have died in the US because of cancer. And I can guarantee that every single person in this room will be affected by cancer at some point in their lifetime. And maybe some of you already have been.

This was my inspiration to start the Cancer Support Team: to support kids on campus who have been affected by cancer, and also to support cancer patients in every way we can.

The cancer team has already raised almost five thousand dollars for cancer, and this past weekend we participated in a cancer walk in Greenfield.

There are a number of ways you can get involved in fighting cancer, and helping prevent any more of these stories from happening.

Whether you want to commit to joining the fifty of us who are part of the cancer team, or make it a one-time thing, there is force in numbers.

This month, we will be selling t-shirts and also holding a hair-cutting event if you would like to donate your hair to cancer or even shave your head to show your support.

As most of you are aware, this month was breast cancer month. But tomorrow is the first day of November; I would like to bring attention to the most fatal cancer, lung cancer. The lung cancer color is white. Please show your support by participating in an all-school white-out. Thank you.

In these bodies we will live, in these bodies we will die
Where you invest your love, you invest your life
In these bodies we will live, in these bodies we will die
Where you invest your love, you invest your life. . .

—*Awake My Soul*, Mumford and Sons

On bended knee is no way to be free
Lifting up an empty cup, I ask silently
All my destinations will accept the one that's me
So I can breathe…

Circles they grow and they swallow people whole
Half their lives they say goodnight to wives they'll never know
A mind full of questions, and a teacher in my soul
And so it goes…

Don't come closer or I'll have to go
Holding me like gravity are places that pull
If ever there was someone to keep me at home
It would be you…

Everyone I come across, in cages they bought
They think of me and my wandering, but I'm never what they thought
I've got my indignation, but I'm pure in all my thoughts
I'm alive…

Wind in my hair, I feel part of everywhere
Underneath my being is a road that disappeared
Late at night I hear the trees, they're singing with the dead
Overhead…

Leave it to me as I find a way to be
Consider me a satellite, forever orbiting
I knew all the rules, but the rules did not know me
Guaranteed…

—*Guaranteed*, Eddie Vedder

the mask and the music

Tuesday, November 15, 2011

"If music be the food of love, play on." —William Shakespeare

What we play is life." —Louis Armstrong

"If I can't dance, I don't want to be part of your revolution"
—Emma Goldman

As of 11/11/11, I had completed my thirty-three radiation treatments. This was oddly bittersweet. On the up-side, the daily shlep of heading north and south on I-91 for an hour each way is over, and it reminded me why, as much as I loved working for Dartmouth, spending two hours a day commuting was not for me. Thanks to the hard work of Barb and many friends, we had a drive-pool to make it all happen, as I was told I would be quite tired after treatments. Car time with friends can be invaluable, and it was. (Thank you all...in addition to your love and support, I-91 from exit 5 to Lebanon, New Hampshire, was that much safer without me on the road.)

On my final day, I gave Lake Champlain chocolates and a card to the sweet, kind women at the registration desk: Rosemary, Judy, and the others. And the same to my radiation team on the Trilogy: Ed, Duke, Kerry, JB, Krista, Becky, and many more who guided me daily through the routine of laying me on the table, locking me down, and calibrating the machine. I will miss them, for they made what could have been a complete drag much more tolerable. At the end, I was handed a "diploma" and my radiation mask, which will be kept as a totem, or perhaps as a macabre Halloween costume. Incidentally, I have two friends who have been treated for throat cancer who have the same mask contraption. We would make quite a trio.

I do wonder what certificate they have for those who don't pass with high honors: "Mark Green has barely completed the prescribed radiation therapy with a substandard grade, and did so with infantile resistance and the worst attitude shown to humankind we have seen in many, many years. The team wishes you good riddance. Next time, try using your microwave oven and see how that works." I'm sure there can be some gallows humor backstage from time to time.

When I walked in the door wearing the mask, the dogs went berserk.

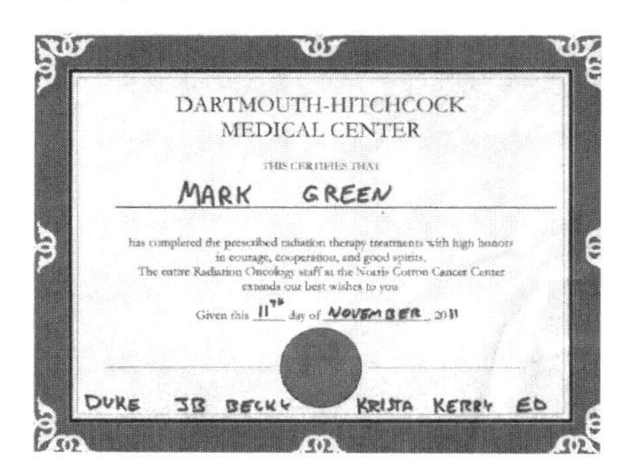

DARTMOUTH-HITCHCOCK
MEDICAL CENTER

THIS CERTIFIES THAT

MARK GREEN

has completed the prescribed radiation therapy treatments with high honors in courage, cooperation, and good spirits.
The entire Radiation Oncology staff at the Norris Cotton Cancer Center extends our best wishes to you

Given this 11TH day of NOVEMBER 2011

DUKE JB BECKY KRISTA KERRY ED

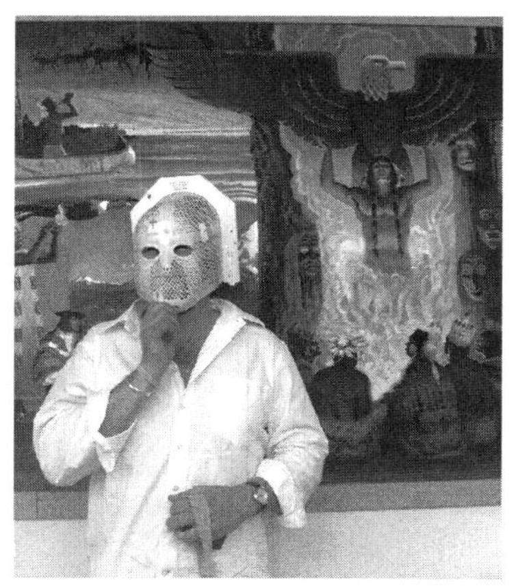

The Mask.
MURAL BY SOL LEVINSON.

Next steps: my headaches are actually heating up, literally, and I'm told that this week through next will be the peak of my fatigue as the cumulative effects of the radiation take hold. Sleep remains an issue (I'm getting very little) as my body fights the combination of radiation fatigue and the steroids I take to help reduce swelling of the brain. Most body parts can swell way beyond their normal state with little effect, but the brain, being encased in a skull, has little room to expand without complications such as seizures or worse. Incidentally, female skulls are slightly thicker than male skulls with an average thickness of 6.5mm for men and 7.1mm for women. What both genders could do with that little nugget of data…

An MRI will follow next month, acting as a benchmark for all future MRIs, which I will have every three months at the outset. It's likely there will be some changes, as "artifact" from the two surgeries and radiation will result in a new landscape. The subsequent MRI in March will be the one we will hold our breath for as we ascertain if new cancerous cell growth has occurred. If it does, we put on our crampons and start the climb anew. Radiation is a one-time thing. Chemo is not an option because of the blood-brain barrier. Additional surgeries are possible, as well as clinical trials. I know my Sherpas, climbing partners, and team are with me in love and support. I remain a lucky man. I understand, but do not always embrace, the usage of battle metaphor when dealing with illness. But it is a good war, if there is such a thing.

A close friend, an oncologist at DHMC, told me that on an emotional level, the hard part begins now, as we learn to live with the disease. The dust of this cancer will always hang in the air, but some of the cinders will settle now that the intensity of the past three and a half months has lessened. I have memories from my childhood of waking up in the quiet of a Sunday morning, just lying in bed, birds singing, with the sun streaming though my window, the sunbeams illuminating the dust coming in, floating like so many feathers.

I'm starting to work full time again and am eager to get my life back on the road, literally. The holidays are upon us. The snows will be coming soon. It's now time to simply live and laugh and love as if every grain of sand in that damned hourglass is as precious as the one behind it…

The Mask and the Music II

Music. It's my life-food. It's carried me out of despair. Lifted my body up. Calmed the torrential storms in my head. Helped me win races and bike long distances, brought me back to earth, and sent me into the stratosphere. Music has helped heal a wounded heart and has been a catalyst for falling in love.

Studies have proven that cows will produce more milk if they're serenaded with Mozart than if they're in a silent barn. (Incidentally and unsurprisingly, they also produce less milk if heavy metal is played. Iron Maiden, perhaps.)

Goosebump moments happen daily. It could be the single-note wail from a Neil Young rocker, it could be a strain of Mozart, Haydn, or Maria Callas. The plaintive wail of an Appalachian folk tune, Dock Boggs on banjo, a cello, a hymnal, a viola, a piano, a shape-note song, a Gregorian Chant, a Georgian folk song, Miles Davis, Monk, Ella, Josephine Baker, the Uilleann pipes, a hand drum, African drums, or Bill Monroe's mandolin. The list is endless.

What does this have to with cancer? Everything. At Dartmouth-Hitchcock, musicians play in the lobbies. (In addition to a very well-defined art program) In Brattleboro, the Hallowell Singers have received international acclaim for their beloved work with end-of-care hospice patients. Music helps heal, just as good diet and exercise are essential whether one is healthy or struggling.

The musical experiences that have molded my heart are too numerous to mention. But I owe deep thanks for my love of music to my late grandfather, my mother, my father, and my Abington Friends School music teacher Cathy Roma (now Founder/Director MUSE Cincinnati's Women's Choir, Co-Founder, Co-Director Martin Luther King Chorale, Minister of Music at St. John's Unitarian Universalist Church and Professor of Music at Wilmington College).

I remember hearing Andres Segovia with Grandma Green, countless Joan Baez concerts, jazz, bluegrass and folk festivals, symphony concerts, ballet performances. I am a distant relative of Jascha Heifeitz but sadly did not acquire his musical fortitude. And I have recordings of my great-grandmother singing Yiddish folk songs.

Like so many immigrant populations, the need and desire to assimilate was often challenged by the tug of the homeland and with it song, food, customs and traditions, eventually percolating into the cultural stew that made, and continues to make, America a dynamic and ever shifting multi-cultural jambalaya of sound. (A paella of song! A stir-fry of harmony!)

I recall as if it was yesterday, school secretary Helen Conkey playing harpsichord for Handel's Messiah in the Meeting House of our Quaker School (founded in 1697, there is still "graffiti," or rather names and dates, carved in the backs of the upper-level pews dating from the 1700's), or visiting as a whole class, classmate Jason Charles Walker's father's Baptist Church in downtown Philadelphia for a gospel concert. These moments were indelible and moved me even then, at a young age. Goosebumps.

My grandfather was an amateur luthier, and I recall his workshop in the basement of his upstate New York home, with tables of bent and carved wood, banjo tuners, mandolin parts, drawers of ebony and ivory for inlay, the rhythm of the ace machine, the smell of musty wood emanating from the f-holes of a 1918 Gibson. Homemade guitars, banjos, banjolins, a double-necked mandola/electric guitar. These gifts still give...they live and breathe.

In 2004, Dr. Karl Paulnack, pianist and director of music division at the Boston Conservatory, gave a now widely shared welcome address to the parents of incoming students:

> "If there is a future wave of wellness on this planet, of harmony, of peace, of an end to war, of mutual understanding, of equality, of fairness, I don't expect it will come from a government, a military force, or a corporation. I no longer even expect it to come from the religions of the world, which together seem to have brought us as much war as they have peace. If there is a future of peace for humankind, if there is to be an understanding of how these invisible, internal things should fit together, I expect it will come from the artists, because that's what we do."

"Life... is a state of mind"

—from *Being There*

Thursday, November 17, 2011

> "Most people think life sucks, and then you die. Not me. I beg to differ. I think life sucks, then you get cancer, then your dog dies, your wife leaves you, the cancer goes into remission, you get a new dog, you get remarried, you owe ten million dollars in medical bills, but you work hard for thirty-five years and you pay it back, and then—one day—you have a massive stroke, your whole right side is paralyzed, you have to limp along the streets and speak out of the left side of your mouth and drool, but you go into rehabilitation and regain the power to walk and the power to talk and then—one day—you step off a curb at sixty-seventh street, and BANG, you get hit by a city bus and then you die. Maybe."
>
> —Denis Leary

I woke up at 12:30 am with a start. I said to myself, "Okay, Mark, its time to cure this cancer." The words fell out of my mouth, and now I write in the wee hours of the morning, wide awake once again. I had this bizarre notion that I had to call Alfred to get me to the Bat-Cave and suit up. Delusions of grandeur I suppose. I always liked Batman and his mysterious tortured-hero persona. And the Batmobile... and all those gadgets....the Bat Suit...

> "I don't use drugs; my dreams are frightening enough."
>
> —M. C. Escher

I'd fallen asleep somewhat troubled. I was doing the math of cancer survivorship in my head, a futile exercise. I had told myself to swear off statistics. But I went there.

Sleep has been a major complication what with the cocktail of medication for both the swelling of my brain from radiation combined with the emotional weight of what swirls above and below and around us. Last night, in an another attempt to get more than three hours of sleep at a stretch, I took hydromorphone for pain, two Lorazepam, and an Ambien. I told Barb, "Please don't let me wake up like Heath Ledger," a beautiful actor who sadly passed much too soon as a result of an unintentional overdose. (Now that I write this, I realize his last role was the Joker in one of the latest Batman films… strange)

The result? Two hours of sleep. I'm up, lit like a lightbulb, wired and ready to run a race. And this after starting to taper the steroid dexamethasone, for swelling. Now I know how Mark McGwire and all those super-human athletes did what they did. I've been doing thirty push-ups and thirty sit-ups before bed to try to exhaust the energy in my system. My medications, while often necessary and useful for many and a lifesaver for some, have wreaked havoc on my whole being, and I look forward to eliminating them completely. But it could always be worse…so rather than complain, I just let them do what they need to do and grin and bear it.

Like my mother, my body seems to have a natural, organic chemistry that resists chemical intervention. We have high tolerances, I suppose. Nothing seems to touch the headaches or the sleeplessness. Warm baths, candles, meditation all help shift my motor down, but sleep, I suppose, will come in due time. I would bet that sugar pills, a placebo, would have the same effect, which has been nearly none. My body seems to metabolize my meds in a way that renders them ineffective. I guess that's better than having a proclivity toward addiction, like I have with bacon, chocolate, and pretzels.

I was in the basement attending to my ongoing effort to organize my library of 2,367 music CDs, which had escaped my maniacally obsessive (and uncharacteristic) compulsion to sequence them by genre and then alphabetize, when a large mass of warm air forced me to sit down. The wave slowly but forcefully pushed my body to the floor. And the tears poured, out of nowhere. This has happened on a few occasions in the past four months. Like a bolt of lightning, when I'm alone. Music, a photograph, the smell of a wood fire, or a beautiful landscape often act as triggers. A good bawl is a healthy physic.

I'm 44. My children are 15 and 12. Without traveling too far down Macabre Lane—as I have every hope and intention of pushing this cancer's ultimate destiny as far back as possible—it dawned on me that, realistically, I'll be very lucky if I live to 65. That's the hopeful number. Given the rarity of this type of cancer in adults, I've come upon only two longitudinal studies, and, well, they don't look so great. And yet any number of medical setbacks or, hopefully, advancements in treatment can happen between then and now. A LOT can happen in cancer research between now and twenty years, let alone in the time it has taken me to write this sentence. I don't dwell on this too often, but I believe it's a necessary and natural step in accepting this disease and beginning to strategize how to live my life to its fullest. At least I know it will include bacon, chocolate, and pretzels, although my meat intake is dwindling as per cancer-diet recommendation. And bacon, even if it's as fresh and as local as I tasted the other day at Putney School (the pigs were raised on the farm...YUM) is not an indulgence I will partake in too often.

Many friends and family have lost loved ones to cancer. Fathers, mothers, brothers, sisters, grandparents, children. What knocked me down was the notion that I'm fortunate to have both of my parents living, yet I face the very real notion that by the time my children are in their thirties—perhaps married, perhaps not, perhaps with children, perhaps not—I may not be here.

Yes, I know, any of us may not "be here." We simply don't know when the "when" will happen. But as one cancer-doctor friend said gently when I asked him point blank to tell it to me straight: what is *up* with this brain cancer?: "Mark, you were dealt a very rare and strange card."

Just putting this down in words gives me pause. What does this mean? In the most practical sense, it means that we will enjoy every moment in a manner never experienced. Everything counts. I know it sounds cliché. It means that the will and drive to succeed at my job knows no bounds, as landing back at Putney has been my long-desired career arc and goal all along. Being there fills my heart. It means that my desire to give back to my community and promote the greater good has been amplified. That's why I've already initiated several projects to raise awareness for cancer, and brain cancer specifically.

My relationships, which were strong, have only been made more so. Deeper, more open, more rewarding. Unresolved issues have been left to slough away as I prioritize what's important. My tolerance for the petty is even less than it was. This piece—the hyperawareness of the seemingly small issues made unnecessarily large—can be illuminating, absurd, mind-boggling, and sometimes hilarious. Alas, we all have our neuroses large and small. Who am I to judge another person's meltdown?

My phone calls to my parents and sister are longer, my ability to focus more intent. And while some might be surprised to hear this, I feel freer to speak my mind. Silence like a cancer…grows. As I've said, every grain of sand…each granule…counts.

On the civil service front, I recently took part in a national study on brain tumors by responding to an hourlong telephone survey and submitting a saliva sample via UPS (don't worry, they have special lab mailers for blood, tissue and saliva samples lest anything bursts on our collective holiday packages) for MD Anderson, the largest cancer center in the world. MD Anderson is where I went this fall to meet with top physicians in the field of ependymal brain cancer, especially the notable Dr. Mark Gilbert. As a recently diagnosed cancer patient, I'm consulting on a documentary film project based on the must-read *Emperor of All Maladies, A Biography of Cancer*, by Dr. Siddhartha Mukherjee, and helping to get the producer in front of some of the top people at Dartmouth-Hitchcock. And I was asked to allow one of my blog posts to be used for the annual fund appeal at Norris Cotton Cancer Center. This blog's purpose is not only to help me process my journey, but to share with others in the hope that it may help those walking through this dark and confusing tunnel. Perhaps it will inspire others to act. I have links on several websites, including the National Brain Tumor Society and CERN (Collaborative Ependymoma Resource Network) and was recently published in the CURE Newsletter.

Because brain cancer is so rare, there simply isn't a profit motive for pharmaceutical companies to invest heavily in research, technologies, medicines, clinical trials, and the like. With this in mind, I'm also working with an extraordinary organization, ABC2 (Accelerate Brain Cancer Cure), founded by the late Dan Case, who passed away at age forty-four with four children and a wife from brain cancer, and his brother, Steve Case. Steve was CEO of Time Warner/ AOL and Dan, a highly respected and successful investment banker and Chairman of the Board of JPMorgan H&Q. As they explain on their website, "In 2001, Dan Case was diagnosed with brain cancer. Discouraged by a lack of information and limited treatment options, Dan, together with his brother, Steve Case, and their families, founded Accelerate Brain Cancer Cure. We are a non-profit organization that partners with leading entrepreneurs, scientists and researchers to find a cure for brain cancer."—ABC2 Website. I am thrilled to be involved with this dynamic group.

Additionally, my daughters and I are working to establish a National Student Cancer Support Network for students in public and independent schools, which has been given a hearty endorsement from Pat Bassett, president of the National Association of Independent Schools.

There's a Shaker saying I admire: "Hands to work, hearts to God." I will never be quite certain about the God question—that's a whole other journey—but the phrase is fitting. We have much to do here on this funny little planet. Why not make a difference and have fun? Selfless acts can fill the heart and raise the spirit.

The hard stuff begins now—the living-with-cancer part—for this will consume our lives in ways unforeseen. The path ahead is unclear, but we are all holding hands, tightly.

For some reason, I keep coming back to one of my favorite films of all time: *Being There*, written by late author Jerzy Kosinski (The Painted Bird, Steps) and directed by Hal Ashby...and this scene... Peter Sellers...absolutely brilliant...

"Laugh as much as you breathe and love as long as you live."
–Unknown

So long, farewell, Auf Wiedersehen, good night...a statistical jettison (the race is on)

Tuesday, November 22, 2011

"Statistics are like a bikini. What they reveal is suggestive, but what they conceal is vital."
—Aaron Levenstein

WITH A RESPECTFUL NOD to *Harper's Magazine*, my "Index." Synthesizing vast amounts of data results, inevitably, in variables and discrepancies. Data shifts further when race, gender, socioeconomic status, and ethnicity are taken into account. I had sworn off statistics, as I am not a number. But when I feel like digging deep, when curiosity and hunger to know more about this cancer claw at my heart and mind, I go there. Less so now. And even less, I hope, after this jump into the deep water.

In the hospital, during the initial trauma, they had to wrest the phone from my clutched hand—I was known to be up in the wee hours of the night, scanning my iPhone for answers and data. Looking back, it was not a healthy exercise, for it left fear, sadness, and even more unanswered questions, all while in the induced haze of postsurgery. I don't advise going there, as I did; you'll be stuck in your own avalanche of information anyway.

We're not a statistic. Life is a variable. That said, grabbing the bull by the horns again, I wanted to face down these numbers. Own them, name them, put them on my plate, digest them, and then purge them.

Mark's Index

Revenue in 2009 for United Way, the largest nonprofit in the US: $4.2 billion
2009-2010 fiscal year earnings, Susan G. Komen for the Cure: $400 million

Amount George Soros, leading philanthropist, contributed in 2010: $332 million

Net worth, Bill Gates: $56 Billion

Highest-paid CEO: John H. Hammergren, McKesson Pharmaceuticals; compensation: $131.2 million; net income (TTM): $46 million

2010 National Cancer Institute funding, brain cancer: $156 million

Funds raised by ABC2, Accelerate Brain Cancer Cure since 2001: $16 million

Gross receipts, opening weekend, *Harry Potter and the Deathly Hallows, Part 2*: $169 million

Call of Duty: Modern Warfare 3 video game sales, first twenty-four hours of release: $400 million

Revenue in 2011 of Wal-Mart, ranked number-one Fortune 500 Company: $421.85 billion

Enough cancer cells for one experiment, including shipping: $300 to $500

Cost of one pound of Kashmir Mogra Cream Indian Saffron: $7,680

Cost of Avastin, a drug for lung and colorectal cancer, for one year: $100,000

Year President Nixon signed the US "War on Cancer": 1971

Cost of War on Cancer (research) since then: $100 billion

Leading cause of death and numbers in US in 2006: heart disease, 616,067

Second-leading cause of death and numbers in US in 2006: cancer, 562,875

Population of Portland, Oregon, in 2010: 583,776

Largest stadium capacity in US: University of Michigan, 109,901

Annual government funding for National Cancer Institute over past six years: $4.9 billion

2010 military budget: $663 billion

Cost of wars in Afghanistan, Iraq, and Pakistan in 2011: $1.7 trillion

Number of deaths from these engagements: 236,000

Number of US citizens diagnosed with lung cancer in 2007: 203,536

People who died from lung cancer in 2007: 158,683

Cost of smoking in direct health care costs: $96 billion

Number of chemical compounds created by burning one cigarette: 4,000; number of additives: 599; known carcinogens: 51

Estimated new cases of invasive breast cancer diagnosed in women in the US in 2011: 230,480

Estimated people (55% male, 45% female) in US diagnosed with a malignant brain tumor in 2010: 23,720

Number of breast cancer survivors in the US in 2011: 2.6 million

Number of brain cancer survivors in the US in 2004: 124,000

Lowest five-year cancer survival rates in order: (1) pancreatic, (2) liver, (3) esophagus, (4) lung, (5) stomach, (6) brain

Approximate number of people who will die of primary brain cancer in 2011: 13,000

New cases of children with primary brain or central nervous system cancers in 2011: 3,000

Leading cause of cancer death among children and young adults under twenty: leukemia

Second-leading cause of cancer death among children and young adults under twenty: brain cancer

Rank of brain cancer as leading cause of cancer-related deaths among adult males up to age thirty-nine: 2

Rank of brain cancer as leading cause of cancer-related deaths among adult females up to age thirty-nine: 5

Most commonly diagnosed cancers among men: (1) prostate, (2) lung, (3) colorectal

Leading causes of cancer death among men: (1) lung, (2) prostate, (3) colorectal, (4) liver

Most commonly diagnosed cancers among women: (1) breast, (2) lung, (3) colorectal

Leading causes of cancer death among women: (1) lung, (2) breast, (3) colorectal

Different types of brain tumors: 120+

Beer known as the "Holy Grail for Hopheads": Dogfish Head 120-minute IPA

Percentage of adults with cancer whose primary cancer is brain cancer: 1–2%

Percentage of adults with brain cancer with ependymoma as their primary tumor: 1-2%

US adults killed by lightning in 2011: 26

Odds of being killed on a 5-mile bus trip: 500,000,000 to 1

Chance, according to NASA, of anyone on Earth being hurt by a satellite's death plunge: 1 in 3,200

Annual average of adults in US diagnosed with ependymoma brain cancer (all stages, I-III): 300

Number of brain cancer treatments approved by the FDA in the past thirty years: 4 (last one just approved this year: NovaCure's NovoTTF-100A device)

Number of FDA-approved drugs in 2010: 21 in 2011: 35

Money spent on weight-loss drugs in US, annually: $1.3 billion

Number of weight-loss drugs on the market: 200+

Percentage of adults with ependymoma located in spine: 60%; located in brain: 40%

Median age of those diagnosed with brain cancer (2002): 55

Median age of death of those diagnosed with brain cancer (2002): 64

Lives saved from cancer research from 1990 to 2004: 500,000

Colorectal cancer cases prevented due to screenings: 60,000; lives saved due to colorectal cancer screenings: 32,000

Good news? Indeed there is, mixed with the bad. According to the National Cancer Institute at NIH, from 2003 to 2007 "in men, incidence rates have declined for cancers of the lung, colon and rectum, oral cavity and pharynx, stomach, and brain while rates have risen for kidney, pancreas, and liver cancers, as well as melanoma of the skin. In women, incidence rates decreased for breast, lung, colorectal, uterine, cervical, bladder, and oral cavity cancers, but increased for kidney, pancreas, and thyroid cancers as well as for leukemia and melanomas of the skin."

However, the fact that these data are already four years old gives me pause, as I believe the landscape has changed yet again. And the elephant in the room? Brain cancer and cell phone use. As of now, many studies and evidence do not ascertain any concrete evidence of a link, but in my heart I feel there is something to the fact that incidences of brain cancer, especially for those between 20 and 29, continue to rise. This may very well be the biggest health scandal since doctors endorsed tobacco commercially and tobacco companies knowingly hid data about the effects of smoking.

There are very few studies, three to my knowlegde, of ependymoma.

Goodbye, statistics . . . so long, farewell, auf wiedersehen, good night. Send me on my way. . . the race is on . . . and Happy Thanksgiving! XO

Sources include: Accelerate Brain Cancer Cure, American Brain Tumor Association, American Cancer Society, Brown University, National Brain Tumor Society, Centers for Disease Control and Prevention, Collaborative Ependymoma Research Network, MD Anderson, National Cancer Institute at the National Institutes of Health, Reuters, Washington Post, Wikipedia.

Elm Lea Farm, Putney School, Putney, VT

Friday, November 25, 2011

Thanksgiving Day, 2011

"I love sleep. My life has a tendency to fall apart when I'm awake, you know?

—Ernest Hemingway

Monday, November 28, 2011

"O bed! O bed! delicious bed!
That heaven upon earth to the weary head."
—Thomas Hood, *Miss Kilmansegg and Her Precious Leg*

When I woke up this morning my girlfriend asked me, "Did you sleep good?" I said, "No, I made a few mistakes." —Steven Wright

Sleep continues to be elusive. The so-called battle with cancer is a steady, sometimes maddening drone that hums along the background of my daily routine, sometimes quietly lurking, at other times a cacophonous roar, and once in a while an earthquake of the highest magnitude.

But the current dissonance of sleeplessness, akin to the industrial noise of the MRI machine, has taken center stage. Sleep is, without question, the starting point for all healing, and faced with its disruption and lack, I find myself caught off-guard by its power.

"It's not the snoring I mind—it's the talking noise you make during the day."

I've never needed much sleep. Prior to "all of this" I'd started to slip into a fairly healthy sleep routine without any assistance, after years of on-again, off-again struggle. Sleep issues affect not only you but also your partner, and the entire household for that matter. Even the dogs are thrown off guard. They look at me with an expression that says, "What the hell are you up for at this hour? Why is Mark installing weather stripping in his underwear at four in the morning?" There's a reason interrogation techniques involve sleep deprivation, for such tactics can truly drive one mad and make one do mysterious things.

I know that if I go to bed before 11:00, I'll be up too soon, and if I head to sleep anytime after midnight, I won't get the rest I need. I seem to operate quite well on five to six hours of sleep. My motor always idled at a high RPM. I cherish the quiet of the early morning, and the days are never long enough to do the things I need and love to do. Besides, power naps of five to twenty minutes can recharge my battery for hours.

I participated in two different sleep studies over ten years ago to address insanely loud snoring and fatigue. The average snore emanates a sound between 60 and 90 decibels, with the loudest snore on record attributed to a 63-year-old grandmother in the UK, who operates her "nose trumpet" (a term used by my daughter Libby) at 111.6 decibels, louder than a low-flying jet. By comparison, the average conversation takes place at around 60 decibels, while a vacuum operates at approximately 70 decibels.

The researchers ruled out sleep apnea, but my asthma contributes to some upper-airway obstruction. They were astonished at both the decibel level of my snoring (I'm not certain of the actual measurement) and my "sleep latency" period: the time between being awake and sliding into deep sleep, which for me was often less than one minute. To this day, I'm asleep as soon as I hit the pillow.

I was issued a CPAP (continuous positive airway pressure) machine, which made me look like a World War II fighter pilot, or like the Gimp in *Pulp Fiction* wearing some bizarre, kinky get-up. It also seriously disagreed with my claustrophobia. I think I sold it at a yard sale.

One doctor (NOT a Dartmouth-Hitchcock doctor) with whom I consulted, who seemed a bit too eager, wanted to carve out my soft-palate, do something with my tongue, and remove my uvula. "But doctor, I like my uvula!" I cried. When he leaned his face into mine and exclaimed, with some irritation, that "there are a lot of people waiting in line for this and you better act now," I raced out of the room, fully expecting to see him chasing me down the halls of the otolaryngology department, wielding a scalpel and screaming my name. I was reminded of the sketch from Monty Python (I must warn you: this is graphic, not for the faint-of-heart and requires a twisted sense of humor).

Ultimately, I swore off pharmaceutical and surgical remedies and chose instead to focus on improving my mental state, diet, sleep habits, and weight. The result had been, until now, a better sleep with less-frequent and somewhat quieter snoring.

And yet here I am, back to square one, facing an unexpected and seemingly invincible side-effect. Actually, there is no "side" to this part of the illness. It surrounds me, envelops me, and swallows me whole. The "sleep issue" is a Hydra, and I'm no Heracles: it seems that each remedy is met with another problem grown anew, much like the multiheaded beast. The mind fights with the body in a never-ending wrestling match, and I generally disdain taking medications that make me feel "off," as I'm "off" enough already.

Insomniacs of Note:

Napoleon Bonparte, Robert Burns, Charles Dickens, Alexander Dumas, Thomas Edison, Benjamin Franklin, W. C. Fields, F. Scott Fitzgerald, Judy Garland, Cary Grant, Catherine the Great, Franz Kafka, Abraham Lincoln, Amy Lowell, Groucho Marx, John Stuart Mill, Marilyn Monroe, Sir Isaac Newton, Marcel Proust, Theodore Roosevelt, William Shakespeare, Mark Twain, Margaret Thatcher

"In a New York Times interview, (Heath) Ledger told Sarah Lyall that his recently completed roles in I'm Not There and The Dark Knight had taken a toll on his ability to sleep: "Last week I probably slept an average of two hours a night. … I couldn't stop thinking. My body was exhausted, and my mind was still going." At that time, he told Lyall that he had taken two Ambien pills, after taking just one had not sufficed, and those left him in "a stupor, only to wake up an hour later, his mind still racing."

"In talking with Interview magazine after his death, Ledger's former fiancée Michelle Williams also confirmed reports the actor had experienced trouble sleeping. "For as long as I'd known him, he had bouts with insomnia. He had too much energy. His mind was turning, turning, turning—always turning."

Sleep is elusive for many. It's estimated that over 70 million americans suffer from sleep disorders, and that one out of three adults will experience insomnia at some point. We know that Michael Jackson struggled with the sticky tentacles of the insomnia octopus before the roof caved in and rained an acid rain of propofol, lorazepam, and midazolam. It appears that this was managed poorly by his caretakers. But it also appears that he too was driven to desperate measures. Factors for insomnia include stress, fatigue, and other health issues, and sleep disorders contribute to obesity, heart disease, and diabetes. The estimated annual health care costs of sleep disorders are over $16 billion annually.

"I couldn't sleep."

Sleep is indeed a multibillion-dollar industry. I once had dinner at the now-defunct Lever House on Park Avenue with the former CEO of Sepracor, the manufacturer one of the top-selling prescription sleep drugs, called Lunesta, reported revenues of $1.22 billion in 2007. According to a CBS news item: "At one time, Sepracor spent nearly $300 million a year advertising Lunesta—the largest ad budget on the entire planet."

I'd never taken a sleep aid before, but since the surgeries and radiation treatments, sleep has been a rabid animal that I've been unable to capture. The first time I took any sort of medication for sleep was last year when I flew a red-eye from Seattle and a friend with whom I was staying, who travels extensively, suggested I take an Ambien. "Make sure you have enough sleep time as you won't remember much, if at all, especially if you wake up. People have been known to sleep-eat, sleep drive, etc. Have fun," he smiled.

To this day I have absolutely no recollection of how I managed to change flights in Detroit at 3 AM. I do recall waking up feeling like a jellyfish (not that I would know what a jellyfish really feels like), drooling, and that I was in a zombie-like trance. It was just like some of my lesser moments in college. And the sleep eating? That was nothing new. But since then, Ambien can't touch me. I tried a few times and all I could muster was a maximum of four hours of sleep. Other meds leave me groggy.

In studies of cancer patients, 30 to 50 percent of those surveyed experienced insomnia (compared to 15 percent in the general population) due to the physical and emotional side-effects of surgery and radiation and the mental weight of the cancer diagnosis itself.

I've tried late-night soothing mechanisms, including setting my iPhone to calming, meditative music; streaming a book on tape (preferably a boring one); white noise from a fan (which I need anyway); and a glass of warm milk with honey or chamomile tea and maybe a banana. What the body needs is serotonin levels to rise, and foods like bananas do the trick. (The Daily Meal is a terrific site for foods that help sleep).

Other suggestions include the seemingly obvious: avoiding alcohol and caffeine, not drinking too much of anything including water prior to bedtime, and avoiding late-night spicy foods. Oh, and, ahem, staying off the computer, which not only awakens the brain and body further but, studies have shown, can confuse your circadian rhythm because the light from a screen mimics the sun.

I take melatonin before bed (20 mg, which is higher than most people take), as part of a wider cancer-related supplemental regimen that includes tumeric (800 mg), vitamin D3 (5,000 mg) and fish oil (5,000 mg). A fellow brain cancer survivor suggested that I also take borage seed oil (3,000 mg), resveratrol (150 mg), lycopene (20 mg), green tea extract (1,450 mg), milk thistle (600 mg), and genistein from soy (50 mg).

Additionally, my intake of cancer-fighting foods now includes more kale, a wonder green if there ever was one. I am perfecting the art of making kale chips. Shameless but earnest commercial plug: buy now famous Vermonter Bo's swag at Eat More Kale—it's a curious bumper sticker, a t-shirt, a global movement, a religion and is setting the world on fire. The latest news, which I hope garners Bo more business, is a ridiculous battle with junk-food chain and corporate bully Chik-Fil-A over trademark dispute. Go Bo! Other food items on my cancer menu: mangos, sweet potatoes, broccoli, spinach, tomatoes, tart cherries, berries of all types, garlic, apples, pineapple, pinto beans, and salmon, salmon, and more salmon. I'm also severely limiting, if not eliminating, fried foods, sugary foods, red meat, and processed foods.

I've just begun my journey into complementary medicine. The doors have been swung wide, and in the coming months, I plan to delve into acupuncture and massage therapy. I've already seen an excellent naturopath, and had one infusion of vitamins to help my body regain its balance after treatment. While it's too early to see results, it seemed harmless enough, so I approached it with a "why not try?" attitude. My doctors at DHMC were open to alternative therapies but rightly suggested I wait until after the radiation treatments, lest anything interfere.

Always open to new ideas, I've tried a few alternative therapies in the past. Some I found to be completely and utterly devoid of reason as my cynical/skeptical side took hold, while others have been very beneficial. Half the battle, I believe, is in the mind, so while I may avoid some forms of alternative medicine, I pass no judgment on those for whom such therapies work, science-based or not. After all, like many people, I've had both positive and negative experiences with the modern medical establishment as well. I'm fortunate to have had the expertise at Dartmouth-Hitchcock and the terrific alternatives available at Sojourns Community Health Clinic where Barb is a PT.

What I find most intriguing is how important the messenger is—how critical it is that there's trust between patient and caregiver. My initial irritation with some forms of alternative treatment has everything to do with the particular practitioners, some of whom I found a bit too flaky for my taste. Then again, the aggressive doctor who wanted to perform a radical surgery (which was later proven not to work) left just as bitter a taste.

For example, when a social worker showed up the day of my diagnosis to assess our situation and recommend a therapist if needed, I told her I didn't want a soft-spoken, touchy-feely, flowy, new-age, "how does that make you feel" sort. I wanted someone with the proper credentials who was warm, accessible, practical, and down-to-earth with a get-it-done attitude and a sense of humor about life. And even though I'm not sure I need someone to talk to at the moment, I'm meeting with someone as a preventive measure, and to ensure that I have someone I can work with if needed.

I've shared with my daughters many times that should they find the need to talk to someone, we'll make sure it happens and that we might do the same preliminary visit for them. Their teachers, advisors, and heads of schools have been right on top of checking in with them, their mom Laura and myself. Fortunately, both girls are comfortable with adults, have great communication skills, and are okay with talking about their feelings in general— but I don't want to assume that they're fine. How could any of us really be fine? But we're faring well, and we all try to keep the door open.

In short, I think it's beneficial to approach all treatment—western, eastern, or something totally new—with a healthy dose of skepticism and analysis. It's up to us to be informed and listen to our gut. Don't be afraid to ask for help, ask questions, or to get a second, third, or fourth opinion. Follow your heart and listen to your inner voice, especially if it gives you pause.

Into the wild I walk. My next MRI, on December 6, will provide a baseline for all future scans. Whatever the next MRI reveals, it will certainly look different than the one prior to the surgeries and radiation. There may be what they call "artifact": dead tissue, debris, undigested pretzels, M&Ms. The titanium screws and hardware stay. The swelling should be mostly gone by then. So the real moment of truth will happen sometime in February. If things look the same as the scan from December, we breathe deep. If they don't, well, we just breathe deeper and keep on walking.

Finally, I will share what I've found to be the best medicine. Along with the joy of spending time with family and friends, having a good meal, meditating, playing music, writing, walking in the woods, and snowshoeing or skiing (something we have already been able to do thanks to the Halloween snow), my primary escape has been the bath. Warm, calming, quiet baths, perhaps with a candle, a glass of wine, soft music, and a book. I tell the family I'm off-duty, and create an "environment." I float away…

I've even taken to making my own bath salts, as prepared versions can be rather expensive. I'm perfecting the recipe: coarse sea salt, mineral salt, epsom salts (which help the body replenish potassium and enzymatic activity), milk powder, and whatever oil either calms (lavender) or invigorates (eucalyptus). My first version used lavender oil and buds, but left me with a bathtub that looked like it had been infested with bugs, as the buds stuck to the entire tub and plugged the

drain. Perhaps there's a market for "Moose's Bath Salts." I just need a picture of my namesake in a tub, so if you have a large tub…
Laugh. Love. Live.

MooseBath, LeAnne Sowa

"I Wanna Be Sedated"
The Ramones

Twenty-twenty-twenty-four hours to go, I wanna be sedated
Nothin' to do and nowhere to go-o-oh, I wanna be sedated
Just get me to the airport, put me on a plane
Hurry hurry hurry before I go insane
I can't control my fingers, I can't control my brain
Oh no no no no no
Twenty-twenty-twenty-four hours to go….
Just put me in a wheelchair, get me on a plane
Hurry hurry hurry before I go insane
I can't control my fingers, I can't control my brain
Oh no no no no no
Twenty-twenty-twenty-four hours to go, I wanna be sedated
Nothin' to do and nowhere to go-o-o, I wanna be sedated
Just put me in a wheelchair, get me to the show
Hurry hurry hurry before I go loco
I can't control my fingers, I can't control my toes
Oh no no no no no
Twenty-twenty-twenty-four hours to go…
Just put me in a wheelchair…
Ba-ba-bamp-ba ba-ba-ba-bamp-ba. I wanna be sedated
Ba-ba-bamp-ba ba-ba-ba-bamp-ba, I wanna be sedated
Ba-ba-bamp-ba ba-ba-ba-bamp-ba, I wanna be sedated
Ba-ba-bamp-ba ba-ba-ba-bamp-ba, I wanna be sedated

Mama tried. The roots of guilt, the guilt of roots

Saturday, December 3, 2011

"A guy comes back from a retreat and tells his friend that he's achieved enlightenment. To which his friend replies, "Wait until you have to spend the weekend with your parents."

A wild ride resulted when a [illegible] Plymouth station wagon went out of control along New Second Street east of High Avenue about [illegible] p.m. Wednesday, police said. The wagon, driven by Mark Richard Green, [illegible], of the 100 block of Walnut Park Drive, Philadelphia, had been proceeding north on New Second Street when it left the road, downed a traffic sign on the right side, then rolled back across the road and diagonally across High Avenue and into an evergreen tree, police said.

The car reportedly bounced back, turned around and rolled onto its left side before bouncing down onto its four wheels again. Officers said Green was treated for minor injuries at Rolling Hill Hospital. There were no citations.

Years after I allegedly started to grow up, which presumably began toward the end of high school and beginning of college, I shared with my parents my thanks and love for all they had done for me, and then expressed sincere apologies for whatever hell I'd put them through. I emphasized that, for the most part, any and all actions that gave them pause, incurred unforeseen expenses, or made them consider military school (a far cry from the loving, pacifist embrace of Abington Friends School) were never intended as acts of rebellion.

"I was just having fun," I said. In high school, I had great friends and solid grades. I was class president, student council president, cross-country team captain, wrestler, thespian, chorus member, journalist, and self-appointed environmental crusader. My friends and I, were just trying to have fun. "Duh Mom. Duh Dad." "No, Mark. Duh Mark."

But it seemed that for everything I accomplished to make them proud, somewhere along the twisted path of teenagedom, I would occasionally take a wrong turn and do something to make them very unproud: wreck a car, have a party, or push the car down the street in neutral, engine off, to visit a girlfriend at 2:00 am. Invariably, no matter how smart I thought I was, my mother the bloodhound would find me out. That solitary beer cap that had slipped into the cushions of the sofa. The fact that the car was parked, oddly, ten inches closer to the garage than it was the night before. Or the fact that in my senior high school yearbook page, I had very uncleverly published a photo of my friends...in our living room at a party held while my parents were away for the weekend (she recognized our artwork on the wall, behind the conga line). Rats, foiled again! How was she so damned smart? It didn't help that as dean of the upper school she often managed to find things out before I thought she would.

As any teacher, parent, psychologist or neuroscientist knows, or soon discovers, the very last part of the adolescent brain to develop is the prefrontal cortex, which helps determine cognitive flexibility and cause and effect. (for a terrific Frontline special, watch Inside the Teenage Brain) The adolescent brain, despite having reached its full size, is nowhere near full developmental capacity as it undergoes a tidal wave of growth. One need only watch *Jackass* or any group of boys in eighth or ninth grade to verify this seemingly stunted developmental growth, which for some never seems to really take off.

I think of the multiple lives (if I do in fact have at least nine) that I managed to sacrifice during the course of several car wrecks, playing catch with shovels and a gasoline-soaked softball, falling through a plate-glass window while standing on a ladder two stories up, or blowing myself up in college while incorrectly firing a propane-powered raku kiln (in that episode, I was observed running madly across campus to the infirmary, clothes and hair smoldering, before I was sent to the burn unit in Syracuse, an hour away).

After Hamilton College called my parents to share news any parent dreads ("Mr.Green, your son has been in a kiln accident"), my father had already booked a direct private flight. My mother called my friend Doug, who assured her that there was no need to charter a flight and that the burns were mostly first-degree with some second-degree about my face and hands. Sobbing and fearful that I was permanently disfigured, my mother was inconsolable and Doug sought to calm her down. "Mrs. Green, I assure you, Mark will be fine and there is no need to come all the way up from Philadelphia. "OK" she said, "but how does he look?" After a lengthy pause, Doug exclaimed "He's fine. He just looks a little more like your husband now." After another pause she started laughing and all was well.

The next day my friend Doug came to pick me up as I stood outside wearing a hospital gown, jeans and cowboy boots. I had implored the hospital to let me go as I was losing my mind. Hands and head bandaged, still wearing the gown, we headed straight for Dowling's Bar in Kirkland for wings and Saranac beer. As I opened the door to the bar, Jim Dowling, proprietor, large, bushy beard, his arms akimbo, asked loudly "where the hell did you escape from?" With Van Morrison on the jukebox and the pool table free, all was well again.

This cancer offers me a chance to pause and reflect on the past 16,178 days of my life, or at least as much as I can recall, in ways I never imagined. Shortly before the diagnosis, I'd been reflecting on my past with a more focused energy and decided that being "middle-aged" is (1) what you make of it, (2) a state of mind, and (3) the point in your life where you begin to look back as much as you look forward.

As much as I am looking optimistically (albeit with equal measure of fear, uncertainty, and trepidation) to the future, one of the many slide shows scrolling past my screen is of my family, my parents, and my past. And one of the many emotions percolating to the surface from time to time is guilt. What matters are left unresolved and need purging, like the radiated, dead cancer cells still floating around in my brain and causing me terrifically painful bouts of headaches and insomnia? Have I made amends with those I have hurt intentionally or unintentionally, or vice-versa? Is it even worth walking down roads that have long been cordoned off, washed away, or rerouted?

Guilt. It comes in many forms, with much of its roots in the heavy-handedness of religion and culture. Guilt is a potent genetic hand-me-down, and walking backwards down the path of my youth I think, "Ma, Da, I'm sorry!" I know we're all "way past that now." I wasn't an exceptionally difficult or problematic child; I just wanted to grow up faster than time would allow, and my concept of "growing up" itself was immature at best.

As for the unresolved, I continue to reflect and make amends, either within myself, or if possible with those who are still accessible, recognizing that some wounds, healed or not, leave scars too deep to be erased. Hopefully, we've all grown from those painful experiences and moved on. Time indeed does help heal many things—as we view events from a new angle, we're able to gain perspective.

I have one issue on the table involving a severe violation of trust from someone I thought was a friend who acted inappropriately toward my own and other children nearly three years ago. That event, barring an unexpected apology, will always simmer in the background as conflicting notions of frontier justice and extending an olive branch come to mind. I know that his cowardice ensures that he is living in his own hell as he lives a lie. And yet there is the larger part of me which simply wants him to admit his wrongdoing and that he has received the help he needed. But this issue, I recognize, needs to be brushed off the table. No closure here.

As one friend shared as she moved through a painful divorce, "You can't go backward. You can only move forward." And as another friend said as she walked into and wrestled with her own cancer-forest, "There are some things that simply can't be fixed, and you have to move on, let it go, and keep walking toward the sun."

"Jewish guilt" is a stereotype rooted in the intensity of the connectedness and emotionalism of family members in the Jewish culture. Similarly, one might argue that Catholic guilt has its roots in the draconian nature of Catholic school and the notion of repentance. When I asked friends where they thought the roots of guilt were buried, most replied either religion or family.

In addition, many Jewish families are matriarchal, and the power of the Jewish mother, also a stereotype, can't be overlooked. There's nothing more powerful than my own Mother's LOD (an acronym for "Look of Disdain," "Look of Dismay," "Look of Disgust," or the most lethal, "Look of Death.") With this nuclear weapon, no words need to be spoken. My grandmothers had similar mystical powers of guilt-inducement. Mind you, my mother and I are both intensely emotional (father is the calm, quiet, cerebral, sometimes brooding member of the family). And she's also a doting, loving woman who's been too devastated by my two brain surgeries and cancer diagnosis to even go near this blog and I understand and accept this completely. She also played a critical (literally) role as I lay withering in the hospital before the initial surgery. I suggested she put herself out for hire as she was an exceptional advocate.

The matter of religion in general and its role in this "event" is another matter entirely, and I find myself, as ever, searching, rejecting, and embracing bits and pieces of spirituality from many sources, faiths, and friends. This is a time to go with what I know, as well as a time for discovery. Quaker, Jewish, Christian, Buddhist. A piece of music. A sunrise. A tree. A hike up the mountain. At the end of the day, my church is the outdoors. My bonds are made within several small communities, from my high school class of under fifty students, many of whom I have known since elementary school, to my college residence in an alternative co-op, to the many small villages, residential schools, and neighborhoods in which I've lived and loved.

Of all the intense emotions wrought from this disease, I find the subject of religion and its role the most complicated. The majority of my apprehension comes from the arrogance of the entire religious complex and those who take it upon themselves to tell you what you should or shouldn't do to heal thyself. To each their own path.

Guilt, and its role in the healing process, is for me an exercise in reflection and a realignment of priorities. When we get whacked in the head with the baseball bat of life (or death), as we all eventually will, it's natural to stand up, try to get a 360-degree perspective from wherever you are, take stock of what's good in life, and let whatever gnaws at your heart slip away.

The beloved Abington Friends Meeting House, Est. 1683.

"And remember, no matter where you go, there you are."

—Confucious

"Happiness is a way of travel—not a destination."
—Roy M. Goodman

Thursday, December 08, 2011

Bing Crosby: "Accentuate the Positive"

The Zen of Groucho: "I, not events, have the power to make me happy or unhappy today. I can choose which it shall be. Yesterday is dead, tomorrow hasn't arrived yet. I have just one day, today, and I'm going to be happy in it."
—Groucho Marx

The feeling of being pounded as if pelted by hundreds of bean bags and the welling up of tears came out of nowhere. When these moments occur, as they seem to with increased frequency, there's no better metaphor than a tsunami. I see myself standing on a beach, hypnotized by what's about to occur. I know it's coming, and there's no way to stop the wave. And then it comes, and I'm buried, drowning, tossed about in the churn of detritus and darkened waters. The waves usually form when I'm alone, walking in the woods, driving in the car, or running into a friend who's going or has gone through the same ordeal. Words needn't be spoken. The water drowns out the sound anyway.

I had to stand up and walk across the room to the sink. It was too much. I stood there, back to Barb and our fantastic nurse practitioner, Roberta Silveira, APRN, MSC, and gathered myself, holding the sobs at bay. The news was good, and so were the tears. Bloodwork was fine, with an elevated white blood cell count as a result of the continued healing from radiation. The MRI, (an amazingly beneficial instrument with its share of claustrophobic and aural torture) which took about an hour, revealed no indication of new cancer-cell growth. While such growth would have been unlikely anyway so soon after the surgeries and radiation, the scans looked good. As you can see from the images, I also have a nice empty space in my head (I was expecting to see a mouse on a wheel). It's now filled with cerebral spinal fluid, or so I'm led to believe. The amazing elastic brain.

My "team" consisting of Roberta and the equally amazing neuro-oncologist, Dr. Fadul have been, and will continue to be, my caretakers. I am lucky to have such magnificent, human, humane people in my life.

This MRI is now the baseline, the "new normal" for all MRIs to follow. I'll have an MRI every two to three months for the next year or so, given the aggressive stage III and relatively unknown nature of this kind of brain cancer in adults. I have asked for the installation of a USB hub in the back of my head but have yet to find any willing parties. I was hoping I could simply store information on various flash drives: film, photos, music, databases for work, etc. My guess is that this notion is not that far off from soon becoming a reality. Imagine the possibilities. Cooking? "Where is my Italian cuisine flashdrive?" Or better yet, forget the USB and just go wireless and use the "cloud."

This "bad craziness," as a friend put it, has certainly focused new and captivating attention on elements of life that had previously held only fleeting interest, namely cancer and the brain.

Historical brain images that come to mind are those of the pseudoscience of phrenology and those fantastical maps.

> "The basic idea upon which phrenology rests is that the form of the head represents the form of the brain and thus reflects the brain's relative development. The Austrian physician Franz Joseph Gall—very much interested in the works on physiognomy by the Italian Renaissance scholar Giambattista Della Porta—formulated his phrenologic theory at the end of the eighteenth century.

At the beginning of the nineteenth century interest in phrenology grew rapidly. People used the advice of phrenologists for all sorts of things, including the diagnosis of mental illness or psychological afflictions. Phrenology seriously attracted the likes of G. W. F. Hegel, Honoré de Balzac, the Brontë sisters, George Eliot, James Garfield, Thomas Edison, Walt Whitman, and Queen Victoria."
Missouri University Life Sciences and Society Symposium (March 2010)

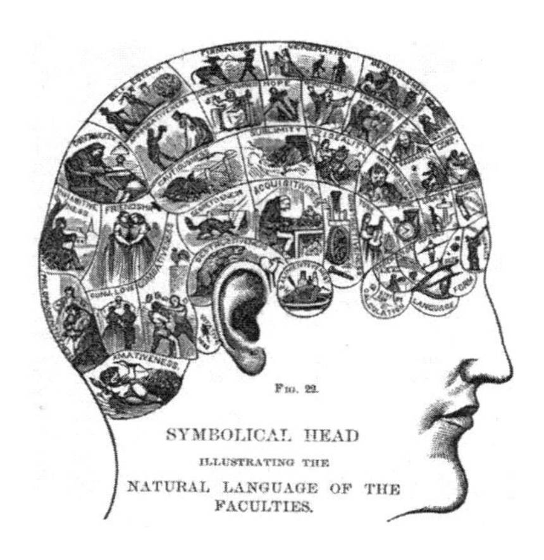

On a whole other level are the images collected by Dr. Carl Schoonover in *Portraits of the Mind*. When I look at the empty space in my brain, I'm startled by its ability to modify and compensate. (As I mentioned before, *The Brain That Changes Itself*, by Dr. Norman Doidge, aptly addresses the incredible elasticity and compensatory abilities of the brain.)

In the meantime, after four months of terror, tears, fear, hope, despair, joy, and love (in no particular order), we learn to wait with this devilish, beguiling disease. I continue to try to find new footing as I wrestle with headaches, insomnia, and coping with this new reality. My depth of gratitude for support and love from friends, family, and community is without end. I will carry on. We will carry on. Smile. Laugh. Love.

sun, sun, sun, here it comes...

Friday, December 23, 2011

As we slide into 2012, with the holidays upon us, I simply wish to share my thanks and deep appreciation for the support of family and friends during what has been a profoundly trying time. This "new normal," however unwelcome, has been all the more bearable because of this love.

In less than five months, I've endured two brain surgeries, experienced thirty-three radiation treatments, filled my body with medicines I'd rather not have had to take, and gone through nights of insomnia, days of fatigue, and steady headaches. Until the next MRI, in February, we don't hold our collective breath—we breathe. Deeply.

But the most difficult challenge makes all of that mundane: understanding and accepting the magnitude of this disease and what it means for friends, family, and most significantly, my daughters.

While cancer is no "gift," I can say with certainty that these events have been a catalyst for some very meaningful and healthy reflection. I've learned, and continue to learn, much about myself, friends, cancer, and the capacities of body, mind, heart, and soul. It's as if I've been stripped naked. Cancer peels away the veneer of life and allows you to see the intricacies of the grain. Relationships have grown stronger. Honesty is easier: I feel I can speak my mind more freely than ever before. Some days I'm leaden, as if my body is truly filled with lead. Other days I feel like I'm floating, light as a feather, feet never touching the ground.

A recent study revealed that those who are predisposed to anger, grumpiness, or irritability become even more so when drunk, and that those who are generally happy become even more exuberant. I think the same might be said for what happens when one deals with a calamitous event such as this.

I've always had deep respect and appreciation for people who take on the challenge of aging, injury, or disease with a positive outlook, even when their bodies, and sometimes their minds, are deteriorating. This isn't to lay blame or guilt on those faced with chronic pain or disease who become permanently angry, depressed, or sad. But certainly having—or trying to have, when possible—a positive outlook helps calm the spirit.

I recently met with a friend who'd had a very large brain tumor removed nearly two years ago, resulting in some paralysis and loss of sight. After enduring countless hours of physical therapy and rehabilitation, he's now living on his own and has become a licensed massage therapist. His outlook has always been positive, facing challenge with humor and even a little sarcasm to help heal the emotional scars of such a life-altering event. We spoke of the sad days, the lonely times. The change in the nature of some friendships, some for the better, some for the worse. The challenges, physical and emotional. But we both agreed that while sadness and anger is a natural, normal reaction, there's little time to waste crying in our collective bowls of oatmeal. There's still too much to live for and look forward to.

I absolutely love the Christmas season. Much has to do with my love of winter, my own childhood memories, the holiday music, the trees, the parties, the lights, the traditions. Handel's *Messiah* and Tchaikovsky's *Nutcracker*, Capra's *It's a Wonderful Life*, or *A Charlie Brown Christmas.* It is a time to get sentimental and revel. Yes, there's the dark side: the smarminess, hypocrisy, and crass commercialism. But you'd have to be a complete curmudgeon to loathe all of it. I suppose the world needs curmudgeons to keep things on the level. But it's the essence of the holiday spirit, that of giving thanks and giving back, that's at the root of all of this warmth.

> "Santa Clause has a red suit, he's a communist. And a beard, and long hair, must be a pacifist. What's in that pipe the he's smoking?"
>
> —Arlo Guthrie

On that note, I wish to give back, not just in this season of giving but as a self-proclaimed lifelong mission from here on. The fact that 95 percent of those with anaplastic ependymoma brain cancer are children makes this cause all the more meaningful. There's a saying in the world of fundraising: "Don't give until it hurts, give until it feels good." In addition to my beloved day job raising funds for the Putney School, I've volunteered for several projects to push awareness of brain cancer, and cancer in general, to the front lines. I'm helping ABC2 (Accelerate Brain Cancer Cure), assisting on a film project based on Dr. Mukherjee's book "Emperor of all Maladies, a Biography of Cancer," and supporting my daughter Hannah's efforts to start a national cancer support organization for high school students. Libby wishes to do the same within her school. Recently, I offered my blog to the Norris Cotton Cancer Center to use as they wish. Much to my delighted surprise, they issued the appeal below for their annual fund drive. They've already seen an increased response rate and contributions.

The girls and I are heading to see family next week and then to New York City for the new year. On New Year's Day, along with friend Buck and his family, we will partake in a cleansing of sorts—although I'm not sure cleanse is the right word—when we jump into the frigid waters off Coney Island for the annual Polar Bear Swim. Finally, I leave this year of 2011 with the salve of James and Yo-Yo. Here Comes the Sun…indeed.

Thank you. Happy holidays and a most happy new year! Live. Laugh. Love.

> "New Year's is a harmless annual institution, of no particular use to anybody save as a scapegoat for promiscuous drunks, and friendly calls, and humbug resolutions"
>
> —Mark Twain

my own private idaho

Tuesday, January 10, 2012

> Life is not a journey to the grave with the intention of arriving safely in a pretty and well-preserved body, but rather to skid in broadside, thoroughly used up, totally worn out, and loudly proclaiming: Wow.... What a ride!!!
>
> —Hunter S. Thompson

When people ask how I am, I usually respond good-naturedly with "I feel great. Tired. But great." The reality is that I'm living in my own private Idaho (not only a reference to a terrific film by Gus Van Zant, but, according to The Urban Dictionary, means "living inside an Idaho potato", or a very small space. Metaphorically, it refers to someone who is not paying attention because he is daydreaming, or under the influence, or otherwise wrapped up within his own very narrow sphere of interest or frame of reference."

I try not to allow this potato-space to fill up my head too much, but when I do I become immobilized. Leaden. The future becomes worrisome. But for anyone who's run a race, climbed a mountain, or otherwise pushed themselves to their limit, you know you must not stop. You... have...to...keep...going. The motto for my grandfather's 94th Infantry, 302nd division, was "The Command is Forward." Yes it is, grandpa. Yes it is.

One way I've faced the dragon is, to steal a phrase, to "just do it." The sad irony is that this slogan, perhaps one of the most recognizable catchphrases in the history of advertising, was inspired by the last words spoken by murderer Gary Gilmore before being executed by firing squad. His final utterance, "Let's do it" was later appropriated by advertising agency Wieden + Kennedy for Nike. Brilliant. Sick, but brilliant.

"Just doing it" in my case has meant pushing myself perhaps a bit too much—my body is now screaming at me to get more rest after the busyness of the holidays. I also spent time with my family in Philadelphia, where oddly my illness was never brought up. It wasn't that we were avoiding anything, it was, as my mother shared at one point, simply too hard to "go there." I attended a mini highschool gathering where friendships of old were sparked anew as if it was yesterday.

New Year's weekend we traveled to NYC where I celebrated the new year in Times Square with my daughters Hannah and Libby and Hannah's friend Lily. The night before we stayed up into the wee hours with friend Buck and his band. New Year's eve, at around five o'clock, we headed into Manhattan from Brooklyn. We all had fun but it was also a completely absurd folly: two million people crammed full on nearly every street. The sea of humanity was amusing, enlightening and disturbing all at once. The following day we went swimming in the frigid Atlantic with thousands of like-minded crazy people in Coney Island to celebrate the first day of the year. Two days later we were skiing at Okemo mountain with -10 wind chill. Days later I was nordic skiing at Grafton Ponds with Hannah's team and old friends. What a great and fitting way to start the year. Just do it has left me enriched, albeit with a few torn strands of muscle, due in part to a lack of regular exercise and from the side-effects of the steroids taken for swelling and inflammation. (Bucky is at 2:36!)

Despite all this, I remain intact physically and emotionally. While I continue to meet with experts in the field for consultation and continue to work toward a healthy regimen of meditation and physical activity, my days are mostly what they were before the calamity. The next big day is February 28, when I have my next MRI, along with a general exam and blood work.

Meanwhile, the polluted water of the New Hampshire primary will soon recede and flow to another state, carrying with it the usual political flotsam and jetsam: the hate, hypocrisy, fear mongering, war mongering, posturing, lies, promises never to be fulfilled, and the deep-seeded, sometimes cloaked, sometimes naked viciousness directed toward women, children, teachers, the environment, science, health care, the poor, minorities, and immigrants.

I refuse to watch the news coverage of the primary with any regularity, as it all seems so shallow and meaningless. Just noise and talking heads. A mindless waste of outrageous sums of money. (I seem to recall my father owning a fake brick fashioned from foam to throw at the television whenever Nixon was on.) Politics presented as sport, like the Superbowl or the Kentucky Derby, driven by ratings, ad revenue, and presented by Ken and Barbie dolls masquerading as newsmen and women. Substance in the news seems to be a rare commodity. Where art thou Walter Cronkite? Murrow, Huntley, Brinkley? Jennings? Brokaw?

So I keep my chin up and move forever forward, trying to laugh each day as deeply as possible, dance whenever an opportunity presents, breathe as intently as I can, strive to help others, and inhale the beautiful, brisk air of winter. And thank goodness for the B-52's! (may I admit a continued crush on Cindy Wilson?) Were they actually singing about the primaries in "Rock Lobster"? I think so. Happy New Year!

"Here comes a stingray
There goes a manta-ray
In walked a jellyfish
There goes a dogfish
Chased by a catfish
In flew a sea robin
Watch out for that piranha
There goes a narwhal
Here comes a bikini whale!"

Of mice and men and Freihofer's: "we'll all float on ok"

Sunday, January 29, 2012

"To a Mouse, on Turning Her Up in Her Nest with the Plough"

But, Mousie, thou art no thy-lane [you aren't alone]
In proving foresight may be vain:
The best laid schemes o' Mice an' Men
Gang aft agley [often go awry]
An' lea'e us nought but grief an' pain,
For promised joy.

—Robert Burns, 1785
Scottish national poet (1759–1796)

After graduating from Hamilton College and turning down several offers to teach, I chose instead to move to Burlington, Vermont, with three other completely confused and adrift but well-meaning friends. Of the jobs I took during my "experiential post-graduate" year, one of the more memorable moments was working as a roll-sorter at Freihofer's industrial bakery in South Burlington.

The training lasted a good ten minutes. Along with a few other cheeky college-aged kids, I was lectured on safety procedures, provided with hairnet and earplugs, given a release to sign, and taken on a cursory tour of the expansive facility. We then entered an enormous, brightly lit room where, shouting over the roar of machinery, the supervisor explained the morning's job.

Pointing toward one of the machines, complete with gears, chutes, and a conveyor belt, he yelled to us that in five minutes 50,000 fresh, mechanically baked sub rolls would shoot from the trap high above. Our task was simple: identify which rolls, traveling at fantastic velocity, were defective, while at the same time turning any upside-down rolls right side up. I could hear my grandmother sighing and exclaiming, rhetorically with that Jewish-Guilt-Laden lilt in her voice, "For this we sent you to college? Oy vey iz mir!" ("Oh woe is me" in Yiddish)

Suddenly, with bells ringing, buzzers buzzing, and lights flashing, the door above our heads slid open, and in an instant thousands of the soft, chewy loaves came pouring out like ants on a burning log. I glanced at my compatriots, some slack-jawed, others fixed with an intense gaze as if in a battle for their lives. Me? I started laughing uncontrollably. It had come to this. My summer was not going well despite living in a great city and seeing a lot of friends. My living arrangements had deteriorated with my housemates and I was becoming tired of the lack of consistent employment. And there I was, sorting submarine rolls with a manic fervor. In between the laughter I think I was also crying. "There's no place like home... there's no place like home." Calling for Auntie Em was to no avail.

Needless to say I did not parlay my good fortune in roll-sorting into a career, and, after an enriching winter of skiing and waiting tables as well as being accepted to the Peace Corps, which I had also deferred, I called the head of the school that had recruited me and took a teaching position. My experiment in "real life" living had ended. And I never looked at a roll the same way again.

Since my diagnosis, I've sought out and been met with an enormous amount of information about my disease. To suggest that when the trap door of cancer was opened, I was met with 50,000 submarine rolls, each representing new information about cancer, the brain, or brain cancer would not be an exaggeration.

Since the first craniotomy, the fire that already burned within had been turned up to maximum capacity. As someone who dives into almost anything head first (usually for better, sometimes for worse), my hunger for knowledge, now related to all things neuroscience and oncology, is boundless. These rolls I am happy to sort, and to eliminate those that are defective.

As with any health-related topic, there's an enormous amount of information and misinformation available. From the moment I was wheeled into my hospital room after surgery, I wanted to know everything about this disease: what it was, how it happened, how to prevent it, what was being done to find answers and cures, who was at the forefront of research, where the experts were, and so on. When I was told it was incurable and that it will recur, words that I can't seem to shed, I viewed it is as challenge, not a threat.

The doctors, nurses, technicians and support staff at Dartmouth-Hitchcock have been nothing short of exceptional. I've been blessed with the good fortune of living within an hour of world-class medical care. I was able to fly to Houston to consult with the exceptional doctors at MD Anderson, and I continue to meet new players in this "great resistance" movement against cancer. However, they are not machines and cannot possibly know all there is to know, especially given the speed at which information is now relayed.

I feel deeply compassionate toward those in the world who are less fortunate, who in many cases have few or no options at all. Thanks to my employer, I have excellent insurance. The swelling from my expanding tumor, had it not been removed, would have killed me within a matter of days. It was killing me. And then there is the cancer. The overall cost of my continued care, including two surgeries and radiation therapy, would have surely bankrupted me and my family. When Blue Cross Blue Shield of Vermont called me to "check in," I was immediately suspicious: what were they after? What should I tell them? I soon realized through continued conversation with my assigned representative Colleen, that they truly did care. I felt embraced by this legion of health care professionals, much as I felt by the community that is the state of Vermont. I was so impressed I contacted the CEO who promptly replied with his own gratitude. It is not often, he shared, in his embattled industry that they receive a letter of thanks.

The ongoing health care discourse, which continues to rise in nasty fervor during this campaign season, leaves me sick to my core. (Visit January 5, 2012 *Washington Post* article for a good mythbusting article on alleged "ObamaCare.") I'm not a policy analyst, nor am I well-versed in the finer details of this issue, except to argue that while Obama's initiatives are by no means the perfect solution, those who seek to dismantle it don't seem to offer any sound alternatives. The dividing line for many seems to be this: health care is a right, not a privilege. Sadly, I think many believe otherwise, and take a Darwinian "survival of the fittest" position. And to make matters worse, we've created an industry that appears to be more focused on "disease care" than health care and is driven by financial incentive above all else. It's all backwards, this focus on treating the symptoms and not the cause. An entirely healthy population is simply not as profitable, at least not with our current model. Thankfully, discussion of preventative medicine and the blending of Western and Eastern modalities, while still nascent, is becoming part of the fabric of conversation and debate.

In the case of brain cancer and many other diseases, if there's not enough money to be made developing new treatments there's little incentive for biomedical companies to pursue further research or development.

It is with these ideas in mind that I have delved into finding out as much as I can about brain cancer and cancer in general. The spelunking has only begun to crack the surface. We have miles to go, down deep, before we sleep.

Of the many things I've learned in the past six months, the most profound realization is that no matter how experienced, kind, talented, or prestigious your health care providers are, they do not have, nor should be expected to have, all the answers. Emergent models of personalized, adaptive therapies are slowly gaining ground, replacing the traditional backwards, if not completely detrimental, one-size-fits-all model of treatment. Hopefully, each individual will follow their own path of learning and decide, in concert with their doctors and health care practitioners, what's best for them.

Of course, the risk evolves and can increase when patients err on the side of deleting standard protocols that generally have a known result. Steve Jobs spurned surgery for nine months following his diagnoses of what is historically a treatable form of pancreatic cancer. His family was deeply upset by this. Ever an independent and deeply spiritual thinker, Jobs was intent on seeking his own paths for healing. Only too late did he admit that he wished he hadn't delayed operation. While I understand that we have a personal responsibility to those who love and support us, I feel it's unfair to judge what anyone chooses to do with their health—because in the end, it's *their* end, not ours.

From the deep, powerful, and ongoing discussions I've been fortunate to have with leading researchers, doctors, investors, and professors in the field of neuroscience and cancer, I now realize we are at a watershed moment in the history of cancer treatment. I've emailed, Skyped, phoned, and met with some of the most fascinating, exciting professionals in the field. I am now a cancer groupie.

No expert I, an English major with a minor in studio art, who knows little about science let alone cancer aside from my religious reading of *New York Times Science Times* section on Tuesdays and *WIRED* magazine, so my apologies for any errors—but a few of the terms we' ll be hearing more and more about include the following: eco-oncology, biomarkers, neutraceuticals (food as medicine), cellnomics (understanding cellular phenotype and function), adaptive therapies, exosomes (microvesicles containing protein and, as recently discovered, RNA; a great article entitled "Exosome Exploration," *The Scientist*, July, 2011), and orthotopic xenotransplantation, in which cells are inserted for research into another organism, usually laboratory mice, born with no immune system. I will share more in a later post about my ever evolving cancer diet which is now incorporating supplemental melatonin, green tea extract, turmeric and vitamin d.

As for the process and politics of advancing new therapies and treatment, it takes an average of fourteen years and $1.2 billion from inception to FDA approval for a new drug to get to market. In a soured economy with decreased, flat-lined, or modest increases in budgets for cancer research and treatment development, companies have become exceedingly risk-averse both in funding and in research models. Incentives for grant funding don't inspire innovation but rather the safely traveled road. Many ideas fall into what is known in the field as the "Valley of Death"—those which become lost in the chasm between scientific discovery and the doctor's office."

ABC2 (Accelerate Brain Cancer Cure), one of the most aggressive and exciting cancer organizations, isn't sitting on top of an enormous war chest of money. Rather, they've raised an impressive $17 million in just over ten years for immediate dispersion to leading researchers and facilities as well as for-profit entities. Their mission, inspired by Dan Case's incredible intelligence and savvy, is simple: "to invest in research aimed at finding the fastest possible route." Taking a venture capital model, they seek to "buy down" the risk for companies as an incentive to invest in new brain cancer therapies. Amazingly, only three brain cancer treatments have been approved by the FDA in the past thirty years. ABC2 seeks to provide leadership, leverage, and impact now, because there's no time to waste. The sandglass does not have endless grains.

In addition to supporting the work of the fine individuals associated with ABC2 in any way I can, my blog has been utilized for the Norris Cotton Cancer Center's annual appeal; my letter of thanks to Sojourns Community Health clinic was used for their annual effort; and both of my daughters have formed groups in their schools to address cancer concerns and the need for support. As a Dartmouth student raising funds for veterans of the Iraq and Afghanistan wars shared with me: "raindrops fill lakes."

And what of mice and men? (I love Steinbeck.) We shall not let these plans go awry. In my conversations with leading research scientists and doctors, I've been made aware of the possibility that I may have my very own line of "Mark Green mice," who will sacrifice themselves for the cause. My cancerous brain tumor cells will be inserted into tiny mouse brains for the purpose of study and research, and perhaps help find treatment or a cure for ependymoma. (Though I don't think they'll have tiny wire-rim glasses.) There are "mouse hospitals" across the country and around the world housing literally hundreds of thousands of mice—many born with no immune system, thereby furnishing a "blank slate"—who are the recipients of similar treatment for hundreds of diseases. One, located at Columbia University, called the Olive Laboratory, is solely dedicated to researching pancreatic ca ncer. This certainly challenged my ill-informed knowledge of the importance of research, even when it means using mice for laboratory experiments, and I admit to a certain lack of discomfort on the subject. Are we, at the core, really more valuable than a mouse? I simply don't know.

I've written before of my belief in animal omens and spirits in the Regnum Animale. The bees stinging me directly on my head after surgery, the recurrent bear dreams, the suicidal squirrel. I suppose one of the qualities that differentiates us from other species is our ability to rationalize. So either I can feel guilty for my hand in the xenographic transplantation of mice or thank them for their noble, if unwilling, sacrifice.

Oddly, in this month of the mouse, I encountered *mus musculus* omens by the dozens this weekend. As I prepared our garden shed for rehabilitation into a much longed-for writers cottage/music-jam room/yoga retreat/man-cave, to be insulated, electrified and finished with rough-sawn Vermont pine, I took to cleaning out the entire structure, formerly used for bike and ski storage. (1,000,000 thanks B for your patience)

Sitting atop a shelf was a box containing a small, unused satellite dish. When I pulled it down and rested it on a chair, I noticed several holes and gathered that these portals had been created by mice. I opened the box and let out a loud shout as a dozen or so mice came pouring from the heavily nested domicile, jumping across my body as if spring-loaded. Beneath the mounds of string, pine needles, chewed towels, and who-knows-what-else was a fully occupied mouse nest. They scattered out and into the woods. They are owl fodder now.

So I tip my hat to my future brain cancer mice, whoever you are. Thank you. We'll all float on, ok.

The Burns poem was written after he uprooted a mouse's nest while plowing a field. The poem is an apology to the mouse, also immortalized by Jethro Tull in "One Brown Mouse."

To a Mouse, On Turning Her Up in Her Nest with the Plough
(Americanized)
Small, crafty, cowering, timorous little beast,
O, what a panic is in your little breast! You need not start away so hasty
With argumentative chatter!
I would be loath to run and chase you,
With murdering plough-staff.
I'm truly sorry man's dominion
Has broken Nature's social union,
And justifies that ill opinion Which makes thee startle
At me, thy poor, earth born companion
And fellow mortal!

I doubt not, sometimes, but you may steal;
What then? Poor little beast, you must live!
An odd ear in twenty-four sheaves
Is a small request;
I will get a blessing with what is left,
And never miss it.
Your small house, too, in ruin!
Its feeble walls the winds are scattering!
And nothing now, to build a new one,
Of coarse grass green!
And bleak December's winds coming,
Both bitter and keen!
You saw the fields laid bare and wasted,
And weary winter coming fast,
And cozy here, beneath the blast,
You thought to dwell,
Till crash! the cruel plough passed
Out through your cell.
That small bit heap of leaves and stubble,
Has cost you many a weary nibble!
Now you are turned out, for all your trouble,
Without house or holding,
To endure the winter's sleety dribble,
And hoar-frost cold.
But little Mouse, you are not alone,
In proving foresight may be vain:
The best laid schemes of mice and men
Go often askew,
And leave us nothing but grief and pain,
For promised joy!
Still you are blest, compared with me!
The present only touches you:
But oh! I backward cast my eye,
On prospects dreary!
And forward, though I cannot see,
I guess and fear!

torn and frayed…

Tuesday, February 21, 2012

And his coat is torn and frayed,
It's seen much better days.
Just as long as the guitar plays
Let it steal your heart away,
Let it steal your heart away.
—Mick Jagger and Keith Richards, "Torn and Frayed"

SINCE THIS BLOG is part health confessional, part personal purging of tales old and new, some sordid, some enlightening, I thought I might begin by sharing that the march toward February 28 (next MRI) slogs ever onward. My life, in between the laughter, tears, fear, and anticipation about all that is yet to be, will be measured in three-month increments: when the MRIs are held and we check in on the state of affairs within my brain. Most of the time, I simply carry on. As the dust from this dust storm settles, and the chaotic din of the initial event is filed away in the memory bank, the realities of simply finding a way to live with cancer have proven to be a physical and emotional mountain of a challenge. Frighteningly, several dear friends have also been diagnosed with cancer in the last few months, two of them with dire prognoses. As I dig in and continue my late-night conversations via Skype, phone, and email with leading research scientists, doctors, and others in the forefront of the resistance movement (Occupy Cancer?), I return to a phrase shared by a leading professor of neurosurgery and neuroscience who almost never, ever uses the "C" word but instead refers to each of our own "personal hyperplasia"—implying that cancer has become too much of a catch-all term fraught with generalizations and misinformation that only adds to the confusion and fear. Cancer is indeed a very personalized and unpredictable affair.

In the meantime, along with many of my peers, I experience the slings and arrows (as well as the joys) of day-to-day living. When I was young, I would hear relatives and family friends in conversation and think, "When I'm that age, I hope my friends and I never spend our time talking about what ails us." Surgeries, breaks, tears, exams, tests, sores, medicines, and the like. How sad and boring! That I now have a pill box containing seven compartments for each day of the week only conjures up memories of my grandmother Ethel, standing before an old porcelain sink in her fuzzy slippers and nightgown, doing the math of medicine.

My friends and I do, in fact, have many other things to speak of: children, community, music, home improvements, cars, technology, arts, skiing, hiking, bicycling, politics and religion (which, sadly, seem to be one in the same these days), concerts, food, and of course, sex. (see politics and religion) The topic of health, however, continues to worm its way into more and more conversations, taking center stage as we all age.

Such conversation was evidenced by recent discourse among friends. During a nordic ski weekend at the Craftsbury Outdoor Center in Craftsbury, Vermont, where we have gathered with other families for many years, eating excellent family-style meals, staying in renovated dormitories and skiing into the night in what the late, great Vermont Governor Aiken referred to as "God's Kingdom" or the "Northeast Kingdom," we shared what has become an annual review of our collective aches and pains.

One friend with a broken collarbone had a TENS unit strategically delivering mini-shocks to interrupt and confuse the nerve pathways that inform pain. Four of us had cheilectomies performed on our large toe joints due to bone spurs (osteophytes) from what is sometimes called "skier's toe." The injurious bone is simply carved down to ease the friction and irritation of regular movement. Old injuries rearing heads, new injuries added to the list. Bad falls and wipeouts, including one entanglement in a barbed-wire fence. And yet we all forge ahead, driven by the inspiring beauty of the snow-covered Vermont backcountry, the joy of being together, and the aim to stay fit.

Between us all, we had a very fine palette of injuries: ruptured tendons and ligaments, broken collar bones, arthritis and many other injuries both sports-related and as a result of mundane events such as slipping on the ice. And then there were the other discussions, among them the indignity of prostate and cervical exams and the forced cleansing before a colonoscopy, for which I'm now preparing. (I have to drink a *gallon* of that stuff ? I can't *eat*?!)

I'm supposed to have one every year but time slipped away and it has been several years. Normally a colonoscopy isn't needed until someone is in their 50s, but I've been identified as carrying the Lynch syndrome HNPCC gene (Hereditary nonpolyposis colorectal cancer), a genetic condition that increases risk of colon and other cancers, including those of the endometrium,ovary, stomach, small intestine, hepatobiliary tract, upper urinary tract, brain, and skin.

I do hope Dr. Rawls is there to help... And woe to Homer's doctors...

Thanks in part to the work of news anchor Katie Couric, whose husband died of colon cancer at the age of 42, her husband, the late John Paul "Jay" Monahan, and their family, millions of people are now getting regular colonoscopies, resulting in a marked downturn in deaths from the disease. In 1998, when Jay, a father of two and noted attorney who also provided legal analysis for MSNBC, NBC News and CNBC, passed away from colorectal cancer at the age of 42, his wife and the family wanted to ensure that this disease would not kill more unsuspecting people and did so by helping raise awareness of the importance of screenings, Couric even had a live colonoscopy on national television, an event that coined the term "Couric effect" to describe the impact a celebrity spokesperson can have on public behavior.

The Jay Monahan Center for Gastrointestinal Health at New York Presbyterian Hospital/Weill Cornell Hospital stands as testament to Jay's life and his faithful friends and family.

So what about brain cancer? Certainly every cancer needs at least its fifteen minutes of fame. Susan G. Komen (Planned Parenthood debacle not withstanding—shame on you Karen Handel, Nancy Brinker and Cliff Stearns) has given, thankfully, breast cancer countless hours of "fame" resulting in the prolonged or saved lives of thousands, if not more, women.

I've come to believe, based on my own ongoing research and conversations with leaders in the field of brain cancer, that we're nearing the top of the mountain. Rather than treating only the symptoms, we'll soon be able to attack mutations at the very earliest stages of cell development through the use of biomarkers and by looking at cancer through the cellular, genomic lens.

And what of the title "Torn and Frayed"? Oh yeah, I've completely shredded both of my shoulders with complete rotator cuff and shoulder tears: the right shoulder from falling while ice skating, and the left side from simply rolling over in bed. I am not unconvinced that my years of asthma medication (steroidal) and the dexamethasone after surgery did not contribute to muscle weakness, leaving me susceptible to tears. This merely adds to my laundry list: two torn knees, one ruptured quad muscle (unrepaired), and one ruptured bicep tendon.

The "Being Patient with High-Maintenance Patient" award certainly goes to Barb, who has endured more than her share of my moans and complaints of aches and pains, and until recently my high level of irritability, which has since undergone a sea-change as I realized I was slowly becoming even more difficult to live with than I was before and was going to scuttle everything we'd worked toward with my bouts of moodiness and unpleasantness. I had to change and refocus on the positive. While I don't run away from or deny the negative, I'm working to channel those negative ions into a safer place.

And while the pain from these tears is often excruciating (I bought my own "TENS" unit, helping me get through the night), I take it in stride. "Bring it on, Demon Body Spirits!" I shout. If I can deal with cancer in my brain and chronic headaches, who cares about a few more tears here and there...I can still ski and bike. My javelin career? That's finished. I have miles to go, however, before I sleep. Soon, it's off to California with Hannah and Libby for the August vacation that wasn't..."hanging ten" off the shores of La Jolla may need to be reduced to hanging two or three...

Meanwhile, Lewis Black provides me with a smile thanks to one of his many apoplectic rants (10.22.08: "Cancer Sucks")

And a nod to Keith and Mick . . . Torn and frayed.

i'm fixing a hole…

Wednesday, February 29, 2012

"I'm fixing a hole where the rain gets in
And stops my mind from wandering
Where it will go

I'm filling the cracks that ran through the door
And kept my mind from wandering
Where it will go

And it really doesn't matter if I'm wrong I'm right
Where I belong I'm right
Where I belong"

—Lennon and McCartney

Yesterday was a landmark occasion: MRI, blood tests, and a visit with the remarkable Dr. Fadul. The MRI came out looking good, in that no visible tumor growth was noted. The doctor was very pleased.

Amazingly, the hole in my brain will remain, which is the cause of some physical imbalance, left-side deficit… but no big deal. This, along with two "full-thickness tears" of my rotator cuffs, is of no consequence at this point as long as I can see, hear, touch, taste, and smell. The whiteness around the margins of the hole, now filled with CSF (cerebral spinal fluid) where the tumor was removed, is leftover irritation from surgery and radiation. While the diagnosis of "incurable and recurrent" remains, that the radiation itself sometimes results in other harmful effects including radiation-induced cancer not showing up until 5-10+ years later, and the Dr. confirming once again that this was a rare cancer especially for an adult (explaining my childlike tendencies) . . . at least now I can breathe a little more deeply. Relax a little more. Let the anxiety and fear melt away as best I can. My next MRI will occur in May. In the meantime, have a "headache clinic" coming up to deal with that element.

Libby, Hannah, and Barb were with me all along yesterday, as they have been from the start, with the anxiety accumulating like so much snow...the moment of truth was upon us, and one of the more moving moments, in addition to hearing the scan results, was between the MRI and the visit with Dr. Fadul, when we wandered into the hospital chapel, a small, quiet nondenominational space with a beautiful, twenty-foot stained glass window of a New England nighttime sky (designed by beloved Vermont artist Sabra Field) intended to symbolize faith and hope.

We sat there in silence with the gray-blue light of the winter sky pushing through the glass, holding hands, each of us with tears welling in our eyes. What news would this bring? What did the immediate future hold for us, and how would we manage?

I realized then and there how rare it was for us to simply sit together, silently, with the people we loved. No words were needed to understand what we were all feeling: love, fear, sadness. But most of all, we had faith and hope. The Milky Way led us there...the Milky Way led us there...

Ode to Bicycles

April 3, 2012

I was walking
down a sizzling road:
the sun popped like
a field of blazing maize,
the earth was hot,
an infinite circle with an empty
blue sky overhead.

A few bicycles passed
me by, the only insects in that dry
moment of summer, silent,
swift, translucent; they
barely stirred the air.

Workers and girls were riding to their factories, giving their eyes
to summer,
their heads to the sky, sitting on the
hard beetle backs
of the whirling bicycles
that whirred as they rode by
bridges, rosebushes, brambles and midday.

I thought about evening when the boys wash up,
sing, eat, raise a cup
of wine in honor of love and life,
and waiting at the door, the bicycle, stilled, because
only moving
does it have a soul, and fallen there
it isn't
a translucent insect humming
through summer but
a cold skeleton

that will return to life
only
when it's needed, when it's light, that is,
with the resurrection of each day.

—Pablo Neruda

I rode my bike last week for the first time since my ill-fated century ride last summer. As I flew down a Vermont hillside, tears of joy washed over my cheeks and the wind cooled my face. I was at peace.

Last summer was my third 100-mile Prouty. The Prouty, the premier event of its kind in northern New England, involves thousands of participants, hundreds of volunteers, and has raised over $14 million for the Norris Cotton Cancer Center at Dartmouth-Hitchcock, one of only forty comprehensive cancer centers in the country. In addition to riding your choice of 25, 35, 50, or 100 miles and even a two-day 200 mile option (The Ultimate—bless you, Charlie Boswell!) one can also walk or row for the cause.

The Prouty was not my first large ride. Two summers before, I completed the 112-mile Harpoon/Vermont Foodbank ride and a few length-of-the-state centuries with the now legendary Joe Cook, a good-natured attorney and bike enthusiast/addict who has quite a following. But I became so enamored with the Prouty that I joined the board of the center's Friends organization, albeit for a brief term, as my work made it difficult to attend the meetings. and in a strange twist of fate, I am now indebted to all things Dartmouth-Hitchcock and Norris Cotton Cancer Center. A heartfelt thank you, Jean, Susan, Rebecca, Catherine and the entire staff.

Learning how to ride in a pack, known in bicycle jargon as a peloton, was a new experience. Prior to jumping into these long rides I was usually a solo rider, save for an occasional trek with a friend or two and a few regional group rides. The politics of the peloton are as important to understand as its physics: you must stay in formation, front wheel within inches of the person in front of you. You must not be "squirrely," lest you invite a disaster of especially painful, expensive proportions. You have a duty to warn those behind you of oncoming hazards (potholes, excessive gravel, roadkill, babies crawling across the road) with proper hand signals. Most of all, you must assume the lead at some point or be left aside, with the stigma of "wheel-sucker" permanently attached to your once-good name.

The purpose of the peloton isn't social, although certainly the camaraderie is a useful incentive to pedal. It's simple science: someone who rides in the middle of a line can conserve up to 40 percent of their energy as they settle into the slipstream. The rider in the front of the pack is working the hardest, not only breaking wind, as it were, but pulling those behind. Riding with thousands of other riders, it's usually okay to jump into a line if you feel you can keep the pace, but again, at some point you must be prepared to assume the position (of being the lead, that is). At six-foot-one and two hundred pounds, I'm usually a welcome presence to buffet the wind.

But last July, something was very wrong. I was terribly "off." Hiding my fatigue, I "Proutied on," meeting up with friends to ride into the wind. I quickly lagged behind and lost everyone altogether. I chided myself for not training hard enough, even though, unlike in past years, I didn't stay up late, have a drink or two, or have a late-night snack. Like many of my friends, I can usually rally and push through the fatigue and pain. But this day was different, and I didn't understand.

I'm not one to give up easily, or to admit defeat until every option has been exhausted. And then there's my Leo pride. But I simply could not power on. At around mile sixty-five I pulled into a SAG (support and gear) stop, a supported area with a repair station, power bars, Gatorade and first aid. SAG stands for support and gear. By then, I was told I would have to get a shuttle back or take a shortcut, as it was getting late and I was beyond the cutoff point to complete the ride lest darkness ensue. There were very few riders, another indiction that I was indeed lagging. Two other riders sitting on the gravel, carried the look of defeat on their faces. One, a lanky teenage boy who found out the hard way that pedaling 100 miles on a fat-tire 29″ wheeled mountain bike was more work than anticipated. The other, a rugby-esque twenty-something who clearly had been drinking heavily the night before and was complaining about his buddies dragging him into this mess, was also waiting for the rescue shuttle.

We loaded our bikes into the back of the four-door pickup and climbed in, none of us making eye contact at first, as our pride masked our defeat. It was as if we were in a cab with thick walls of scratched Plexiglas between us all. The driver, a kind volunteer who took his job seriously, drove on, calling in on the walkie-talkie that he was transporting three bicyclists back to the staging area and finish line.

Finally, we broke the silence and shared our stories of why were such a bunch of lame-asses.

"I should have listened to my friends," said the mountain bike kid. "I should have used my road bike!" he shared dejectedly.

"I'm still hung over," exclaimed the rugby guy. "What an idiot I am."

"I didn't train enough" I told them. "I should have ridden more."

As we barreled down the highway back to Hanover, passing the ones still on the road, we tried to hide our embarrassment. I overheard the driver speaking with some of the other volunteers on the radio. There had been a pileup ahead about ten miles from the finish.

"It doesn't look good," someone shared over the static. I didn't think about it much except to feel sadness that there had been such an accident. But as we approached the emergency vehicles blocking the road I had a wave of fear wash over me. "STOP" I shouted. "Those are my friends!"

I immediately recognized several of my colleagues and the truck pulled over. I told the driver that I was going to see if I could help and that I would bike back on my own, at which point the other two in the truck also got out, taking their bikes.

On the pavement were two of my friends and another rider. One was being slid onto a backboard and the other was about to be placed on a stretcher. Other friends looked on, fear and concern hung in the air. They had somehow gotten their handlebars entangled with another rider and happened to be brother and sister, both excellent athletes and remarkable people. Their children, also exceptional athletes, were riding with them. The brother wound up bruised and battered but OK after flying over the handlebars. His sister, a cancer survivor, did not fare as well and I believe she broke her hip. Several months later she succumbed to the cancer, leaving a beautiful legacy of kindness, friendship, and athleticism.

After the ambulances drove away, we all got back onto our bikes. No one had noticed amidst the frenzy that I had been dropped off.

They just figured I had caught up. I said nothing as I was so stunned by the events which had unfolded. As we pedaled the last ten miles back to the staging area and finish, knowing a festive scene replete with delicious food, music and free massages awaited, I contemplated the road ahead and the one left behind.

As I crossed the finish line, with the multitudes welcoming every rider with cheers of congratulations and celebration, I felt an enormous lump of guilt lodge in my throat and all I could think of was the scam of marathoner Rosie Ruiz. Walking around the celebratory scene, I now felt doubly awful, physically and emotionally. I had cheated myself and deceived my friends. Near the pizza stand I caught the eye of the hung over rugby guy hanging with his other presumably less hung over friends. He smiled, raised his finger to his mouth and whispered "shhhhhh."

Only a few weeks later I would come to understand just how different that day was. We now know that my brain was beginning to bleed and swell from the tumor and was ever so slowly herniating into my brain stem. It's indeed a miracle that things didn't come to a complete end that very day. By the time I reached the hospital two weeks later, I was told that I was within twenty-four hours of dying instantly.

Bicycling is my first athletic love, shared perhaps with any winter sport, particularly cross-country and telemark skiing. Growing up, bicycling was for me less about exercise than it was about freedom. During my middle and high school days, I'd often bike the 4.36 miles home in Melrose Park, PA to Jenkintown, PA where I went to school. My other option was less attractive: riding with mother, who happened to teach at my school. Commuting with Mom, when I was a somewhat typical, slightly incorrigible adolescent, usually meant arguing with her until we crossed the first speedbump onto campus, when she would then turn to me and say "I'm no longer your mother. I am Mrs. Green. See you at the end of the day," at which time we would pick up our argument where we left off that morning. So riding my bike was a thrill, a joy, and a necessity.

My first major purchase as a teenager, after my first hi-fi stereo, complete with integrated tape deck, record player and am/fm tuner, was a bicycle. If memory serves, it was in 1983, a sophomore in high school and I had spent much of my time at the local bike shop which was run by a crew of very crusty, thickly bearded, wire-rimmed-spectacled revolutionaries. I had set my sights on a Specialized Expedition Touring bicycle replete with multiple braze-ons for three water bottle cages. Outfitted with the proper rear and front racks and panniers, mirrors, frame-fitting pump and handlebar bag, it would be all I needed to begin my two-wheeled journey to who knows where.

Prior to the Specialized touring bike, which would carry me from Milford, Pennsylvania to Boston, Philadelphia to New Orleans and many other destinations near and far, I had my share of banana-seated, high-handlebar cruisers, heavy, steel ten-speeds and at one point a pseudo-aerodynamic steel 12-speed which had cast aluminum covers on the brakes and a flattened handlebar to allegedly "slice" through the wind. Mind you, these were the days of protecting your head with one of three choices: nothing, a hat, or an oversized white Bell helmet with red reflective tape, giving the rider the appearance of being an escapee from a mental hospital.

In college, my first year, with no car to speak of, I again invested in a new bike. 1985 saw the rising tide of the mountain bike coming into its own. 1981 saw the first mass-produced mountain bike, the Specialized Stumpjumper, but initially most bike companies were wary or not interested. I had to get one. In fact, I was one of two students on campus at the time who owned these relatively new commercial inventions. With roots in California, specifically the hills of Marin county and Mount Tamalpais, where counter-culture types would retrofit Schwinns with fat balloon tires and motorcycle parts and fly down the mountains with reckless abandon, mountain biking was still nascent. Mountain biking has origins tied to cycle-cross in Europe where bikes were made more rugged to offer an exercise alternative in winter. Names like Joe Breeze, Ned Overend, Charlie Kelly, Tom Ritchey, and Gary Fisher became part of my knowledge base and I would devour whatever I could about mountain bikes. I even sought out Ned when I lived in Durango, Colorado, where he worked as a bike mechanic.

Mine was a deep green Cannondale with motorcycle-styled hand grips, enormous aluminum tubing, large caliper brakes and a 24″ rear tire with a 26″ in front. That beloved Cannondale was my best friend and saw me through some terrific ups and a few downs.

At one point it was even stolen and later retrieved off the porch of some punks in Utica who had tried to sell it at the same bike shop where it was purchased. It's ALWAYS GOOD to get in with your local bike shop! Case in point, I could argue I owe a very good chunk of my long-term happiness (as well as a depleted bank account) to the folks at West Hill Shop: the mechanics and sales people, the former owners the Quinns and the current owners Jim and Diny.

There's something incredibly beautiful and seductive about the art of the bicycle. Poetry in motion. Even the clothing, especially that of the old-school, appeals. Vintage bicycle shops which quite literally make me tremble include Old Spokes Home in Burlington, Vermont, Landmark Vintage in NYC and Via Bikes in South Philadelphia. I love to watch the Tour de France and admire friends who are superior athletes on the bike.

I continue to be moved and inspired by one dear friend who, in addition to being a champion skier, having most recently competed in the IPC World Cup Adaptive Races, is also a world-class hand-cyclist. Alicia Brelsford Dana, paralyzed from the waist down since an accident in high school, she didn't let her physical challenge stop what she loved doing. She has cycled across the United States, championed in dozens of races, often with first-place results including winning the Vermont City Marathon hand cycle division. She's also an artist, mom, sister, and daughter. I know she's an inspiration to all who learn of her fortitude, and for those who are lucky enough to know her, she's a beacon in the darkness—for me, even more so now that I have my own darkness to face.

Another inspirational friend, with a love of cycling, also enduring the challenge of brain cancer, is someone whom I have never met in person as she lives in England. Anne Feeley started an organization called Brains on Bikes. I was introduced to her through an amazing organization, Accelerate Brain Cancer Cure (ABC2). Two years ago she bicycled from San Francisco to Washington, DC, a total of 3,708 miles, to raise funds and awareness for cancer research. A remarkable individual, she was in training to launch her next project, Brains on Boats and row across the English Channel, when her cancer returned, delaying this noble effort, but I know her mind, body. and faith are strong and I think of her often.

Ah yes, the darkness. How am I? How I am? I'm great. I'm not. I'm up. I'm down. Generally I'm pretty damned good, buoyed by the love of friends and family, but sometimes the cancerous water washes over me in an attempt to drown. I resist. I fight. Treading water physically and metaphorically is no longer possible, with both shoulders severely torn due in part, we think, from the weakening of the muscles from steroids taken after the two craniotomies. So I must learn a new way to swim. I am still trying to excavate and then excise the words "incurable and recurrent." The next MRI is in May.

Blinded by headaches akin to having a white-hot steel rod sliding through my skull, I am about to launch myself into a new phase of pain management that involves severely restricting my intake of sugar and carbohydrates. Acupuncture, which I've never tried, is on the menu. My man-cave/writer's cottage/jam room/meditation retreat project is underway. Work lifts me up. My daughters lift me up. Barb lifts me up. My family lifts me up. My friends lift me up. And yet, the demons of depression lurk, and once in a while clock me on the head as if to say, "Don't forget about us...we're coming for you...." Dementors all. A large part of the so-called battle against cancer isn't just trying to eat right, exercise, and find new cures, all of which are of course critical. No. The biggest battle cancer wages against its victims is against that which lunges for the jugular of the spirit and mines the soul as if by some monstrous auger. The same can be said for any terrible, debilitating disease.

Thank heavens for the bike, because I can't wait to ride again. Bicycling is a salve, an intoxicant, an art form. It helps me forget that there's an octopus inside my brain whose tentacles are at this moment resting between the coral, waiting . . . watching while I pedal on.

"We wanna be free! We wanna be free to do what we wanna do. We wanna be free to ride. We wanna be free to ride our machines without being hassled by The Man! ... And we wanna get loaded. And we wanna have a good time. And that's what we are gonna do. We are gonna have a good time... We are gonna have a party!"

—Peter Fonda as "Heavenly Blues" in *Wild Angels*, 1966

papa

Sunday, April 29, 2012

A million ancient bees
Began to sting our knees
While we were on our knees
Praying that disease
Would leave the ones we love
And never come again
—Regina Spektor, "On the Radio"

I lay my head on my father's side, his threadbare, white t-shirt just the same as it was over forty years ago. He with that warm, rich, Dad smell. Suddenly I let loose with a flood of tears, previously dammed by the concrete of pride and a desire to protect him from the pain already inflicted of knowing the boy he had raised now had brain cancer, and the unspoken agony of physical distance. I'd held back for too long.

When we're most vulnerable, we seek the love and comfort of those closest to us. No one has a monopoly on who that will be. Each relationship has its own particulars. A partner, a spouse, a friend, a relative, a colleague. But because two of my primary triggers for heartache of the deepest, most primal kind are when I think of my daughters and my parents, it's rare that any of us can "go there." Barb has held my crumpled body more than a few times as I let my guard down, becoming a babbling, incoherent mess of fear, exhaustion, and gripping despair. Thankfully, the clouds fade away, the skies clear again, the sun appears, and I carry on as I must. I'm not one to wallow, but I know having a good cry is simply a healthy thing to do. It's a purifier of sorts, a tonic, a purgative, flushing the toxins of stress out of every pore. But it leaves me completely wiped out.

When I think about this illness, I think about my daughters: my beautiful, smart, sweet, strong Hannah and Elizabeth, and my parents, who brought me into this strange universe, to whose lives I owe mine and who are a part of me. In me. Of me. The strong and the weak, the good and the bad. They are more than blood, they are connected souls though the genetic matter that bonds and binds us.

You don't have a soul. You are a soul. You have a body.
—*atributed to* C. S. Lewis

I often wonder, does Obama, with his brilliant, calm, grace-under-pressure manner, ever fall apart? Of course he does. More to the point, has he recently been so doubled over with fear, drowning in his own tears of paralytic agony, that his knees crumble as he cries out for the touch of Michelle's soft, warm hand caressing the top of his head? Can anyone really be so strong knowing that they hold so much power and that the decisions they make every day have an impact on so many?

We push it back, the fear and terror. The tears. We simply must... carry...on. My mother has apologetically shared that she is unable to go "there" and that she has still hasn't had the courage or strength to go near my writing. When I speak with her or spend time with her, it's all she can do to muster a mention of "it," as it is simply impossible for her. At first I didn't understand. Why would Mom, a writer herself, not want to see my work? But it soon became clear. How could she? Why would she want to? She already knows, and yet none of us can know how deep the depths of darkness are, lest we go there and find no way out. While we dance around the perimeter, we're careful not to fall into the emotional sinkhole only to have the dirt and debris fall in with us, burying us alive. We just can't go there. There is too much to celebrate, too much good music to hear, foods to eat, places to see...and then there's life itself.

The tears, which broke with surprising swiftness and were completely unexpected, fell into my dad's shirt as he held my head. My "keppelah" as he used to call it. Flashbacks of him standing in my doorway in the morning, beaming, shouting, "Up and Atom, Atom Ant!" Of helping me ride my two-wheeled bike for the first time. The games of catch. The fishing. The Phillies, Sixers, and Flyers games.

The league softball games he would play at Haverford, mom dutifully packing a picnic lunch as my sister and I lay on the blanket. But most of all, his warmth. His love of my sister and me. Like his own father, a clothing merchant and teacher, my father seems to derive much of his joy from a love of children.

What does it mean to be a good dad? No amount of riches, no level of poverty can trump love. Love must be unconditional. Period.

One year, when Dad drove the five hours from Philadelphia to upstate New York to pick me up from college, U-Haul in tow, a close friend shared a story I've never forgotten. He was looking out the window of his dorm room when my father pulled up, and watched as Dad got out of the car and I ran to greet him with a warm embrace. He said tears filled his eyes because, while he knew his dad loved him, he'd never experienced such a loving, physical display of love with his own father. When he went home, he told his dad they were going out for a beer that very night. At the bar, he did something he'd never done: he told his father he loved him. His father, stoic, of a generation and culture not prone to showing emotion of any kind, said, "I love you, too." The earth moved that day. A new chapter was born. The dam had burst. The ice had been shattered.

While there's no monopoly on suffering, there can be no loss more devastating than losing a child. Disease, war, violence, and accidents claim untold young lives every minute of every day. I was going to add natural causes but how can that be so? There is nothing natural about a child dying. And yet they do, and always will. They say no one should outlive their children. But sometimes people do.

This is all very hard to write about. So I will end with a variation on "if you love somebody, set them free." This is for all men—sons, brothers, uncles, cousins, fathers, grandfathers, friends, colleagues, and neighbors, who by way of history, culture, religion, homophobia, fear, insecurity, politics, or whatever virus has infected your heart and rendered you emotionally challenged, are unable to express feelings of affection:

"If you love somebody…tell them!"

Thanks, Poppa. For believing in me. For going the distance. And most of all, for telling me you love me. I love you.

See lyrics of Cat Stevens' "Cat's on the Cradle"

back down south

Thursday, May 10, 2012

"All I wanna know
Is how far you wnna go
Fighting for survival"
—"Back Down South" by Kings of Leon

No losers here. It was the brain tumor olympics, and every participant, every volunteer, and every donor was a gold medalist. The fifteenth annual Race For Hope was held in Washington, DC, this past Sunday, with over 11,000 participants raising over $2.3 million to help support the fight/war/resistance movement against brain tumors, the second-leading cause of cancer death among children and young adults under twenty, a disease in which only one out of three survive beyond five years and for which there is no known prevention as there is no known cause. Sponsored by two very important organizations, ABC2 (Accelerate Brain Cancer Cure) and NBTS (National Brain Tumor Society), this outpouring is one of the largest (but by no means the only) events of its kind in the US.

I admit to having a peculiar feeling all weekend—a mix of love, fear, hope, and anxiety as I found myself awkwardly cast in a surreal performance. This was my new tribe. Unwilling members all, we were there for one primary reason: to raise funds and awareness of the need to find cures to this incurable disease. I walked among the thousands affected and afflicted. Parents wearing customized t-shirts celebrating their dearly beloved children, some of whom had left this earth way too soon. Others participating in the 5K walk/run, who continued to smile despite their disease. Friends, families, colleagues, all marching, walking, running, hoping toward the Capitol.

The notion of "losing" a battle to cancer (or any disease) frustrates. The word "lose" when combined with cancer implies that cancer won and left the defeated beaten to death. No. There is no losing...even when cancer has infiltrated and spread beyond repair, the spirit, I believe, carries on...winning. Yes, when we succumb, we lose our place as a living being on this earth. Nonetheless, this was indeed an army of brain cancer survivors and their families. Given that of all cancers, brain cancer represents 1-2% of the total, this was a uniquely qualified group.

I met other soldiers leading the charge: brain tumor survivors akin to leading generals on the battlefield, fighting for every living soul and in memory of those who are gone. My brave and loving parents were also there to support and share in the experience, and my dear sister ran her first 5k for the cause. Countless others laid their cards on the table for all to see in the hope that their naked truth will help others understand and support the cause.

There were over 500 teams, including those supporting survivors and those who had already suffered the loss of a loved one and sought to honor their lives by participating: "Kisses for Kayla," "Dr. Bears Brain Tumor Busters," "Keep Calm and Cure Brain Cancer."

As someone who first became involved in fundraising for cancer through my participation in century rides to benefit the Norris Cotton Cancer Center at Dartmouth Hitchcock, inspired by a friend who had lost his father to cancer, it shook me to my core to be suddenly walking in the "survivor" crowd for the opening ceremony of the Hope for Cure. I was humbled as I walked among the children in wheelchairs, the adults, many in a much worse state than I was, mustering all they could to walk with the crowd. Some were blind from their surgeries, others walked with extreme difficulty.

A young couple in front of me walked in a tight embrace, the lanky boy walking forwards, his girlfriend backwards, her face buried into his chest as she wore her yellow survivor shirt. They held each other tight as they cried, "I love you! I love you!" Tears streamed down my cheeks. The crowd went wild, cheering all of us. "Wait," I thought to myself, "you must have the wrong guy. I must be in the wrong place. What am I doing here? This is all wrong."

But I was right where I needed to be and doing what I needed to be doing. And it was all right. It was all right.

"Life is a shipwreck, but we must not forget to sing in the lifeboats."

—Voltaire

Just Breathe

Monday, June 18, 2012

For Barb. Our song.
a few lines from "Just Breathe" BY PEARL JAM

Yes I understand that every life must end, uh huh…
As we sit alone, I know someday we must go, uh huh…
I'm a lucky man to count on both hands
The ones I love…
. . .
Nothing you would take
Everything you gave
Hold me 'till I die
Meet you on the other side . . .

June, 18, 2012

FATHER'S DAY CAME with a particular poignancy. Three days earlier I had my MRI with contrasting dye to allow a visual into my brain to check on any profusion of abnormal blood flow which would indicate possible tumor growth. No signs of this or signs of new tumor growth.

Sigh. Deep breath. It's been nearly one year since the calamity. It's been an exhausting time. My next MRI will take place in September, along with a neuropsych evaluation, as I'm experiencing some deficit in memory ("but how can we tell the difference?"), possibly from the side-effects of radiation. I'm off Facebook. Too much a distraction from what is real and important.

Also working on a book to serve many purposes:

1. To continue to tell the story, many tales yet untold

2. To help others with brain cancer know they aren't alone, and that while some of my experiences will be alien, others may resound with familiarity
3. To help raise awareness of the need for more research and support for brain cancer, which comprises a mere 2 percent of all cancer but remains one of the deadliest
4. To leave a legacy for my children, and their children, and so on
5. And most of all…to help me breathe

Thank you for reading. Helping me breathe.

losing face…book

Tuesday, June 19, 2012

"Friendship needs no words—it is solitude delivered from the anguish of loneliness." —Dag Hammarskjold

It is said (by whom, I don't know) that our best qualities are, at times, our worst qualities. That which makes us good, happy, and wonderful can be the same that brings us to our knees. Lately I've been brought to my knees.

My parents told me recently how every time we went out for dinner, I, age four or five, would "work the floor" as if I were running for office. Weaving in and out of tables, I'd walk up to complete strangers, smile, and ask them how their dinner was.

Fast-forward to forty years later, I've begun to realize that some of my gregariousness actually masks a profound insecurity and insatiable need for attention and approval…from everyone. The problem? Such focus and attention steals me away from the ones closest to me, the ones who truly know and love me and who will be at my bedside when I take my last breath.

Over twenty years ago, I was having lunch with a friend at an outdoor cafe in Burlington, Vermont. As I sat there pretending to listen, I was distracted by the pedestrians walking past. More than a few times, I recognized someone, or vice-versa, and interrupted the conversation to chat. Finally, she had enough. "Mark, are you even listening to me? I feel like you're someplace else." I was caught off guard by her honesty and bluntness. She'd called me out. I sat there, stunned. Hurt. Embarrassed. She was absolutely right. And even though we haven't been in touch since that time, I still recall this moment like it was yesterday. Or today.

A few years ago I went out to lunch with a colleague whose job I now hold. It was a wonderful afternoon, and the French-style bistro was brimming with energy. Even though I knew most of the people in the room, I sat content, wanting to get to know this acquaintance. But I was immediately irritated when nearly every time he recognized somebody walking in the door, he got up to say hello. He was like a kid in a candy shop. He must have gotten up nearly a dozen times. I'd met my match—and seen myself in a mirror. How rude. How off-putting. He wasn't really there, and yet I was.

I've always had difficulty saying no. I never wanted to disappoint anyone. Years ago, my former wife told me that my time spent in search of the newest friend or thrill was pulling me away from the relationship most important to me, or the one that should have been. Thus the "former." And I've been repeating this pattern to no healthy end.

This cancer has amplified every character trait in my body, both good and bad. When I was first diagnosed, the steroids I took for the surgery created a monster: while I wasn't aggressive or angry, I wasn't sleeping more than a few hours a day for weeks on end. I wrote endlessly, with what one therapist called a manic demeanor.

Cancer is so much more than the disease itself. The shock of the two brain surgeries combined with the cancer diagnosis scrambled my soul. Only now, as I face some challenging emotional moments, having overcome most of the physical ones, I'm beginning to realize the deep and damaging effects of the way I've sometimes handled this calamity—and the way others (most with good intentions) want more than I can give, as if my illness is their illness. Cancer has been profoundly enlightening and at the same time isolating. In the end, no one, not even those I love the most and who are closest to me, can truly understand. The same could be said for disease, physical or psychological limitation

I recall a scene from The Sopranos in which Tony's shrewd battle-axe of a mother, Livia, shares her stark, cynical view of life and death with her grandson Anthony, Jr. My parents and I love this scene as it recalls a few relatives long since passed. We have all referred to this piece more than a few times as we grimace and laugh simultaneously.

AJ: What's the purpose?

Livia: Of what?

AJ: Being… here on our planet. Earth. Those kids are dead meat. What's the use? What's the purpose?

Livia: Why does everything have to have a purpose? The world's a jungle. If you want my advice, Anthony, don't expect happiness, you won't get it, people let you down. And I'm not naming any names, but in the end, you die in your own arms.

AJ: You mean alone?

Livia: It's all a big nothing. What makes you think you're so special?

While cancer can indeed be an opportunity for profound emotional and spiritual growth, it can also rip families and friendships apart, as the one "without" can never possibly understand, no matter how hard they might try, what the one "with" is experiencing on a constant basis. When I was in DC, I met another fellow brain cancer survivor, whose fiancee left him three months after diagnosis, surgery, and radiation. She couldn't deal.

When I was 16, I drove my mother's new car to a friends house to lift weights. Mom was asleep at the time, and while I asked to borrow the car, her response wasn't made with cognition. The car made it less than three miles before I, being inexperienced and driving too fast, lost control on a turn, went airborne, overcorrected, and hit the gas instead of the brake. I had no idea why the car wouldn't slow down, and in fact thought I'd suffered some major mechanical malfunction. The car continued to swerve wildly, barreling through a stop sign, blowing a tire, careening down a side street, traveling up an embankment, taking down a pine tree, and rolling back down the hill before finally landing upright, facing the opposite direction on all four blown tires.

My reaction was puzzling. I immediately started to pull everything from the car and place it under a tree. The boombox on which I'd been blasting German pop music had flown out of the passenger window and was lying in the pine duff, still playing. I continued to empty the glove compartment, running back and forth to the tree. My glasses were gone, I couldn't see anything, the damned German pop music was still blaring, and a little girl on a bicycle came pedaling up to see a very bewildered man, bleeding from his nose, blood spattered on his white polo, sitting beneath a tree with all of his belongings set neatly in a pile.

Why did I empty the contents of the car? What was I thinking? I was in shock. Maybe I thought the car was going to blow up. I have no idea.

When I was diagnosed with cancer, I immediately went into shock. What I realize now is that I'm still in shock. I went into overdrive, planning parties, reunions, and, in an obsessive-compulsive bit of bizarre behavior, my own memorial service. What started as a "living will" became an obsession, right down to the selection of music ("Amazing Grace," "Nearer to My God to Thee," songs from Appalachian Journey), flower arrangements (wild), wine (Napa Cab, Oregon Pinot), food (local), and program. The only thing missing were the directions to the venue (which I'd also preselected).

I amassed over 1,000 Facebook "friends," many of whom I didn't even know. Yet I was the loneliest one in the room. I was losing sight of what really mattered. I wasn't reaching out to the ones closest to me, but to the greater world beyond. What was I looking for? What did I need? I still don't know, and I suppose that's part of the adventure of discovery, trying as it may be at times.

The road to recovery is littered with potholes, roadkill, broken glass, and soft shoulders. Drift too far in one direction and you'll either collide head-on with an oncoming car or get pulled off the road and roll down the hill. If you're not paying attention, the bones from a freshly killed raccoon may puncture your tires. Or you may never see the tiny fragment of safety glass that's unknowingly cored its way into the rubber.

For the first time in my life, I've admitted that not only can't I do this alone, but I need some extra help. A coach. A lifeguard. (but not a "life-coach," a term that makes what little hair I have left stand on end, with all due respect and apologies to my life-coach friends. I just loathe the term, not the practice) When cancer arrived at my doorstep, everyone recommended a therapist. When I was in the hospital, a social worker sat quietly in the corner until she had room to speak with me. With her notepad she scratched down a few notes and called me a week later with the names and numbers of a few people she suggested I contact. I had told her then that I did not feel like I needed anyone and if I did, I wanted nothing to do with a "touchy-feely," new-age form of treatment. Nobody in flowy purple linen. speaking in hushed tones, asking me "how does that make you feel?I wanted straight-talk and I did not want to commit for any extended duration. I met with someone as a "prophylactic" for a few sessions but bailed quickly. I didn't "take" to him, nice and experienced as he was.

He himself seemed to be rather unhealthy physically and this concerned me greatly. Was this an excuse to avoid? Perhaps. Perhaps not.

I've now found someone I can respect and work with who isn't afraid to ask tough questions. The goal is to heal—to heal the wounds from past lives, from this current one, and to address anxieties about the future. One sage bit of advice offered by one therapist when I told him I didn't need to see anyone because I had my partner, my family, and close friends, was that it's unfair to expect them to be able to handle everything, and that it's healthy to have an objective outlet. I agree.

So I'm making steps large and small. I joke that I'm ready to undergo a "spiritual high-colonic." I've quit Facebook cold turkey. I must admit, I don't really miss it. For many it is a fun, useful, healthy tool. For others, Facebook represents the Evil Empire, designed to extract critical data for the sole purpose of mining marketing opportunities and dollars. As a parent I have seen it tap into the darkest side of adolescence. It's also fun to see what your own kids are up to. But for me it had become a detrimental distraction from the things that mattered most and the people closest to me. It wasn't that I was "on" for hours, it was the constant drone of distraction feeding an addictive personality. A source of escapism and immediate gratification.

I'm coming clean. My writer's cottage is nearly finished. I'm trying to learn and embrace the art of meditation. I need to calm the noise in my head. I'm pushing stress-inducers off the cliff as much as I can, and playing guitar, mandolin, banjo, and ukulele again with passion. I have a book to write.

I have miles and miles to go before I sleep, but I'm ready for the trail: rocks, roots, and all. I need to get back to the start.

"The Scientist" by Coldplay

Come up to meet you, tell you I'm sorry
You don't know how lovely you are
I had to find you, tell you I need you
Tell you I set you apart
Tell me your secrets and ask me your questions
Oh, let's go back to the start
Running in circles,
Coming up tails
Heads on a science apart . . .

muzzle of bees

Tuesday, July 31, 2012

"Muzzle of Bees" by Wilco

There's a random painted highway
And a muzzle of bees
My sleeves have come unstitched
From climbing your tree

And dogs laugh, some say they're barking
I don't think they're mean
Some people get so frightened
Of the fences in between . . .

As of this evening at approximately 11:00 or so, it will be exactly one year since I nearly slid into the abyss...the dates are etched in memory. July 31, 2011, monthlong headaches devolve into calamity. At 12:05 AM, August 1, I am admitted to Cheshire Medical Center in Keene, New Hampshire, and later rushed to Dartmouth-Hitchcock. August 2, 6:00 AM, my first craniotomy. A 4.3 cm tumor removed. September 6, second craniotomy to remove residual brain cancer tissue. On 11/11/11, the end of thirty-three radiation treatments to my brain. This morning I went to get night crawlers and supplies for fishing. The receipt was for $11.11. It was just after 11:00 AM.

I'm not very superstitious, but sometimes one has to wonder about the "lattice of coincidence" referred to by the character Miller in the movie *Repo Man*: "A lot of people don't realize what's going on. They view life as a bunch of unconnected incidents and things. They don't realize that there's this, like, lattice of coincidence that lays on top of everything. Give you an example; show you what I mean: suppose you're thinkin' about a plate of shrimp. Suddenly, someone'll say like, plate, or shrimp, or plate of shrimp out of the blue, no explanation. No point in looking for one, either. It's all part of a cosmic unconsciousness."

The girls—my teenage daughters and two of their friends—are slowly waking after a whirligig ride of a weekend consisting of sailing on Lake Champlain, eating our way up and down Church Street, taking in the earnest, bohemian street performers, shopping (of course, what with two daughters and two of their friends), attending a wonderful Wilco concert, and camping out at the North Beach campground. It was a great weekend of just being a dad to my fantabulous daughters and enjoying all that the great state of Vermont has to offer. After closing out with a sumptuous brunch at the Skinny Pancake we set off for Pennsylvania, traveling through the lush pastures and apple orchards of Addison County, with the Green Mountains to the east and the Adirondacks to the west. We drove to my parents' camp, where I now have a moment to breathe deep and pause to write. Nothing like a near death experience, nor continuing to live with a deadly disease, to further deepen an appreciation for all that surrounds. Carpe diem indeed.

Last night, as I slipped into the dark, warm waters of this glacially formed, spring-fed lake, the hazy moon casting a soft glow on the lily pads, I felt a great sense of calm with the usual current of fear, humming steadily but softly, like the hum of an overhead power line, inside the porous marrow of my bones. What a year it has been. What a year it has been.

The headaches continue, my moods are not always steady, and my memory chip often feels as if it has been placed too close to a magnet, scrambling things up a bit. This reminds me of a great scene in a recent Breaking Bad—spoiler alert—where Walt and Jesse attempt to erase a laptop stored in the evidence room by loading a truck with a high-powered junkyard magnet and driving up to the building causing a maelstrom of everything metal to attach to the adjoining wall (for a debunking of this myth-making scene *PC-Mag* has a great essay).

It was last July I started a new position at Putney School after a wonderful albeit brief stint (again) at Dartmouth. As rewarding as it was and as wonderful as I found the Dartmouth community, the commute was becoming unpleasant and expensive to my wallet, my body and soul. And my love for Putney has always been strong. It was last July that I failed, feeling weak and out of sorts, to complete the century ride for the Prouty, as I had done the previous two years. Two weeks later "it" all happened. And this year, Barb and I rode the Prouty together, bicycling fifty miles (her first fifty!) and helping to raise funds for cancer research and care. It was a moving, shared experience, brought us closer, I believe and was a symbolic event in many ways. Friends joined The Blue Lobsters, a team formed by Tamra Mooney. Fellow cancer survivor and most wonderful friend Jerry Evarts rode as well, with his entourage as he always has. Tamra made great shirts which we all wore with pride. Her young, highly athletic son Scott raised over $3,000 alone. My eldest daughter, Hannah, interned this summer for the Friends of Norris Cotton Cancer Center, working on the the Prouty, and Libby shared with great poise and beauty her moving experience with all this at her Bat Mitzvah this summer, lending further strength and support with her words. This year I wore a "Survivor" bib. It was an odd feeling. While I have certainly become a brain cancer evangelist, the "survivor" moniker always makes me uncomfortable but I know at the core that such a nod might inspire others, no matter their ailment, to do what they can to help advance the "cause for cure" as it were. Awareness is tantamount.

Words and gestures seem too thin a response to thank everyone for the love and support: Barb, Hannah, Libby, parents, sister, extended family, friends, family and communities all. I can only hope that my expression through words will serve a greater good while continuing to serve as a salve for my heart, brain and soul.

One could argue that any expression of art, be it music, writing, painting, sculpture, theater, or sport (yes, I see sport as an art form), requires a dash of self-indulgence. Sometimes more. But as many in the cancer community have expressed, there's a river of guilt that sometimes exceeds its banks, particularly when we hear of other trauma via natural or man-made disaster. The urge and need here is to give back and find your own heroes.

One hero is an old friend, someone I knew when he was a student at Putney School over twenty years ago. Neil Taylor is now not only a friend but a comrade. Before we reconnected, I had partied with him at a local annual barbecue–softball party in Westminster West. A kind, strong young man, with a great family, Neil's presence would guarantee that the softball would be hit with such force that it would nearly hit the roof of the local elementary school across the road. One would almost expect to find the ball deep in the woods, the leather stripped from the core, seams torn apart.

Then, as it always seems to happen, Neil's life was hit by the lightening bolt of cancer. Brain cancer. The surgery to remove the tumor, the size of a grapefruit, left him permanently blind and with some paralysis. A young man, in his prime, a life changed forever. Yet Neil's strength and courage continues to triumph three years later.

While we have shared private conversations about the devastation from brain cancer and his unfortunate aftermath, the isolation of being blind and all that entails, he has also been an inspiration. I, along with the many friends and acquaintances, watched Neil's rehabilitation unfold, often on the streets of Brattleboro and back roads of Putney and Westminster as he had to re-learn, in ways unimaginable to most, the contours, sounds and smells of his environs. He then became a licensed massage therapist and is now living in his own home, unassisted where he practices his craft. Last week I finally signed up for a wonderful massage. Neil has spoken to area schoolchildren to great reception and the buzz is out about "The Blind Masseur."

We spoke of our wonderful shared oncologist, Dr. Camilo Fadul and the team at Dartmouth. The MRIs, the fears, the challenges. When we spoke of blindness, I said something, I don't recall what—I think it was about connections with other blind or visually impaired people, to which Neil replied "you know, what most people don't realize is that there really aren't that many blind people out there, at least not what you might think. Think about it. Aside from me, who else do you know or when was the last time you saw a blind person?" Food for thought.

In another moving moment, we compared our scars. After he worked on my aching muscles, he moved to my scalp. With great sensitivity, he asked about my scar, as his scar remains tender to the touch. I said "no, it's ok, you can work on that too" as his hands moved across the indented seam which runs across the top of my head.

"Mark, you're my tumor twin!" he exclaimed joyfully, as he first did when I spoke with him about my "situation." Yes, I am Neil. Yes I am. And you are also my hero. Thank you Neil. My tumor twin.

God Willin' and the Creek Don't Rise

Thursday, September 20, 2012

THE CREEK THAT BORDERS the Quaker cemetery at my alma mater, Abington Friends School in Pennsylvania, was always a place of magic and fantasy. This short, narrow run of water seemed to arrive from nowhere and came to a peaceful end in a hundred yards or so by spilling into a small pond just below what was known as the "East Wing" where I attended kindergarten.

The school, founded in 1697, had a cemetery, in which were buried long-deceased as well as more recent members of the Abington Monthly Meeting, including school teachers and administrators and sadly, tragically, even a few students taken much too soon, It was of no particular interest to me during those early days; the headstones were simply part of the landscape. When I moved up into the lower school, and all through middle and high school, I'd have to walk through this beautiful, sacred space, framed by a cathedral of large ancient oak trees, on the way to the weekly Meeting for Worship. Years later, whenever I visited school, I would first do so quietly, unannounced, and head directly to the grounds, mourning those I knew—fellow students, school teachers, and staff—and contemplating those I didn't.

But as a young child, it was the water that held my attention. The loss of innocence, play, and connection with the natural world among children today is a very real and growing problem. Recesses and athletic programs have been cut, parks and green spaces are shrinking, and too often kids come home from school and immediately glue themselves to computers, cell phones, and television. The problem is further deepened by a generation of grossly overprotective parents, who themselves never go into the woods and won't let children out of their sight, let alone allow them to walk home from school, even in bucolic New England villages.

This disconnect has been articulated beautifully by many, including Richard Louv, author of *Last Child in the Woods.* Louv is also responsible for the term "nature deficit disorder," which is connected to obesity, stress, aggressiveness, depression and a lack of understanding about the natural world. (Citing a great article in the 3/29/12 *New York Times*) I feel lucky indeed that I was raised in an environment where my parents, teachers, and school recognized the importance of free outdoor play and made it an essential part of our day and development.

During recess, even in winter, we'd slip on our black rubber galoshes, often lined with plastic baggies, and march out to the creek, smashing as many frozen puddles as we could find, triumphant with every chorus of fractured ice, like so many windows, and play in the cold mud, encrusted with crystalline frosting much like misshapen cupcakes set halfway in the ground. In the spring, when all had melted, the creek, at least to our young eyes, became a roaring river.

One of our favorite pastimes was fashioning small boats out of whatever material we could find and having contests to see whose boat survived the longest on its journey downstream. The most successful boats were usually composed of aluminum foil and decorated with leaves and sticks.

I recently dreamt of that creek and my boat. Styled as a canoe, inspired by the great dragon boats, my craft had a wide middle and was narrowed on both ends in tall swooping curls. I set the boat carefully in the water and followed it along from the bank. The boat floated slowly at first, drifting lazily along, then picked up speed. The faster it went, the more it rocked side to side, taking on water until ultimately capsizing under the imbalanced weight. The dream came to a halt.

Much of the past year has been like that boat. Some days drift lazily along until my boat starts to pick up speed and take on water. I may have capsized a few times, but I haven't drowned. I continue to swim and scramble back into the boat, scooping the excess water out as much as possible until the next set of rapids rise to meet me. I can't help but think that the unseen boulders I keep crashing into are the cause of my intense headaches.

The latest chaotic river run has been in the form of seizures. The first occurred during a work trip to Chicago with the head of the school. A brilliant educator and one of the strongest heads of school Putney has ever seen, she is at the forefront of progressive education and leading the charge. Having awakened before dawn to drive an hour and a half from Putney to catch a flight from Hartford, I was eager to get to our destination in time to have a rest before our afternoon meetings. After landing and checking into the hotel, we did indeed have time to stretch our legs and have some down time. But the bicycles stationed outside the lobby caught my eye.

I dropped my luggage off in my room and raced back down to take out a bike for a downtown spin. Drawn as I am to water, without even looking at a map I found my way to Lake Shore Drive along Lake Michigan. With the wind and sun in my face, I was elated. But I was also tired, it was hot, and I had just flown from New England.

I had also just returned from a rather stressful weekend with my family in Pennsylvania. Basically, the stress was the result of the usual subcutaneous low hum of intrafamilial, emotionally fraught regression that sometimes occurs when one spends time with family, in addition to the continued aftershocks from the earthquake of cancer. This, combined with the dull roar of headaches, only heightened my irritability.

About twenty minutes into my ride, I turned back toward the hotel. As I barreled along the busy streets, I became aware that my left arm felt numb and tingly, and ultimately "disappeared." I realized that I had been pedaling with my right leg, and that the spinning of the crank was simply carrying my left leg along. My entire left side "slipped away" as I tried to stop. I managed to slow down just in time to fall slowly to one side, and ultimately to the pavement, in between two parked cars. "*Damn! No! No! No!* Not again!" I moaned as concerned bystanders watched this odd sight. Some workmen across the street yelled, "Hey buddy, you okay?" They ran over, lifted me up, and dragged me off the street. "You want us to call 911?" they asked. "No, I'll be okay," I told them. "I think I'm having a seizure. I just need to rest." They helped me to a chair at a sidewalk café, where I sat exhausted, watching my left leg and toes quiver wildly. A young family asked if I needed help. I called Barb and left a frightened, tearful message, and then called the hospital in New Hampshire, which instructed me to get to a hospital. I couldn't fathom being stuck in Chicago and creating a scene, and thus, perhaps wrecklessly, I ignored their pleading.

Five minutes later I slowly rose, getting back my "sea legs," and started walking back to the hotel with the bike. I had just five more minutes to shower and get dressed for our first meeting. I met the head of school in the lobby, and we took a cab to our destination. Too proud and slightly freaked out, I said nothing. The meeting went quite well.

After the meeting we stopped for ice cream. I looked at Emily with a combination grimace and smile. "I wasn't going to tell you this, but since we're traveling together, I suppose I should. I had a seizure right before we met in the lobby." She stared at me with a quizzical look that could only be interpreted as "What are you, nuts?" I assured her I was not nuts (to be debated) and that I would be fine (not that I really had any idea) and declared I was ready for our next meeting to take place. She admonished that I needed to rest, and that since I'd already met with the people with whom we were supposed to dine, I need not go and instead should simply take it easy. After some protest, I finally gave up. "I guess you're right. It kills me to miss this meeting, but I should rest," I said, dejectedly. "No," she said, "I know I'm right."

When I returned home, I immediately set up an appointment with my oncologist and had another MRI, which are normally scheduled in three-month intervals to check for new tumor growth. Yet another hour in "the tube" listening to the cacophony of enormous magnets, a sound akin to the opening chords of "Helter Skelter" by The Beatles and a chorus of jack hammers. The results showed no sign of tumor growth but did show pronounced enhancement of scar tissue from the surgeries and radiation. The effects of radiation, especially to the brain, can continue for months or even years after treatment. The dead cells don't really have anywhere to go because of the blood-brain barrier, so instead of being flushed from the body as waste, they just float around like dead leaves in a pond. Ultimately, I assume, they compost.

I carried on, went to work, and started back on Keppra, an anti-seizure medication, first prescribed after my initial surgeries last summer. Oddly, I smile when I say Keppra as it reminds me of my grandmother's use of the Yiddish word "kepele" which means "sweet little head."

Several weeks later I was in Boston when again heat, fatigue, and stress created the perfect storm. My left side slowly began to feel as it were filled with lead and water. My balance was thrown off, and I began cursing the demons. I decided then and there I was going to become fully aware of my body and "talk" to my brain. I was going to fight the onset of seizure with positive thinking. I continued walking, albeit slowly. I felt as though I were hallucinating, or in a bizarre, slow-motion scene of some other dimension à la *The Matrix* or *Crouching Tiger, Hidden Dragon.* I felt the presence of an "aura" (no, I did not see unicorns, rainbows, or the Holy Spirit). Interestingly, people who experience seizures, an electical malfunctioning of the brain, refer to having a perception that something is amiss just before an onset.

My seizures are "focal," or partial, seizures, and have occurred on my left side due to the location of the tumor, which was within the right parietal lobes of the brain. For now, the anti-seizure medication seems to be working, with some modest side-effects including dizziness and fatigue. The headaches, some elephantine in nature, others like an arrow being slowly driven into my forehead, continue despite the medications. Stress, bright flashing lights, excessive noise, and other sensory overloads are to be avoided or approached with a new sense of care and awareness.

Going to the Tunbridge World's Fair last weekend, one of my favorite seasonal events, and, in my opinion, the best of the Vermont country fairs, presented a new challenge. Even the Ferris wheel, the only ride I enjoy, was a challenge. Next year I'll spend most of my time in the historical section or just climb into the pen with the lambs and curl up in the straw.

As I've said previously, these writings have been part purge, part therapy, and part community service, in the hope that others may benefit by knowing they're not alone. Not everyone is comfortable laying everything bare. Some simply can't out of fear that it will hurt their career or that they'll be perceived as unfit. I completely respect their choice. Most of the time, when asked how I am, I respond with a thumbs-up and a smile. "Bully!" as Theodore Roosevelt would have shouted. "Bring it on!" I say.

I am constantly moved by how many tumor survivors walk among us struggling quietly with the physical and psychological debilitation of such a disease. Most of us, on one level or another, have endured the crushing, incapacitating blows of multiple surgeries, radiation, chemotherapy, and side-effects from medication, and yet we continue to attempt to live happy, normal lives. We're raising children, in committed relationships, maintaining friendships, holding down jobs, pursuing passions. But in the background, there's a steady drumbeat—or rather, the thud of some sinister clock with a second hand marching forward like a time bomb.

Lately I've been experiencing a percolating anger at the cancer. This resentment comes from the emotional toll, seen and unseen, that I know it's had on my colleagues, friends, and family, especially my parents, my sister, my partner and, in particular, my two teenage daughters. My daughters have certainly learned all too early that life is not always "fair," that the deck of cards we're dealt is the deck of cards we're dealt...and that we must stick together, carry on, move forward, and do our best to enjoy the gifts we have.

The brain cancer community is a relatively small one, and yet I know I can reach out to comrades from around the world with questions, thoughts, or concerns and receive immediate replies with ideas and gestures of comfort and support. I've gleaned so much valuable information, and continue to learn with, dare I say, an open mind. I do have some extra space up there, now that the tumor was resected.

I've spoken with, emailed, Skyped, met, and befriended a wide array of fascinating, committed people, including doctors and scientists in the trenches and on the cutting-edge of research and discovery, and lawyers navigating the often complex regulatory landscape of insurance coverage, the drug approval process, the clinical trial process, the NIH, and the FDA. My sister, as an editor for the National Comprehensive Cancer Network (a Pennsylvania-based organization that develops treatment protocols for cancer) has been a wonderful point of support. Then there are the biotech explorers and venture capital investors with a personal connection to brain cancer. All contribute in their own way to seek better treatment and help move the scientific community forward toward finding cures for what is, for now, an incurable disease.

The book effort is already underway, replete with stories yet to be shared. The somewhat provocative, tentative title and cover has been chosen and the words are being laid down like the bricks of a foundation. Stay tuned!

Man in a Shed

I WRITE FROM MY NEWLY COMPLETED COTTAGE, formerly a simple ten-by-twelve-foot garden shed, now insulated, wired, and finished with rough-hewn pine board from a local sawmill. The "Cabin"—a dream since my days as a Thoreau devotee—has been realized.

Fighting, as I already have been, with a small army of mice seeking to invade and inhabit my space, I cannot but help think of the scene in the film adaptation of Farley Mowat's novel *Never Cry Wolf* (a favorite book and film—how I long for the Arctic!) in which Charles Martin Smith ritualistically prepares mice for eating in a variety of ways—fried, sautéed, dipped in chocolate—to further deepen his understanding of how the wolves survive, as it was assumed they were to blame for the decline of the caribou herds in the Canadian arctic. I may get very hungry and choose to win the battle of occupation not by trapping the creatures but by eating them.

The Cabin is a space to ensconce myself. To rest, dream, cry, think, not think, yell, laugh, listen, meditate, seek solace, play music, and write. And write I will. And rest I must. And Be.

> "There is nothing to writing. All you do is sit down at a typewriter and bleed." —ERNEST HEMINGWAY

> "I am a drinker with writing problems." —BRENDAN BEHAN

Thank you Wes

Monday, October 22, 2012

THANK YOU Wes, Jill, Gary and Rick. Click here for a great blog from a great man with wonderful friends.

Or copy and paste:
http://www.mwestonchapman.com/mark-green-on-mt-moosilauke-with-the- kilimanjaro-team/

Coming up on one-year anniversary of end of radiation 11/11/11... blog to follow...debate time now!

"If I live the life I'm given,
I won't be scared to die."

—Avett Brothers

Friday, January 04, 2013

"I don't think any of us even knew what we were doing here and why we decided to come. I mean, we were all having a blast and all, it was probably the best day of some people's lives. Maybe even mine, but I can't really remember which was the best day of my life or if I've even had it yet.

"Do we know when it is when it's happening, or just looking back on it? I don't really want to have the best day of my life though because then I'll know that that was it, nothing will ever be better than that, and now the moment's gone. I guess I would just get all depressed after it happened. I don't know really, but I didn't get depressed after this day, I just couldn't stop thinking about it and smiling."

—My daughter Elizabeth "Libby" Green, age 13, on participating in the annual Coney Island New Year's Day Polar Bear swim, January 1, 2012

It's been some time since I've jotted out musings vis-à-vis this funny-sounding medium called a "blog." The word to me sounds onomatopoetic. Perhaps the sound of a frog when it has indigestion after slipping too many dragonflies into its stomach. Or the name of a mythical creature from the swamp, emerging from the murky deep and devouring small children with a gaping mouth and massive drooling bicuspids.

In a promise to myself to keep putting pen to paper, or rather applying my awkward yet adaptive style of hunting and pecking with both forefingers (I never learned to type and my handwriting is horrid), here I am. Oh yes, the book. Yes. The book. The. Book. Yes. So much to say. Stories to share.

What has gripped my thoughts of late with talon-like efficacy among the many torrential downpours of emotion has been a strange and unsettling convergence of events involving the ongoing aftershocks of living with brain cancer, the celebration of my great-aunt Sarah Willdorf 's one-hundredth birthday in Stamford, Connecticut, and the mind-numbing massacre in neighboring Sandy Hook, Connecticut.

Lives threatened, lives extended beyond the norm, and lives stolen far too soon to even comprehend. Tucked within these events, I can't help but seek—what? Meaning? Truth? Or is all just what is? I think Libby was writing of the same question. Darkness and light. Tears and laughter. Love and pain. Just what are we doing here, and is this the best we can be?

> "It's a fool that looks for logic in the chambers of the human heart."
>
> —Ulysses Everett McGill, *O Brother, Where Art Thou*

I feel as if I'm about to embark on a very important journey. I can't explain anything more. It's just a feeling. I know it's sparked by some new fires being lit in my heart, mind, body, and soul. I sense a nascent enlightenment, catalyzed by years of self-inflicted pain that I must shed. The tracks of my ice skates are finally cracking the fragile surface: risk evolving into recklessness, caution to the wind, carefree-ness sliding into impulsiveness. I don't seek perfection in this journey, only progress. If our best qualities are also our worst, I seek to make the best better and the worst fall away and slip beneath the ice into the… Deep. Icy. Cold. Blue. Waters.

A friend, also a cancer survivor, said that cancer doesn't make whatever challenges you had in life disappear. To the contrary, whatever was going on in your "pre-cancer-state" eventually bubbles to the surface, like an underground geyser, often with more intensity. Depending what those things are, this can be either blindingly beautiful or catastrophically upending. And geysers are hot and powerful. Scalding steam thrust from the earth's core. A violent, earthly purge.

I''m unable to reference much in the world of popular film, art, music, and literature about cancer. There's surprisingly little given the numbers of those with the disease. Sontag, Hitchens, and Solzhenitsyn, of course, are a few that come to mind. There's a television series called *The Big C*, which I haven't seen, and the film *50/50*, which was *meh*. The scene of Elizabeth dying of cancer, George Clooney's wife in *The Descendants*, was more irritating than moving because I resented my emotions being manipulated; the camera seemed to linger over her dying body much too long. *The Cancer Ward, Illness as Metaphor,* and *Mortality* are good starts, as is the sublimely executed *Emperor of All Maladies: A Biography of Cancer*, by Dr. Siddartha Mukherjee. Then, sadly but gratefully, there are the thousands upon thousands with cancer or who have endured the loss of a loved one who write, paint, draw, sing, play, sculpt, sew, cook, and otherwise express themselves not only as an outlet for their creativity but as a way to process pain and fear. All that anger, fear, and sadness must be managed and translated into something good, if possible, in some fashion.

Others are inclined toward the physical: participating in competitions, running, walking, hiking, bicycling, or swimming toward a cure, relishing the esprit de corps and camaraderie. Or just for the sake of exercising, no cause attached. Some take part in the political process, lobbying, writing letters, visiting their representatives, working tirelessly to press the cause and seek more funding and research. And many choose to endure their cancer quietly, privately. Each follows the path that's right for them.

But in popular culture, certainly the day-to-day coverage, little is shared about the havoc the blanket of cancer covers. A cyclone of financial, physical, emotional, sexual, spiritual, and psychological mayhem. Thank goodness there's a dearth. A reality TV show about cancer would be dreadful. There is no such thing as reality TV. The whole notion is oxymoronic. Reality TV is not real, it's television. Pixels carefully manipulated for maximum effect with no regard for anyone or anything but the voyeuristic, salacious and often profoundly sad, exploitative nature of such shows. And of course, ratings and revenue.

Stories of heroism and courageousness are another matter and are important for cancer's storyline. They offer hope, inspiration, and faith. That I'll take. But they often belie the struggles behind the scenes. It's sort of like the ironic lie of a family photo album. When was the last time you saw a family photo album where all the pictures were of the unhappy times? What if you had an album capturing every family blow-up, each domestic argument? The tantrums. The accidents. The foot in the wall. The spaghetti tossed to the ceiling. The burned dinners. That wouldn't be very much fun now would it? (actually, it might be) A real cancer story would be difficult to achieve in a thirty-minute segment with commercial breaks. Thank goodness for public television and independent film.

I've left the Putney School, a place very dear to me, but most happily have joined the terrific team at Accelerate Brain Cancer Cure, based in Washington, DC. I can now honestly say that I've quite literally dedicated my life to finding treatments and cures for brain cancer, currently an incurable disease with very few options. The moving story behind this small but effective organization can be found here. I hope to carry Dan Case's legacy forward and beyond as I spend part of my time working from home in New England and part of my time evangelically pursuing avenues of funding for the cause. I have miles to go before I sleep!

Living with cancer is like:

- Waiting for Jack Nicholson, as Jack Torrence in *The Shining*, to smash his way through your door with a fireman's axe screaming "Heeeere's Johnny!"
- Being served a birthday cake with trick candles that don't ever blow out.
- Swimming in shark infested waters.
- Having a hornets nest nearby at all times.

That said, when times get tough, I think of what Teddy Roosevelt would say: "Bully!" Or perhaps Winston Churchill: "A pessimist sees the difficulty in every opportunity; an optimist sees the opportunity in every difficulty." "Never give in, never, never . . . "

I just spent a lovely holiday break with my daughters in Quebec, nordic skiing at Mount Sainte Anne and celebrating New Year's in Quebec City. Nothing like being surrounded by a historic fortress with French-Canadian folk music blaring from a frigid stage and everyone as happy as can be. The Quebecois are fun-loving people no matter what the temperature.

At the ski center, gliding along a single-track trail with nothing but a canopy of snow-covered evergreens above and the soft snow under my skis, I paused often to take the cold air in as deeply as I could. My heart, mind, body, and soul were one. I was happy. I was at peace.

The journey has already begun, but I have new mountains to climb, trails to ski, and many rivers to cross. Happy 2013!

Great Uncle Morris and Great Aunt Sarah at their camera shop on Madison Avenue. Jacqueline Kennedy Onassis was one of their favorite regular customers

With my girls at The Nutrcracker Ballet in Boston.

Quebec w Eric Aho.

Bliss. Photo by Libby.

"Music is the language of the spirit. It opens the secret of life bringing peace, abolishing strife."
—Kahlil Gibran

Thursday, March 07, 2013

Thank you Sam, Bela, Jerry, et al for lifting my spirits whenever I hear this song...it's 12 minutes of bliss.
("Same 'Ole River")

The journey continues. Perhaps Michael Corleone said it best: "Just when I thought I was out, they pull me back in."

What sobriquet shall I find to assign to the latest evolution of that which grows within? Only ones with nasty epithets come to mind. That which shall not be named. Acronyms work well. SFC. Stupid f*%#ing cancer. I must amuse myself with what one fellow cancer comrade refers to as his "personal hyperplasia." Alas, cancer is indeed us. Isn't battling cancer really a twisted war against one's self ?

Those "bad" cells—haven't they been there all along like some deep-sea, luminescent angler fish floating in disguise beneath coral, waiting to spring out and swallow victims whole? As far as we can discern, my cancer, like most cancers, didn't come from "outside," but rather with a genetic mutation either inherited or created at the very beginning of my cellular formation.

I do know that these mutants lack the normal mechanism, or "switch," that triggers apoptosis, natural cell death. I also know that too much angiogenesis, the growth of new blood vessels, can create a problem, as cancer cells crave new blood sources to grow as much as they crave sugar. What's in my databank arsenal? Bad: stress, fatigue, sugar, processed foods including meats, simple carbs. Good: curcemin, broccoli, green tea, leafy greens, exercise, the usual course of action for healthy living multiplied.

So the good doctors now believe, given the latest MRIs, that the tumor has returned. It's possible that what's appearing is necrosis of cell tissue from radiation, but things are looking like tumor. They're also of the belief that I may very well have what is known as a grade III mixed glioma, a diabolical blend of two types of rare brain cancers: ependymoma, as originally believed, and astrocytoma. This makes things a bit more…complicated, and the outcome of my next surgery, intended to be a biopsy on March 15, will determine the next course of action. I've already received the maximum radiation treatment possible. Chemotherapeutics might include Avastin or Temodar.

My experience at Dartmouth was exceptional, what with two successful surgeries, fine patient care, a supportive community and one of the most sensitive, caring physicians I have ever known, Dr. Camilo Fadul. Once again I hope to ride this summer in The Prouty for the Friends of Norris Cotton Cancer Center. But as my condition becomes more complex, and given my new understanding and ties to the brain cancer universe thanks to my work with Accelerate Brain Cancer Cure, I'm now under the care of some of the most experienced physicians in their field at Massachusetts General Hospital.

So like a boxer in the ring, I may have been knocked down again, but rise again I must and rise again I have. After a week of skiing, ice climbing, and horseback riding in Colorado with my younger daughter Libby, and another weekend of skiing coming up with the entire family, I'm renewed and ready for the next chapter. I feel strong and empowered.

It's perplexing to my therapist, who's asked me on several occasions, why I don't talk about my cancer very often. I tell him, "What's there to discuss? I have brain cancer." If it were only so simple.

I'm in therapy, more so, I believe, to dig deeper into some of the mysteries about my life lived thus far and how I can improve myself with whatever time I have left. It's a good time to get my house in order for Barb, my family, and friends and to work to right the wrongs I've done to those closest to me and heal.

And it's when I'm most down, when I crumble, that I think of the love and support of Barb, my family, and friends which at the same time lifts me up.

It's within the space of the quiet times where I experience the most grief and fear, intertwined with a rising sense of hope and love. Listening to music or skiing the quiet, untracked, hidden trails of northern New England helps cleanse and renew. And spring is en route.

"Before you love, Learn to run through the snow, leaving no footprint. "

—Turkish Proverb

from "The Snow Man"
BY WALLACE STEVENS

One must have a mind of winter
To regard the frost and the boughs
Of the pine-trees crusted with snow;

And have been cold a long time
To behold the junipers shagged with ice,
The spruces rough in the distant glitter . . .

Histologic nebulousness evades category

Friday, March 22, 2013

Spring is nature's way of saying, "Let's party!"
—Robin Williams

The brain is hot these days. The continued evolution of our understanding of the most mysterious and complex of all organs rolls along at a rapid pace. The convergence of biology, chemistry, technology, and other realms of knowledge relating to the gray and white matter inside our skull rages like so many rivers combining into a torrent (bit?) of information.

A recent *New York Times* article brought news that "The Obama administration is planning a decade-long scientific effort to examine the workings of the human brain and build a comprehensive map of its activity, seeking to do for the brain what the Human Genome Project did for genetics."

Beneath the twenty-two bones and three membranes lies an organ, the largest of any mammal related to body size, weighing on average around three pounds, with 100 million miles of blood vessels. 100 billion neurons (the gray matter) are organized into 100 trillion total connections. The white matter is made up of dendrons and axons, the network needed for sending signals. The brain is not coiled but folded, and if laid out flat would cover about 2.8 square feet. The brain is the fattiest organ in the body and is 75 percent water. I didn't know this when I ate sauteed goat brain in Puerto Rico many moons ago. Yum.

How funny, and not necessarily ha ha funny, that I hadn't thought much of the brain, my brain, or any one else's for that matter, before "this." One could argue that I hadn't done much thinking to begin with, as I bounced and careened through life, a mostly fun roller coaster ride with rickety, wooden Coney Island rails. Until now. There's nothing like a little humility of ill-health to slap your soul into orbit. And all I can come up with for the moment is "Holy smokes, I am a lucky man." It's been a week since surgery and I'm up and about, albeit with some pretty good bouts of headache and some unsteadiness. But why complain? What would be the point? Barb, my parents, daughters, family, friends, and the incredible team at Massachusetts General Hospital were the wind in my sails once again. Perhaps I can sail with a full wind for a while before the next storm.

I was mobile two days after this, brain surgery number three in two years' time, giving the nurses a hard time by pretending to drink from my bedside urinal, containing not what was intended but apple juice instead. Unlike several people on the neurosurgical ICU ward, I could talk, see, hear, touch, and taste.

After the surgery, some of the leading pathologists analyzed the tissue, which will be further studied at a genetic level. In the notes: "Findings consistent with recurring glioma but specific tumor type elusive although trending towards mixed ependymoma/astrcocytic as it would be unusual for ependymoma alone to recur so quickly."

I'll know more when I see my neuro-oncologist next week and discuss results from mutation testing. I believe he'll provide a menu of options, including chemotherapy: temozolomide, Avastin, and so forth. We shall see.

In the meantime, I'm moving toward a modified Atkins/Ketogenic diet. Life is indeed too short to not enjoy great food, but life indeed will be shorter if I enjoy some foods with more indulgence than necessary. Incidentally, a bottle of red wine has fewer carbohydrates than an apple, as hard as this is to believe. Go Willamette Valley Pinot! Fresh feeling.

The world is mud-luscious and puddle-wonderful.
—E. E. Cummings

A little Madness in the Spring
Is wholesome even for the King.
—Emily Dickinson

Sugaring Time

Wednesday, March 27, 2013

Fisher's Sugarhouse, Rockingham, Vermont

I WALKED INTO THE INTIMATE, mystical confines of Fisher's sugar house, maple steam hanging in the air, a sweet sauna. From old, low timbers of the old barn dripped the dampness of spring. The Fisher family and friends gathered, a springtime reunion, some with Vermont accents as thick as the spring mud, Vermont's fifth season. Memories flowed, bringing quiet tears, of carrying my then-toddler daughters in my arms to inhale the maple, teaching them the ancient ways carried over from native populations long passed. "Forty gallons of sap makes one gallon of syrup, Daddy!" they would exclaim with delight. Pee Wee, a stout firefighter with a horseshoe mustache held court over the sample bucket, passing around tiny paper cups of fresh, warm syrup. Heavenly sweetness slipped down our throats. Arnie, a multigeneration farmer, exclaimed without irony that he was a diabetic and thus couldn't even enjoy the fruits of his labor, at least not to eat. Another relative stoked the fire while he skimmed the froth off the top as the sap boiled down.

This moment, captured last weekend, filled my heart with great elation. I contemplated my own mortality, my life here on this funny little planet. Cancer does that to you, with a steady drumbeat. Those moments when you're frozen in your tracks and realize the beauty in things great and small. I had no reason to turn up Pleasant Valley Road, a beautiful backstretch between Rockingham and Saxtons River, but something pulled me there. I saw the cars, the smoke rising from the rusted chimney, and I knew. It was a Vermont homecoming.

The art of making maple syrup, like life itself, when lived to its fullest, is about boiling something down to its sweetest essence. It's a science, a craft, and then there's something else: faith and hope. Faith and hope that when it's all done, all we have left is the sweetness.

Arnie Fisher

"One thing's for sure,
we're all gonna be a lot thinner!"
—Han Solo

Monday, May 13, 2013

Drum sound rises on the air, its throb, my heart.
A voice inside the beat says, I know you are tired, but come.
This is the way.
—Rumi

Lately I've been thinking about my days in terms of the trash compactor in *Star Wars*, in which Princess Leia, Chewbacca, Han Solo, and Luke are nearly crushed to death as they try to escape enemy fire from stormtroopers while aboard Death Star I. The walls of time, which during moments cause my knees to buckle, sometimes feel as if they're inching forward in a manner unstoppable. And for you *Star Wars* aficionados, you may recall Luke being dragged under the sewage and detritus by a large reptilian "Dianoga." It's an easy metaphor to say this beast is the cancer. Will someone please hand me a light-saber?

The third craniotomy (the term alone has a medieval gruesomeness to it) went exceptionally well, despite the tumor having spread toward the superior saggital sinus, the central outflow for blood in the brain as it circulates through the entire body. Dr. Cahill felt confident that he resected the new tumor growth successfully. And I now have an updated diagnosis of "mixed glioma," consisting of a fine blend of ependymal and astrocytic tumor cells. Well, isn't that just a fine picnic?!

I'm about to begin my second round of chemotherapy, Temodar. It'll be five days on, twenty-three days off for a year. The medicine ultimately exits the body in twenty-four hours. I just learned that my dosage will also increase. With the first course, I experienced some fatigue, a burning sensation throughout my body that eventually dissipated, and some discomfort from the anti-nausea medication. These are cytotoxic drugs after all, so of course there will be some effect. I think the packaging even warns against handling the pills and avoiding contact with the skin. I can only imagine the internal effect these scientific poisons have. Mind you, Temodar is one of only a very few FDA-approved drugs for brain cancer.

I found this wildly bizarre and amusing gem created by a fellow brain cancer comrade, Alex Moore, which recalls some very distant memories of cowering behind the couch in my parent's simulated woodgrain paneled basement watching Ultraman. It also reminds me of a favorite Beastie Boys video, Intergalactic, inspired by the same genre of Japanese Tokusatsu television. (One Beastie, Adam Yauch, died last May of salivary gland cancer at 47 as did a dear acquaintance only a few weeks ago.)

"A million ancient bees began to sting our knees."
—Regina Spektor

Most irritating, and sometimes frightening, is the seizure activity and the "aura" effect on my left side. Keyboarding can be a cumbersome task, especially if I'm fatigued, but most of all I worry when the seizures are more intense. They begin with a sensation like an attack of bees, starting with my left foot (not ironically one of my favorite films), traveling up my leg, and on two occasions, up the left side of my head. All I can say then is "Please, please no, not now."

Eventually the activity ends and my body calms down, but given the electrical storm occurring within, I'm left exhausted. Imagine a torture device involving a car battery and cables attached to your legs. My sympathy has been amplified as never before for those who've suffered strokes, accident victims, and those with cerebral palsy and other neurological symptoms that disallow control of their own bodies. I know that these symptoms, now better managed with Depakote, 1,000 mg in am, 1,500 mg in pm, are often precipitated by fatigue and stress. I can also feel them coming on, so at least I can batten down the hatches and prepare for the neural overload.

But like our friends in the trash compactor, I try to find new ways to slow the progress of this disease. Anything to hold back the walls from closing in—if not in body, then at least in soul and spirit. I realize I need to dance, write, bike, swim, cook, fish, sing, skip, laugh... more.

There is much to be thankful for, and much hope as well. As one compassionate, brilliant brain cancer doctor, Henry Friedman, shared in an interview with Dr. Sanjay Gupta, "I don't want to see my patients die with dignity, I want to see them live with dignity!"

Lately I've been relishing the success of working for Accelerate Brain Cancer Cure, the joy of witnessing Hannah and Libby evolve and mature, spending time with friends and family, and digging deep down into the spiritual core of not only what it means to live, but what it means to die. This is often heavy lifting, but I am an eternal optimist, and at the end of the day I just want to dance. Turn up the damned music!

Embarkation

Sunday, June 16, 2013

Riders on the Storm
"Expose yourself to your deepest fear; after that, fear has no power, and the fear of freedom shrinks and vanishes. You are free."

—Jim Morrison

It feels a bit odd to quote *The Lizard King* but with the recent passing of The Doors keyboardist Ray Manczerak, I have been spinning some Doors as of late. Jim was indeed a poet.

There's a profound empowerment in feeling powerless, once fear is shed. The letting go. What matters most isn't matter itself. We are all mortal beings, and no more important than the spider crawling quietly in the corner of the shower. We are all squashable.

Our complex relationship with Mother Nature is borne of this dichotomy and of the very realness that, in the end, Mother Nature will always prevail.

Floods, tornadoes, earthquakes, hurricanes come and go. They steal lives, destroy our homes, and while we know they will come again, we rebuild. But in the end, Mother Nature always prevails.

Genetically manipulate our food supply? Mother Nature will find a way to circumvent this and wreak havoc with our attempt to quite literally reshape living organisms.

And what of disease? Most specifically cancer? We have indeed been able to change the course of history, save untold lives and eradicate many lethal diseases. But again, we remain fragile, vulnerable beings, and Mother Nature finds a way to remind us that we are mere mortals.

What I'm learning about cancer has continued to rock my world as we enter a new era. One of the most promising developments is learning not to fight with the forces of nature (think of the mayhem hewn by our creation of the Dust Bowl, with shortsighted farming practices combined with an unfortunate series of weather events), but to work with nature in partnership to alter the course of the genetic mutations that cause cancer in the first place, using the body's own natural defense mechanisms. After all, cancer is us.

In the meantime, I prepare for surgery number four to remove a growing cyst and more tumor growth, as the chemotherapy wasn't taking.

There are some intriguing options we continue to explore, and I will know more after tomorrow.

I remain focused and strong—perhaps even more so after reflecting upon all things natural and powerful. Mother Nature fill my heart.

Born a poor young country boy
Mother Nature's son
All day long I'm sitting singing songs for everyone.
. . .
—John Lennon and Paul McCartney

"I will take a little bag of prairie dirt. I cannot take the sky."

—from *What You Know First,*
BY PATRICIA MACLACHLAN

Sunday, July 28, 2013

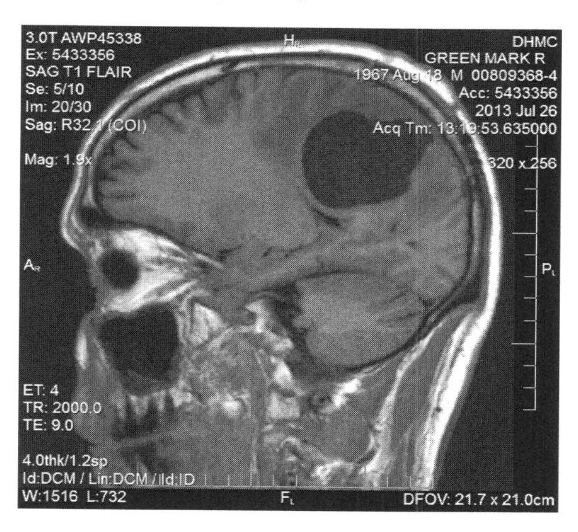

I HAVE ON ONE BOOKSHELF a collection of favorite books from the early times of raising Hannah and Libby. Fond memories of the family: Laura, dogs ZuZu and Gracie curled up in bed, the girls squealing with anticipated delight as the familiar story lines unfolded. "Caps! Caps for Sale! Fifty cents a cap! shouted the peddler." Or the tactile serenity of *The Snow Tree*. The lupine beauty of *Miss Rumphius*. The mettle of *Katy and the Big Snow. The Wild Party of the Barnyard Dance. Tikki Tikki Tembo. We're Going On a Bear Hunt. The Christmas Reindeer.* And many more. But there is one book, *What You Know First* which pulls my heart right out front.

With simple text and exquisite artwork, the story is as much about going away as it is about going somewhere. It is about loss, fear, wonder, love, family and the longing for a sense of place. It is one of my favorite books and also one of the saddest I know.

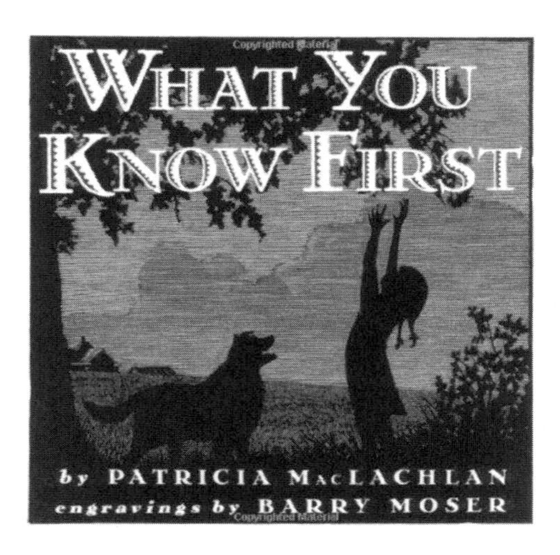

I am a passionate person. Our best qualities can also be our downfall. I have to be careful lest I get swept up and carried away by the high tide, left to drown in the ocean. Or just simply pulled every which way by rip currents, ultimately dragged over the coral, smashed against the rocks. When I was a child, on the beaches of Avalon, New Jersey I was once swept away by a rip current. I remember seeing my family ashore and realizing that I was being carried off. I yelled to them. They could not hear me. I was getting tired from fighting the water's force. A calm washed over me. I had this sensation that I was about to let go. Not give up, but to let go. To slip into the deep. And it was OK, This dream state was interrupted when I was rescued by a lifeguard. I was probably eight or nine.

Letting go. The egg. That was grandma Bennett's egg. She was a china painter. The date was 1972 so I was 5 when she painted it for me. I have other items she painted from her large shop of china, imported from Japan, France, Portugal and her travels around the world. But the egg was special. This and a small mug with a dutch boy with my name she had painted for me. Somehow, over all these years the egg and the mug survived.

I don't know what to make of omens except to say I suppose we find messages and meaning when and where we need them most. When the egg casually, and, as if by its own force, rolled off of my bureau, I watched in slow motion as it fell and smashed to the wooden floor. I put the pieces in a bag. Rather than try to glue it back, I think I might bury them. Omen? My health continues to challenge, vex, harrass as one might discern from the images indicates a fourth surgery, a cyst now removed and build up of CSF (cerebral spinal fluid) causing pressure. I will know more soon. The challenge is that because of the uniqueness of the tumor (grade III anaplastic astrocytoma/ependymoma) there aren't any clinical trials nor treatment protocol.

Recently I spoke with a woman at a conference who was walking in the same direction as I. Within two minutes she asked if I had taken the Lord Jesus as my Savior after finding out about my cancer. I kindly shared that I had not done so but that I thought that he sounded like a pretty cool guy from what I had heard. She didn't miss a beat and then asked me where I sought spirituality. I replied that this is a life journey, that I was willing to consider any point of view, that my Quaker schooling and Jewish upbringing informed some but not all of my views and that my place of peace is in nature, on a ski trail, a hiking trail, sleeping beneath the stars or floating in the ocean. Nature was my cathedral.

Expecting her to take me further down the Jesus road, she simply smiled, shared that when we are in the natural world we ARE in the presence of God. That sounded good to me, whatever God means. Finally, as we reached the doors to the conference she shared that she had had open heart surgery and that she felt that this health challenge had been a wake-up call and opportunity for her to get right with the lord. Amen to that sister. Amen to that. LET THE MYSTERY BE! (David Byrne and Natalie Merchant.)

"It became necessary to destroy the town to save it"

Friday, August 16, 2013

"It became necessary to destroy the town to save it."

THIS FAMOUS QUOTE from the Vietnam War was attributed to an unnamed US officer by AP correspondent Peter Arnett in his writing about the city of B n Tre. "He was talking about the decision by allied commanders to bomb and shell the town regardless of civilian casualties, to rout the Vietcong," Arnett explained in the *New York Times*.

Okay. The gloves are off. I'm about to willingly kick the crap out of my body in order to save it. Healthy cells as well as mutated ones will be sacrificed. I'm home after my fifth brain surgery, in which they inserted a shunt to drain the pressurized buildup of what the doctors called "sludge," a not-to-be-enjoyed concoction of cerebral spinal fluid, dead cancer cells, and active cells both cancerous and non. I can actually feel the tube that snakes its way from the back of my head into my abdomen. Wow.

Intravenous chemotherapy will be the next mountain to climb. They're recommending a combined therapy of carboplatin and bevacizumab, widely known as Avastin, a drug that slows the growth of new blood vessels that the monster cancer cells need to feed themselves. Microcellular vampires!

The side effects of carboplatin, a part of the family of alkylating agents first discovered to have cytotoxic effects after the use of mustard gas in World War I appear to be no picnic. I continue to try to push the evilness of this disease over the cliff and look to the good. News junkie that I am, I'm finding it more difficult than in the past to absorb the daily tragedies of murder and mayhem and instead seek sources of inspiration and hope. Not that I'm about to wallpaper my home with images of unicorns and rainbows, or puppies and kittens (yet), but this shift in focus certainly lowers my stress level.

I've taken to decreasing the din of the day. Buzzers, ringtones, text and calender alerts have been muted or turned way down. I am, for the first time I can recall, taking the time to just sit. Think. Meditate.

In a visit today, my neurosurgeon explained that it will be important for friends and family to keep track of any overt or subtle changes in my demeanor, as those with my disease in a similar location of the brain often become unaware of changes in their own personality or temperament. He shared that one patient was found sitting on the couch in his home unaware that he'd been doing so for ten hours. This would be painfully ironic—sitting for any length of time has never been a skill I mastered.

Hope and inspiration are not hard to find. Friendships, family, community, tales of courage, struggle. Art, music, nature.

When I'm really, deeply down and out, there are moments I pull from the past that to this day leave me with profound emotion and lift me up again. Moses Jaenson's cover of R. Kelly's "I Believe I Can Fly" at his eighth-grade graduation in 2008 at my children's former elementary school, The Grammar School in Putney, Vermont, is one of those moments etched forever in this manner. Thank you, Moses.

"the ability to just sit there… that's being a person"

—Louis C.K.

Friday, September 27, 2013

"I felt in need of a great pilgramage, so I sat still for five days."
—Hafiz rendering, Daniel Ladinsky

As I push through to my upcoming third blast of chemotherapy, three things aligned for me recently: the card above, which my daughter Libby chose at a gift shop; a video below, from Conan O'Brien's show, featuring comedian Louis C.K. in a terrific rant against cellphones, as well as musings on sadness, nihilism, just "being," and life in general; and a recent first-time-ever experience with yoga classes.

As a child, when we took road trips—either to upstate New York to visit Grandma or to Kentucky or Maryland to visit aunts, uncles, and cousins—my sister and I would sprawl out in the back seat of our massive brown Chrysler Newport and just lie there, staring up through the large windows at the power lines as we sailed along in our massive boat. We were left to read, nap, play auto bingo, color in coloring books, or just daydream (I would later recall long hours sitting in the back of this same car as we waited for what seemed like an eternity for gas during the gas crisis). I'm sure we had a fight or two, especially if either of us crossed that imaginary border between the seats. Our visual entertainment was whatever was outside the window. Music was limited to scratchy FM radio.

The beauty of it all was that there were no LCD TVs in the car, no iPads, gameboys, smartphones, or even iPods. The windows were our "screen." Our imaginations the CPU. Today, shutting things out, down, or off is a challenge for us all. Even while pumping gas now, we're assaulted by the cacophony and visual headache of twenty-four-hour marketing. Screens on the gas pumps? At the checkout counter in grocery stores? Please *be quiet!*

Everything is just so damned loud. I'm sure having multiple craniotomies and now chemotherapy, resulting in the infamous affliction of "chemo-brain" (a double whammy, since the chemo itself is for my brain), has only enhanced my sensitivity to this unpleasant aural riot.

I recently attended two yoga classes different in methodology and resulting in two entirely different reactions. I knew little beyond the fact that there are many different practices, and that many friends do Bikram Yoga, also known as hot yoga.

The first one, led by an experienced instructor who was very kind and patient, was a bit of a crushing blow. Many things conspired against me. My usual course of daily headaches were already starting, my two torn rotator cuffs didn't take well to some of the more physically intense poses, and I was intimidated by the regulars with their yoga-appropriate mats, pants, tops, and so on. I bailed. This dude's body would not abide.

The second session, at a different location, with a different guide, was a blessed event. A young woman had just started her practice nearby after moving up here from Georgia with her husband, and I had seen her poster on a community bulletin board. The class was held inside the very spiritually soothing space of a yurt set in a lush field. Wood, canvas, a skylight, and candles. She helped me breathe. Deep breaths. After the session, I had never felt better. I felt alive, enriched, awake, and calm.

The alignment of Hafiz rumination, Louis C.K., and yoga created a welcome triad of moments in time that help me put one foot in front of the other, thank the sunrise, and focus on the gifts that life offers when one has been given a diagnosis such as brain cancer. A pilgrimage to be taken within the mind, body, and soul.

"If there ever comes a day when we can't be together, keep me in your heart. I'll stay there forever."

—Winnie the Pooh

Sunday, November 03, 2013

If we are the pins, and the bowling ball is the cancer, I'm growing weary of how many strikes are being thrown—as if the ball, an indestructible Death Star with three finger holes, rolling along the finely waxed lanes, holds some steroidal, otherworldly force. The pins are knocked violently down, the ball returns, and everything starts all over again.

Without digging into a statistically futile construction effort to prove a point that needs no fortification, let's just agree that the din of the cancer death-dirge hums darkly along as if written by Chopin ("Funeral March"), Gorecki (*Symphony of Sorrowful Songs*), or Britten (*War Requiem*).

Since the summer I've spoken with two college friends who've been hit with breast cancer, resulting in a double mastectomy for one, metastasis to that brain for the other. Another neighbor was diagnosed just a few weeks ago. Last summer, I held the hand and stroked the forehead of a longtime friend who passed away only a few months after her diagnosis of pancreatic cancer. Normally vivacious and full of energy, she whispered, "I'm so tired, Mark." A few days later she was gone.

Being part of the cancer community, and specifically the brain cancer community, is incredibly tragic, as those diagnosed, especially with stage IV (glioblastoma multiforme), and even more particularly children with brain cancer, have a very poor prognosis. It's the children that make one freeze. Pediatric cancer is the leading cause of death by disease among children. This is where the gloves really come off.

We lost another brave child just recently, Gabriella Miller. She was only ten. There's been an inexplicable rise in childhood cancers, with leukemia and brain cancer the most lethal. Something is very wrong.

But with every storm comes hope for change. Last week, I had the moving joy of sharing and celebrating the achievements of another brave child, Madeleine Baet, of Manassas, Virginia, who, along with her family, has joined the fierce army to slay the cancer dragon. There's Anya Zvorsky, of New Cumberland, Pennsylvania. And so many more.

My daughters have also jumped in to join the fight, supporting efforts to find cures for cancer and helping me get through each day with love (and patience). This winter, Hannah will be climbing Kilimanjaro as part of a fundraising effort on behalf of the Norris Cotton Cancer Center.

And then there's BethAnn Telford, of Team BT, who has dedicated everything to and for the children. A brain cancer survivor herself, she has inspired me to look beyond my own predicament to help others. The children don't even have a chance. Working for Accelerate Brain Cancer Cure has been a gift. That said, our CEO, Max Wallace, often says that our ultimate goal is to be out of business—when we cure brain cancer.

> "As devastating as it is to be afflicted with brain cancer, it is heartbreaking to see an innocent young child have to go through the same pain and suffering. This is why I fight hardest to raise awareness for pediatric cancer, especially brain cancer."
>
> —BethAnn Telford, eight-year warrior

"Mirth is God's medicine.
Everybody ought to bathe in it."
— Henry Ward Beecher

Wednesday, January 15, 2014

Writer and stage IV non-Hodgkin's lymphoma survivor Robert Kessler wrote a remarkable piece in his blog recently, in which he took a stand in defense of blogging and took issue with a rather insensitive assault on stage IV breast cancer survivor and blogger Lisa Bonchek Adams. Guardian writer Emma Keller and her husband, Bill, a former New York Times editor, had accused Adams of oversharing. This got my chemo-infused blood boiling in defense of my fellow blogging cancer brothers and sisters.

We all manage challenge differently. Some see it as an opportunity for growth, some retreat, some paint, compose, perform, some suffer greatly, some just "roll with it," some take up arms, some just want to party like it's 1999. Some try to check off their bucket list (if they have the time, resources, and health to do so) as they acknowledge that something has moved the clock forward prematurely. It's not daylight savings time anymore. It's just savings time. And some write. Publicly and privately.

Robert's post incited me to get back to the keyboard. Since my initial diagnosis of stage III mixed glioma brain cancer in the summer of 2011 and subsequent five craniotomies, radiation, shunt installation, ongoing chemo regimen of Avastin/Carboplatin, and seizure management, living with cancer is more or less just a fact of life. Eventually, the Carboplatin chemo will need to be stopped, because over time the kidneys become overtaxed. The bills from co-pays and deductibles keep coming, the headaches and fatigue change like the weather, and as long as I keep giving something back to the amazing institutions that have helped and continue to help save my life, the waters are steady. The tumor is still there, lurking. It hasn't shrunk, nor has it grown. We're keeping the needle in the middle, the dam fortified, the waters at bay. My younger daughter and I had the good fortune to Nordic ski in Quebec, as we have every year (she an average of 20 miles a day; I much, much less), while my older daughter's fundraising climb up Kilimanjaro raised over $11,000 for the Norris Cotton Cancer Center. Proud poppa am I.

One aspect of my coping strategy is to tap more readily into the elements that provide nutrition to my heart, body, and soul. Music. Food. Friends. Family. Laughter. My work.

I have music on throughout the house at all times, usually Vermont Public Radio's classical station (yes, I am a proud sustaining member!).

I love food. I love it more. I want to travel. I want to travel more. I truly do want to live each moment in the moment, as best I can, for as long as I am physically and mentally able.

Friends far and wide, close and merely acquaintances, give me wind in my sails. My community, from the post office to the local café to the pub to the brain cancer community, offer a lift.

A walk, a ski, a snowshoe in the woods fill me. And, when I remember, just being silent, maybe watching intently the birds at the feeders.

One of the elements of my living a happy life is avoiding stress and finding humor in between the crags of the day-to-day and that which vexes. I'm fascinated by the science of laughter: the healthy chemical changes happening within the body when laughter takes hold. Example? A few weeks ago, during a particularly icy and snowy time, I got in my car, my dear black VW Jetta Sportwagen, started up, and began to back out. There were some crunching noises that I assumed were chunks of ice built up in the wheel wells. I continued my exit rearward, thinking if I simply powered out of the garage I'd break free of whatever was causing resistance. The sounds became louder, until I heard what I thought was a torrent of glass raining upon the roof. It was exactly that. I had driven backwards through the multipaneled garage door, shattering every pane of glass, destroying every wooden panel, ripping the whole damned thing right off the tracks.

I had no idea what I'd done, nor the extent of the damage, until further inspection. I winced and let out a "What the...?" Then I started laughing. The whole scene was absurd. What else could I do? It was the healthiest response I could muster, and it helped calm me down. "Whatever," I said to myself. "Whatever."

> "Today we fight. Tomorrow we fight. The day after, we fight. And if this disease plans on whipping us, it better bring a lunch, 'cause it's gonna have a long day doing it."
>
> —Jim Beaver, from *Life's That Way: A Memoir*

Hannah atop Kilimanjaro "Every little thing's gonna be alright."

Me and Libby, Mont Sainte Anne, Quebec

"Many men go fishing all of their lives without knowing that it is not the fish they are after."
—Thoreau

Sunday, April 6, 2014

"Not all those who wander are lost"
—J. R. R. Tolkien

When I was around twelve or thirteen, I placed a map of Alaska from an issue of *National Geographic* next to my bed. Pinned through the dark scores between the faux walnut paneling, the map, along with that issue, became a dreamscape of grizzly bears, vast terrain, soaring snowcapped peaks, and salmon-filled rivers. I imagined planes equipped with pontoons landing on remote lakes, or planes with skis gliding onto the frozen tundra. I delved into what became one of my most memorable books during those formative years, John McPhee's *Coming into the Country*. I knew then that I wanted to become a bush pilot. Reading his other books equally captivated and inspired, but this one left me hungry. I've always been hungry. And restless. And now, with another lightning bolt hurled my way (damn you, Zeus, give me a break!), my hunger for life and living has only increased.

Tuesday was a rough day. Aside from the usual bother of the early-morning commute to Dartmouth for a 6:00 am MRI (a necessary lifesaving device of aural claustrophobic torture) and the din of hospital life, I was told soon after that the scan showed "significant" tumor growth and that they were not going to administer chemotherapy, as the Avastin/Carboplatin combination was not having its desired effect. The tumor, a unique grade III mixed glioma with astrocytic and ependymal cancer cells, is now being treated as a GBM, a glioblastoma multiforme. "It's time to get your affairs in order," I was told. My hourglass suddenly needed more sand.

It was timely, then, that two days later I happened to visit a therapist whom I hadn't seen in awhile—a cancer survivor herself, and one learned in the ways of Buddhist practice. We shared moments deep and light. "Cancer is a great opportunity for spring cleaning," we laughed. At one point, when speaking about being or doing something audacious, I said, "So little matters now," to which she replied, "You can't even impress yourself." She went on to say,

"You're free to experience life without the burden of needing to build something. You're just *experiencing*."

The day after I learned of the results, I put my beloved Dartmouth, made-in-Maine, carbon road bike up for sale, as my balance had deteriorated too much to risk a fall on a skinny-tired bike with clip-in pedals. For the moment, thankfully, I can still use a mountain bike. The week prior, I had attempted to telemark ski at Stratton Mountain. Telemark skiing, another love, in which the heel isn't fixed to the metal-edged ski, is used for backcountry or lift-service skiing and requires balance and strength I no longer have due to the cancer's insidious effects on my right parietal lobe. Same goes for skate-skiing, a form of Nordic cross-country in which the skier moves in a skating fashion. So hang up my skis I must, lest I meet my demise through an immovable object such as a tree or boulder. That said, I can still snowshoe and cross-country ski in the traditional, "classic" fashion. I continue to work, and my passion to raise maximum funds for Accelerate Brain Cancer Cure has only increased. Our largest event, held on Sunday, May 4, in Washington, DC, stands to raise over $2.5 million for brain cancer research, and I along with my colleagues continue to reach out to those touched by this disease who may wish to support our initiatives.

Tuesday I head to Massachusetts General to see my neurosurgeon and another accomplished neuro-oncologist for consultation, and within the next week or so I fly down to Duke for another consultation about possible enrollment in clinical trials, perhaps involving immunotherapies that use the body's own immune system to fight the spreading cancer. I must also eliminate or significantly reduce sugar and carbohydrates, which help feed the cancer—something I've already been doing but can do better.

I will continue to fight the fight, not just for myself but for my friends and family. Holding on to hope. To exceptions to the rule. There are many examples of people who far outlive any prognosis. Cancer or any calamitous health event impacts like a meteorite not just the afflicted but all those in that orbit. It's a scorched-earth affair. The steady drumroll of cancer beats on as I continue to learn of others being struck. Without fail, every time I go to Dartmouth I run into friends who've just been hit. In one instance, I even shared an infusion suite (a misnomer if ever there was one) with my dear former uncle-in-law. At the moment, thinking of the drum metaphor, the insanity of this unfortunate card we've been dealt is best captured by the mayhem of Animal the Muppet, with apologies to and in remembrance of Keith Moon. Stupid cancer.

"What will our children do in the morning
if they do not see us fly?"
—Rumi

Fly I must, and fly I will.

Riding that Bluegrass Train: Dona Nobis Pacem

Thursday, May 22, 2014

I'M ON THE TRACKS. Train is coming. The tumor is growing. The previous chemo isn't working. I'm trying another round. The trip to Duke proved that, because of the location and heterogeneity of the cancer, I'm ineligible for clinical trials involving such recently reported experiments as injecting the polio or measles virus directly into the tumor site. Surgery is not an option. Too diffuse. I'm told it's "Like an iceberg where we can see the top, but because of the nature of the tumor we can only see it spreading within the MRI." We must lay more tracks. Do I see John of God, in Brazil? Try experimental medicinal marijuana oil therapy in Colorado (which, while unapproved, shows promise, but is costly and time consuming)? My current new course of chemo, Avastin (again) in combination with Lomustine, can't continue for longer than nine months due to long-term side-effects: white blood cell counts, fatigue, pulmonary function, and platelets. We must lay more tracks. Slow the train.

Go to Hell, Kübler-Ross!

(From Wikipedia: The Kübler-Ross model, or the five stages of grief, is a series of emotional stages experienced when faced with the impending death or death of someone. The five stages are denial, anger, bargaining, depression and acceptance.)

Maybe it's the steroids I'm taking to prevent more swelling from the growth of the tumor, which causes headaches and imbalance, but I can only type with one finger now, using dictation device sometimes, then transferring from iPhone—but maybe it's just me. I'm a pretty happy-go-lucky guy. Pharrell Williams has it right; he makes me want to go get a Curious George "Man with the Yellow Hat" cowboy hat and dance in the streets with his widely popular infectious groove.

But lately, things large and small and often meaningless have begun to irritate. Mind you, I'm grateful for every day I can take a breath or walk with my own two feet or see with my eyes, hear with my ears, taste, touch, feel. I think of those who suffer much more than I ever have and ever will. I'm on a new, different course of chemo which is already having effects on many different things.

Whether it's the girls in Nigeria, the Boston bombing victims of last year, or the crimes in Syria and Crimea… I finally saw *Twelve Years a Slave*, and my rage neared seizure level. The toilet paper roll that you have to pick at to get started, or that's put on the wrong way. Bad service or bad food at a restaurant. Our wounded veterans who have inadequate health care and can't find work. Extreme right-wing party members who want to limit people's freedom to marry whomever they want, prohibit a woman's right to choose or receive equal pay, those who make or act on racist comments, or think global warming is a left-wing conspiracy. Or those who think that, regardless of ongoing school massacres, we should continue with no sensible consideration for gun reform, as if the right to own a high-capacity clip is a constitutional (or G-d) given right. Or whoever designed the aluminum foil brick package that cream cheese comes in.

The latest thing to really send me over the edge? I received a brochure for 24/7 medical alert monitoring system with nice photographs of people who look nothing like me and an ambulance and the call button. (recollections of the commercials: "Help, I've fallen, and I can't get up!"). But my dear friends have helped move my bedroom downstairs and installed handrails in all the bathrooms, reminding me of my late grandmother Ethel years ago, bless her. And that's okay. But in the darker recesses of my brain, sometimes all I can think of is the opening scene of Francis Ford Coppola's *Apocalypse Now*—the bombing of Vietnam with the Doors' "The End" playing in the background. But I'm not morbid, I'm not depressed, and I will stay happy as I always do, or try to do. It's good medicine. Being happy makes me happy. But screaming, crying, and wanting to pick up my car and toss it Hulk-style also comes to mind on occasion.

I had a meeting recently in New York with an incredibly kind woman who lost her husband to a brain tumor. She had kids the same ages as mine, and we talked a lot about our children and our love for them. We held hands and cried right there in the lobby of the hotel, not standard operating procedure for my line of work in fund-raising. (In my other roles in development, I might have met with an angry alumnus who threatened not to give because their poor football team didn't have a winning season or their ineligible child failed to get accepted. Boohoo. "Do you know who I *am*?" they would whine or threaten. It was hard to keep my mouth shut before smiling, heading for the door, and saying with great enthusiasm, "Thank you! I hope you'll consider a gift this year!") The hotel was ironically named The Mark. She said, "Mark, you're a good man, you're a good dad, and your kids will be okay." Later she texted me and said it was nice to meet me, but that she'd given me some wrong advice. She said, "Mark, I told you to stay strong. What I really should've said was stay real and enjoy every moment." Amen. When I was first diagnosed, a dear friend, also a survivor, shared that when she was diagnosed with cancer she went through many emotions, as most people do in some form or variation, but that she came to embrace her illness as a gift. I couldn't be more grateful for the love showered upon me and my family, and wish I could pass it all down the line to those in need. From the prayer shawl knitted by a friend's mother's church in Edgartown, Massachusetts, to the Quaker service being held in my honor at my alma mater, to my friends, neighbors, and colleagues at Accelerate Brain Cancer Cure, and my beloved family. And my two daughters, Hannah and Libby, my pride and joy. Thank you. Thank you. Happy.

Happy.

Grant us peace. *Dona nobis pacem.*

One Headlight

Friday, May 30, 2014

In what is surely one of the most bizarre exhibitions of high school athletic sport, the ritual of making weight before a wrestling match knows little equal. I still recall the sprightly Alex Leeser running around the main building in circles multiple times wearing several layers of Glad garbage bags with duct tape at the wrists and ankles, shaving ounces off his already slight frame before we met our next competitor. I was never very good at wrestling. I enjoyed the psychological intensity of facing an opponent, but I was often outgunned and outperformed strategically, sometimes not knowing what hit me until my nose was being ground into the mat. But it didn't matter; we had a great team and a lot of fun. Well, if I'm striving to make some sort of weight now, I guess I've succeeded. I now weigh 173 pounds, the lowest I can recall since high school. Thanks to a four-year infusion of blue cheese and chicken wings (standard upstate New York college fare) and becoming a new parent, I weighed as much as 215 pounds post-college. I'd like to think it was a case of *couvade syndrome* (sympathetic pregnancy), but I'm not sure Laura would buy that. I was once a size 38. Now? 33- to 34-inch waist. I'm now a size medium to large, down from extra-large. Oh well. None of that matters.

In what was one of the more sobering moments this week, my friends Chris and Eric stopped by. After installing another handrail on the stairs, they put their hands on my shoulders, set me down on the porch, a beer for each of us, and made me swear to a blood oath that I would never again get in my car and drive. My tears and anger flowed, but I knew they were doing this out of love and concern not just for me but for my friends, family, my children, and everybody else out there. It would have been unfair and selfish of me to do otherwise. My declining health, seizures, left-side impairment, and risk of not being fully cognizant of where and in what space I am is too much to risk. Needless to say, this was hard news to take.

I've spoken to many people whose families have endured the struggle of having a loved one with a debilitating disease or other trauma lose their driving privileges. They all said that this was one of the hardest moments. To lose one's independence is to lose a sense of self. Living in a rural area makes this new reality that much more difficult, but I'm grateful for friends and family who are willing and able to help. We are so dependent on car culture, and surrendering the myths and reality of freedom attached to driving is a deep loss. Whether it's flying down the highway with the music on full blast and the sunroof open, just wandering and exploring (one of my favorite things to do), or taking a road trip with friends. But it will be fine. It will all be fine. At least there's comfort in knowing that those around me will breathe a deep sigh of relief now that I'm no longer on the road. Not to mention that, given my past driving record, it's in the interest of national safety.

I will now take a moment of silence to remember the fallen. My 1965 postal Jeep, bought for $400 in Old Forge, New York, which I had painted hunter green with purple trim. My 1987 emerald green Volkswagen Scirrocco (which means "desert wind") that I rolled on black ice in Richmond, Vermont. The Subaru I took airborne, causing great undercarriage damage. The Honda sedan I took into a ravine after sliding on wet leaves. My dad's mustard yellow Toyota Corolla, whose axle I bent after hitting a tall curb. My parents' days-old 1987 Dodge Colt Vista wagon, also rolled and totaled. The 1976 Toyota FJ40 I traded, stupidly, with a friend for his 1993 Saab Turbo, which became known as yet another "Saab" story after multiple alternator problems, a missing reverse gear, and a stickshift that kept coming out in my hand. Or the 1990-something Toyota SR5 that looked like an ugly breadbox held together with annoying bumper-stickers, which was so rusted that when I took it through a car wash before a date in Burlington the foamy water came pouring through the windshield onto my nice clothes. I know there are others, but I can't seem to recall, either by design or true loss of memory.

I recently visited my friend Neil Taylor, the "blind masseuse," whose brain cancer impacted his optic nerve. We call ourselves the tumor twins. Since he also can't drive, I get a ride to his house and we walk down into town together for dinner and a beer. I know I can speak for both of us when I say this is a highlight of our week.

To end: two great road trip songs among the many that make me want to just get in the car. And drive. "One Headlight" is particularly apt. (By The Wallflowers; the other, "Back Down South," by Kings of Leon.)

It was like this

Wednesday, June 25, 2014

It was like this:
you were happy, then you were sad,
then happy again, then not.
—Jane Hirshfield

I sit here at Dartmouth Hitchcock Hospital, looking out at the verdant forests of Lebanon, New Hampshire. Because my left hand has been rendered virtually useless, thanks to the paralytic aftermath of seizures, I'm using the often inaccurate and potentially lethal iPhone dictation function. (For those of you who've tried this, how many near misses and professional or personal fatalities have you had through erroneously interpreted language? You might be telling your mother-in-law that you just bought a new truck, only to have iPhone dictation interpret it as something else entirely, rendering your relationship deeply scarred.) I've been given this great opportunity to reflect in relative peace, despite being interrupted every two hours by nurses and doctors and the drip, drip, drip of the new high-dose chemotherapy I'm having administered (methotrexate, requiring a five-night stay, followed by another five-night stay in two weeks, followed by an MRI to see if it's worked). I write this out of a desire to continue my explanation and exploration of this *mishegoss* (Yiddish for f*#ked-up), uncharted journey. The tumor continues to grow unabated, and while this drug normally doesn't cross the blood-brain barrier, I'm trying it because, given previous studies, it's thought that it may succeed in high doses (it's normally administered for leukemia and lymphoma, among other diseases).

I refuse to think that the road continues to narrow into a dead-end, but that it instead has spur trails that will lead us in new directions. There's no question that the equal exchange between hope and loss of hope has played an interesting war of the worlds within my psyche. Not a day goes by that I don't find something floating across my screen that inspires hope, whether it's a new trial therapy or another potential option, but nearly all of these are in the very early stages of application. I do know that the approval process continues to be sped up, but the advancement of science requires time and resources.

For me, I think Joni's got it right: "We can't return, we can only look behind from where we came and go round and round and round in the circle game."

This blog written in memory of Melanie Delonge, friend, neighbor, my daughter's first day-care provider. You are missed and loved.

"How long have I been sleeping?"
—Jackson Browne

Friday, July 18, 2014

The opportunity to reflect is a gift: what was, what could've been, what might be, becomes part of a deeply tumultuous swirl of emotion from places within I didn't even know existed. Because of this cancer, I've been given this time, this heretofore unwelcome "gift." And there is no one like Jackson Browne to reach inside my heart and pull everything right up to the front, like the deep roots of some primeval tree, to unleash a torrent.

There's a Gaelic word, "keen," and another, "ululo," meaning to wail, and in my private moments I've found myself doing just that—keening, often loudly, late in the night. The emotions that occasionally grip me, that come through the raw fear, act as both a healing function and a purgative. The way different cultures deal with death and dying is fascinating indeed.

After enduring two weeks of chemo in the hospital and a third to begin Tuesday, I'm feeling a little bit like a punchdrunk boxer in the ring: DeNiro in Raging Bull, with fists coming slow, hard, and unrelenting. I know I've referred to the Native American character in "One Flew over the Cuckoo's Nest" who in the end ripped the sink from the flooring and smashed through the wall, releasing the patients from the asylum. While certainly my hospital stays are nothing of the sort, the doctors, staff and nurses all being toprate, Being tethered (and often entangled like a fish caught in a driftnet) to an IV pole day after day, having it wrapped around my legs and arms, having to unplug every time I have to go to the bathroom, trying to get there before it's too late, having it pull on my PIC-lined arm… it's not a friend I wish to be attached to. The notion of tossing the entire IV pole through the plate-glass window comes to mind quite often. Imagine my excitement when I found out that the Au Bon Pain was open twenty-four hours, and that they served lobster salad sandwiches on a croissant. While the methotrexate sessions last about three hours, I'm allowed to move about the cabin after that, when they administer leucovorin to bring the methotrexate down to a safe level for my taxed organs. On one journey, at three in the morning, I somehow managed to detach my entire bag of sodium bicarbonate from my IV pole, causing it to explode all over everything, including my beloved lobster-salad sandwich. The nurse said he'd never seen anything like it in his 10-plus years of nursing. Chalk up another disaster to my restlessness and midnight munchies. Another MRI, more chemotherapy (even though the desired one, a MEK inhibitor, has been denied by insurance), as we try to beat this back. The one thing we can't buy is time. But we're trying.

I continue the journey, without knowing what's around the corner. My anger and tears mix with hope and the strength generously offered from friends, community, family, and my daughters.

> *How long have I been sleeping,*
> *How long have I been drifting alone through the night,*
> *How long have I been running for that morning flight,*
> *Through the whispered promises and the changing light.*

—Jackson Browne

Brittany Maynard Brought Much-Needed Attention to Brain Cancer and Choosing Dignity

October 27, 2014

IT'S BEEN THREE YEARS since my diagnosis of brain cancer. I live my life in the shadow of "stages," like a rocket booster: explosive, progressive, lethal. First it was anaplastic ependymoma, then astrocytoma, now a full-blown GBM (glioblastoma multiforme). I'm five craniotomies in, plus weeks and weeks of radiation, multiple chemotherapies and, most recently, "alternative approaches." At least three times since my diagnosis, I've been told that I have six to nine months to live, or three to six, or less. I've also been told that I am strong, healthy, and that there are always "outliers."

The minute I was diagnosed, my entire being went into overdrive. There was no roadmap for getting through the maelstrom that fell upon our family with such a diagnosis. Sure, there are pamphlets on every rack, and plenty of good advice from doctors. But nothing can prepare you for what exactly to do in such a situation.

Brittany Maynard, the 29-year old woman from California who recently moved to Oregon to avail herself of its Death with Dignity Act — often referred to as the assisted suicide law — was also diagnosed with a GBM. She has chosen to set her own terms as to how and when she will die, rather than let the disease take her on its unrelenting course. Her story has received worldwide attention. She has brought much-needed attention to brain cancer, which remains rare, lethal and incurable. She's also examined and shared broader personal issues about dying and living with dignity, and the choices we may or may not have the freedom, not to mention the courage, to make.

Brittany's public, controversial, and very brave decision has helped me reflect upon my own three years of living with this disease, and the gripping fear I face with each MRI, as I hold my breath and watch the doctor pull up the screen on his laptop.

I can now read these images pretty quickly. I can watch the tumor expand and spread like a slow moving oil slick. There was a period when it seemed to be slowing down, but like the demonic hydra that it is, it resumes its encroachment. I continue traditional chemo but that, too, will soon run its course. Barring a last minute miracle cure, I will be truly at the end of the road.

I continue to try alternative methods with trepidation, skepticism, and hope. I've seen a spiritual medium who heals through channeling "entities," while subjects wear white, drink "blessed water," and follow a series of seemingly arbitrary rules purportedly designed to bestow healing power. To each his or her own.

My high school alma mater, a Quaker school in Philadelphia, held a special service in traditional fashion, to "hold me in the light," a way to channel healing energy in my direction. I've tried taking various supplements, and I've managed to limit sugar and carbohydrate consumption, often facing the nagging question, as a lover of foods of all kinds, "does it really matter when you have a terminal illness?"

I've taken the arduous, complicated and, for the moment, uncharted route of securing medical marijuana, and in particular the oil-based compound CBD, a.k.a. cannabidol. Doing so involved more risk and effort than anyone should have to face in seeking alternative approaches to their own cancer care. I suppose as marijuana laws and policies evolve it will get easier, but as it stands the process has taken up an enormous amount of scarce time, energy, and resources. I have no idea whether there will be any therapeutic effect. We shall see. I will, as I live and eventually die of this disease (no date set), try anything. I welcome any prayer, spirit, or compound that will help me proceed with dignity and happiness.

I have no problem with assisted suicide, death with dignity, or whatever other route anyone feels the need to choose in order to make an awful situation less so for themselves and their families. I have to admit that I felt irritated when I first learned of Brittany's story. I wanted to shout, "WAIT! TOO SOON! TOO YOUNG! THERE'S HOPE!

But in the end, no one else can truly understand the pain, fear, and heartache experienced by a person in her place — or in mine. Without knowing the details of Brittany's tumor progression, without experiencing her suffering, how can anyone truly understand her decision? What are her doctors telling her? Has she exhausted all treatment options? Is it too early? Most important, what is the disease doing to her?

Within the war-torn landscape of cancer, there are no winners or losers. Just people trying to live, and perhaps die, with the universal human dignity we desire.

I wish Brittany and her family love and whatever else it takes to make her final days, however many remain, what she wants them to be.

Mark Green resides in Walpole, New Hampshire and is Vice President of Strategic Partnerships for Accelerate Brain Cancer Cure (ABC2), based in Washington, DC. Founded in 2001 by Steve Case and his late brother Dan, a victim of brain cancer, ABC2 funds high-risk, high-reward research to speed the development of new therapies, trials and, ultimately, a cure. ABC2 has raised over $20M towards this effort. His blog can be found at moosevt.wordpress.com.

If you don't know where you are going,
any road will get you there.
Lewis Carroll

Void if Detached

November 29, 2014

I AM UNDER HOSPICE CARE NOW. My first thought has been "hospice care? At the age of forty-seven? Really? This launch of incredible services which I am only now beginning to understand: A hospital bed has been installed, grab bars, galore.

The furniture has been moved around significantly (thank you friends!), the bathroom modified, physical and occupational therapy tools on hand, and I am welcoming visitors on a careful, stress—free, measured, rotational basis to secure my safety from falling, and to lift spirits. Recently I have been having a recurrent dream that I am standing on the edge of a cliff near the Grand Canyon. Behind me were friends, neighbors, doctors, nurses and all of those employed to provide the care necessary to help me perform daily functions like bathing and dressing. There are times that dream becomes very threatening and I feel like all of these wonderful people are simply waiting to throw me over the cliff, stopwatch in hand. I was initially overwhelmed by what was being offered and didn't understand it all. This sudden and suspicious invasion of my privacy and the management of my time began to become a point of misplaced resentment. But as time moves on and I begin to understand and harness the generosity and hard work of those involved, I get it, and I am very grateful as well as deeply moved by offers from friends and family to check in on my well-being and on my family as well as my eager stomach!

Many years ago, when my grandmother Ethel was slowly dying from emphysema she, ironically being a nurse years ago who had smoked (like so many) in her past, I watched her writhe in discomfort trying to pull her thin flowered print nightgown over her weakened body. But most of all, she just wanted to maintain her dignity. Then, almost until her last breath,which occurred soon after I whispered into her ear, "Grandma, it's okay you don't have to fight anymore, you can let go now."

I had just flown in from Arizona to say my last goodbyes. With the aide standing by, I left her apartment and she passed soon thereafter. And another incident this past summer: I had a fairly sizable seizure when a friend who had recently cared for her ailing father rushed to the scene and the first thing she did was to help me wash my face with a warm wet washcloth. This act was knowing, loving, and caring and it was the best remedy because it had nothing to do with taking pills in that moment but to restore my dignity and it made a world of difference: to try to start up again with a fresh clean face and outlook all within that one small gesture. Needless to say I have a lot to be grateful for.

The End of a Road Well Traveled

March 9, 2015

WITH INESTIMABLE SORROW, we must inform you that Mark Richard Green completed his journey on February 27, 2015. The caring and devotion of all those who were with him during these last months, particularly the wonderful people of the Walpole, NH and Saxtons River and Putney, VT communities and environs, cannot be measured, and no amount of thanks can be adequate. The following appeared in the Brattleboro Reformer on March 5, 2015:

"Mark Richard Green, born August 18, 1967, passed away in Walpole, NH on February 27, 2015, peacefully, smiling and with his joy and passion for life intact. Mark's enthusiasm for life was equalled by the vigour and intensity with which he confronted his illness. He described his fateful journey through his blog "moosevt.wordpress.com."

"A native of Philadelphia, PA, Mark was a proud "Lifer" (K-12) graduate of Abington Friends School, in Jenkintown, PA. There he developed a strong sense of justice, equality and human rights, and a deep passion for the outdoors. He then graduated from Hamilton College (Clinton, NY) with a B. A. in English and a Minor in Studio Art, and earned his M. Ed. at the University of New England, Antioch in Keene, NH.

"His love for friends and family, and in particular daughters Hannah and Libby, sister Kerry, former wife and dear friend Laura Gaudette, Aunt Carolyn, beloved friend Barb Silbey and parents Beverly and Stephen, was limitless.

"Mark loved nature, outdoor sports, music, photography, food, travel and adventure. He visited Costa Rica, India, China, Hong Kong, Taiwan, Korea, Egypt, France and Puerto Rico and he pursued studies in British drama and writing at the University of East Anglia, England.

"He spent several summers working in Durango, CO and was an administrator at Verde Valley School in Sedona, AZ. Some of his most formative times were spent at Twin Lakes in Shohola, PA—fishing, sailing, swimming, skiing, skating, biking and carousing.

"Mark served on the Boards of Friends of the Norris Cotton Cancer Center at Dartmouth-Hitchcock and the Saxtons River (VT) Main Street Arts Center, and as a village Trustee in his beloved Saxtons River. He was also a DJ for the local community radio station "WOOL FM," on a show he aptly named "No Depression," featuring "old time," honky-tonk and "hillbilly" music, and he was proud to be part of The Bread and Puppet Theatre in Glover, VT.

"Mark taught and worked in financial aid and admissions until devoting his talents to fundraising at The Grammar School and The Putney School in Putney, VT, Dartmouth College and its Thayer School of Engineering in Hanover, NH, and finally, for Accelerate Brain Cancer Cure (ABC2) based in Washington, DC, where he literally dedicated his life to the cause of funding research and new treatments and hopefully a cure for the incurable disease which ultimately ended his adventure.

"Mark lived every minute of his life. It was an adventure he shared with his girls and an uncountable number of friends. He was an authentic, special, good man, kind, generous, funny, adventurous and beloved by all who knew him."

The loving comments on his Facebook page attest to the fact that we are indeed fortunate to have had Mark in our lives. Hold him in your thoughts and hearts.

His family and Friends of Mark

MARK RICHARD GREEN ("MOOSE")
AUGUST 18, 1967–February 27, 2015

Some Thoughts and Reminiscences*

If I should mention anecdotes that other speakers planned to tell you—they ought not be discouraged from doing so. Good stories are worth retelling.

Shortly after midnight on August 1, 2011, experiencing horrific head pain, Mark was rushed to Cheshire Medical Center in Keene by Barb Silbey, who then accompanied his ambulance to Dartmouth-Hitchcock after a CT scan revealed a large tumor.

After emergency surgery on August 2, Mark was given what can only be described as a death sentence. But he treated it as a life sentence right up until his last breath at 8:32 A.M., February 27, 2015. Once again, Barb Silbey was with him through the night.

Despite five surgeries, 33 radiation treatments and three years and three months of nonstop chemotherapy (including experimental clinical trials), Mark lived and loved every minute of his life, and shared it with what we now know were hundreds of friends.

He especially, and passionately, loved "his girls," Hannah and Libby, of whom neither he, nor any of us, could be more proud. That they are so wonderful is and will be a lasting tribute to him—and to Laura. They are smart, funny, very pretty, caring, intense and adventurous, they thrive in the outdoors and in school, they read avidly, they seek and meet challenges. He loved them with all his heart and soul, and the thing he cared most about since August 1, 2011 (and before that, too) was whether they would be "ok."

*Delivered at the April 19, 2015 memorial at The Putney School.

Not to worry, Mark. They will be ok.

Mark was by no means perfect, but the good certainly outweighed the less good. He loved people and they were attracted to him. What was it about Mark that made so many people love him? My grandmother would say it was because he was a "zeesa neshama"—a sweet soul.

The unbelievable caring and loyalty of his friends cannot be exaggerated. In no particular order: What Margaret Clark, Eric and Rachel Aho, Laura Gaudette and Dave Hume, Barb Silbey, Chris Harlow and Bettina Berg, Doug and Christina Last, Bucky and Beth McAllister, Charlie and Poppit Boswell, John Jessup and Mary Chamberlin, Ally Lubin, Ann Guyon, Leidy Geer, Dan and Mary Pipes, the Weed family, Karin Mallory, Steve and Nancy Lorenz, Hugh Montgomery, Bill Scarlett, Alexandra Scarlett, Valerie and Mark Kosednar, Tamara Mooney, Mark's Aunt Carolyn Bennett, his lifelong friend Ben Barnett, and all the other incredible people, did for Mark is beyond belief. Also, his Hospice Nurse Aylene Wozmak and caregivers Shelby, Andrea, Ann, Jesse and others I did not meet. He was and we are grateful to everyone for their extraordinary kindness and devotion. I apologize for not knowing or remembering the name of everyone who was on the support roster.

Special thanks are also due to Mark's colleagues at ABC2 (Accelerate Brain Cancer Cure)—especially Max Wallace, David Sandak and Dennis Steindler. Their unstinting support and kindness were incredible. Mark worked at ABC2 because he believed that it could be the source for exceptional research into treatments and, hopefully, cures for the various types of brain cancer. They believed in him, and his work justified their faith.

And extra thanks to Doug Last and Eric Aho for the incredible fundraising campaign which enabled Mark to be home with 24-hour care right up to his last day.

In addition to the medical procedures, Mark did everything he could to fight. He attended a lecture by St. John of God. He went to Colorado to be eligible for "alternative treatment." He visited experts at M. D. Anderson in Houston and at Duke. He had top doctors at Dartmouth-Hitchcock and Mass. General. But he never really complained. An example you may have already heard: after his third surgery at Massachusetts General, when he awakened, we asked what we could get for him; with no hesitation he answered: "lobster ravioli." And after what I believe was his fourth surgery (when a shunt was implanted), he asked his nurse for a brand-new, never-used urinal. When she left the room, he filled it with apple juice. When his doctor and his entourage entered the room, Mark said he was dry as a bone and then lifted the urinal to his lips and drank from it. Needless to say, the reaction was shock and awe. Hannah posted a video on her page.

Of course, there was the occasional—sometimes frequent—and loud outburst, and there were lots of tears, especially in the late stage of his illness, but he never gave up. He was determined to make the most of his life even though he knew that his ticket would not take him all the way to his destination. Shortly before we lost him, he talked about spending a week at the Lake house, and he and I doing another "guys" weekend in Boston. And he was excited about the March 28 benefit concert in Bellows Falls; he bought tickets for everyone—including himself.

I've never known anyone who lived and loved life as much as Mark. He took delight in everything. During his last trip—when Eric Aho took him to Montreal—he was excited not only by their time together and the wonderful meals they enjoyed, but even by the handicapped shower in their hotel room. "That was really great, Dad."

A few highlights of an incomplete history:

After college he first worked as a teller at Vermont National Bank in Burlington, where he was nicely asked to leave because—in his assigned role of providing Christmas holiday music—he piped Bob Marley Rasta music through the branch (he said "it was spiritual"); he worked at a dude ranch in Durango, Colorado; he worked at Bread & Puppet Theatre in northern Vermont; he scrubbed boats in Puerto Rico with Bucky McAllister; he worked at Verde Valley School in Sedona, Arizona (where he was proud to report that David Crosby had used the toilet in his house during a benefit concert); he followed The Grateful Dead around for a few years; he worked at Dartmouth, the Greenwood School, The Grammar School and the Putney School; he visited India, China, Egypt, Taiwan, Korea, Costa Rica, Hong Kong and France (with Hannah and Libby), he spent a college semester in England and if he hadn't gotten pneumonia and come home two weeks early, he would have been a passenger on Pan Am 103; he rode his bicycle from our house in the Pocono Mountains to Maine—sleeping in people's garages and other places he chose not to discuss.

I joined him when he moved from Vermont to Sedona with a huge Ryder truck towing his car. In Bristol, which is partly in Virginia and partly in Tennessee, not exactly a bustling metropolis with wide streets or Starbucks, Mark wanted to cruise around—looking for music—with the multi-ton truck and car trailer. He finally relented, and we checked into a posh motel which had a sign behind the counter: "No refunds after ten minutes." We also stopped and stood on a corner in Winslow, Arizona. Of course, the highlight each day was where we would eat next, and when.

Mark's happiest times were with Hannah and Libby: ice-climbing; skiing in Vermont, New Hampshire, Colorado and Quebec (which was an especially wonderful annual trip); canoeing and kayaking; sharing music, spending most of a terrific, high energy time in France looking for the next restaurant; sunning in St. John USVI; visiting Times Square on New Year's Eve and doing the Polar Bear Swim at Coney Island the next day; watching the girls excel at The Grammar School, Northfield—Mt. Hermon and The Putney School; sharing time together at our Lake house (which is where he first imbibed "Kivas Regal" and liked to ride his mountain bike down a steep hill, through the trees, off the dock and into the water).

He treasured his time at Abington Friends School ("AFS") (outside Philadelphia) and Hamilton College. While at AFS, he trained for college life by hosting parties at our house— on weekends when he said he had too much school work to accompany us to the Lake house. Ironically, he strictly enforced a clean-up rule. We finally found out when we found a Coors bottle cap behind a couch. The deception was bad enough, but Coors? A right-wing beer? He was, of course, deeply contrite—about the Coors.

It was a party of AFS classmates during Thanksgiving weekend that was his last celebration in Philadelphia—orchestrated by Ben Barnett, who also picked up Mark and his caregiver and took them to the party and back home (and who was a frequent visitor in Walpole—once after receiving a 10 P.M. call and leaving immediately).

At this point, most of the memories are good. Even the totaled cars evoke smiles, because it seems he was always able to escape with a grin—even when he rolled over a week-old Dodge Colt Vista and plowed into a tree while driving barefoot and shirtless and changing a cassette, and when he totaled a VW Scirocco in a wintertime Vermont pond and had to swim to safety.

He also survived a kiln which blew up in his face while at Hamilton, resulting in a Medevac trip to a Syracuse hospital. When Beverly called Doug Last to ask what Mark looked like, he reassuringly told her: "your husband." (I've always wondered about that.)

Unfortunately, we must now deal with an "accident" he couldn't walk away from, a tragic ending he couldn't avoid. Mark did not want to leave us. At the end of his wonderful visit with us Thanksgiving week (when Kerry modified her house and her life to assure his comfort), he cried out: "I want my life back. There are still things I want to do."

The hole in each of our hearts can be at least partially filled with memories that can enrich-or enliven-our days ahead. I hope that every tear over his loss may be accompanied by a smile for our good fortune to have had him in our lives. He was truly one of a kind. As his good friend Dan Pipes recently described him—Mark was "one of the goofiest, kindest, (most) irritating and most interesting people I know."

Mark had a larger than life persona. He was kind, generous and devoted to his friends and family. He had unbounded passion for food and music and camaraderie, and intense love for his Hannah and Libby. He was a special, good man. Among the words people have used to describe him are: joyful, compassionate, gentle, energized, mercurial, authentic, funny, sweet, inspiring, intense, free-spirited, Graceful (with a capital "G"), intelligent, spirited, dear, selfless, genuine, "he was everywhere." One good friend wrote to him shortly before the end: "I miss everything about you." All of us will miss something—or many somethings.

Hannah, Libby, Laura and Dave, Barb, Beverly, Kerry, Samantha, Jake and I, as well as guardian angels Margaret Clark and Eric Aho, thank all of you for sharing your friendship, your love and your caring with Mark, and with us.

—Stephen H. Green